Rebels
Pretenders
&
Impostors

J.V. Schley fecit 1737.

LE BARON DE NIEWHOFF,
Soi-disant
Grand d'Espagne, Lord d'Angleterre, Pair
de France, Baron du St Empire, et Prince du
Trone Romain; & reconnu Roi *par les* Corses,
Sous le Nom de

THEODORE I.

REBELS PRETENDERS & IMPOSTORS

Clive Cheesman and
Jonathan Williams

Published for The Trustees of

The British Museum by

BRITISH MUSEUM 🏛 PRESS

For George Cawkwell,
the genuine article

Frontispiece: The 'king of a summer', Theodore
von Neuhoff, who ruled briefly as king of Corsica
in 1736 (see pp. 51–2). The islanders, in rebellion
against their Genoese rulers, were dazzled by his
promises of forthcoming military aid. When this
failed to appear they turned on Theodore, who
escaped and made his way to London. Fleetingly
lionized by English society, he was soon in prison
for debt and died in destitution. He was buried in
Soho in central London, where to this day a pub
is named after him.

© 2000 The Trustees of the British Museum

First published in 2000 by British Museum Press
A division of The British Museum Company Ltd
46 Bloomsbury Street, London WC1B 3QQ

Clive Cheesman and Jonathan Williams have
asserted the right to be identified as the authors
of this work.

A catalogue record for this book is available
from the British Library

ISBN 0-7141-0899-5

Designed and typeset in Photina
by James Shurmer

Printed in Great Britain by The Bath Press,
Avon

Contents

Acknowledgements

This book grew out of a British Museum exhibition of the same name which ran from April to October 1999 in Gallery 69a. It was opened in splendid style by Professor David Cannadine, whose remarkable assertion that he was not David Cannadine at all but in fact the illegitimate son of the Duke of Windsor will long be remembered by those who heard it. During its brief life the exhibition attracted a gratifying number of visitors and some press attention. This encouraged the curators, who are also the present authors, to venture into print. We would not have been able to do so without the help we received from many individuals both within and beyond the British Museum, who assisted us in the preparation of both the exhibition and this book. From the Department of Coins and Medals, we would like to express our profound gratitude to Richard Abdy, Marion Archibald, Philip Attwood, Andrew Burnett, Annette Calton, Susanneh Chan, Barrie Cook, Joe Cribb, Virginia Hewitt, Janet Larkin, Andrew Meadows, Brendan Moore, David Owen, Venetia Porter, Simon Prentice, Luke Syson, Helen Wang, David Ward and Gareth Williams; to Sheila O'Connell, Janice Reading, Angela Roche and Kim Sloan of the Department of Prints and Drawings; to Rachael Bailey and Andrea Easey of the British Museum Design Office; and finally to Stephen Dodd of the British Museum Photographic Service for his unfailingly expert use of the camera under great and seemingly ever-increasing pressures. We would also like to thank the following individuals from other places and institutions for helping us so generously in a multitude of ways: Giuseppe Albertoni (University of Bologna), Lucy Allchurch (Jersey Heritage Trust), Douglas Anderson (Glasgow), David Beech (British Library), Elizabeth Buettner (University of Birmingham), David Cannadine (Institute of Historical Research, London), Michael Crawford (University College London), Patric Dickinson (College of Arms), Andrew Logan (London), Brian McGing (Trinity College, Dublin), Pat Prole (College of Arms), Bernhard Rieger (Iowa State University), Stephen Sack (Brussels), Konstanze Scharring (London), Richard Smout (Isle of Wight County Archives), Katja Sommer (Tübingen University), Guy Stair Sainty (New York), Roberta Suzzi Valli (Rome and San Marino) and Robert Yorke (College of Arms). We make our greatest thank-offerings to Emma Way of the British Museum Company for supporting the idea of the book from its inception, and to our editor, Nina Shandloff, whose patience and persistence were indispensable ingredients in bringing it to fruition.

The division of labour has resulted in Jonathan Williams being responsible for the introduction and chapters 1 and 5, and Clive Cheesman for chapters 2, 3 and 4.

CLIVE CHEESMAN & JONATHAN WILLIAMS
London, May 2000

Introduction

Our story begins with perhaps the most famous case of rebellion in history. The scene is the Garden of Eden, where Adam and Eve were tempted to eat of the forbidden fruit from the Tree of the Knowledge of Good and Evil. The third chapter of the Book of Genesis tells how the serpent made them an irresistible offer, that they would be 'like God, knowing good and evil'. So they disobeyed the commandment of the Lord and were driven from Paradise by the angel's flaming sword for 'the man has become like one of us, knowing good and evil'. There was no pretence possible between God and his creation. Adam and Eve felt their nakedness and – a futile gesture – covered themselves and their shame with a fig-leaf. Rebels both against God and pretenders to His divinity, our first parents set the pattern for those who would follow their example, heedless of the awful consequences.

Obedience to settled arrangements, to gods, their priests and to the lords of the earth, the secular rulers of mankind, was for most of history the

Adam, Eve and the Serpent in the Garden of Eden, from a genealogical manuscript of the 1460s recounting the descent of the kings of England.

generally accepted creed ordering human communities, perhaps until the eighteenth century. Change and innovation were rarely on the official agenda, revolution almost unheard of. Tradition declared what was and was not thinkable, who should be the ruler and who the ruled. The word of tradition was absolute. Yet certain things did change. Cities and empires rose and fell, kings and dynasties, even gods, came and went with them. There were winners and losers in the world of unchanging tradition. But the order of things stayed the same and, despite all appearances, had to be seen to stay the same.

Within this world, in which thoughts of change were not so much avoided as not even imagined, new arrivals, gods or men, of which there were always many, had to find a way to insert themselves into the tradition, to represent their advent or usurpation not as an irruption into its unbreakable skein, but as its fore-ordained, just and heaven-blessed fulfilment. How, in many different periods of history and cultures across the globe, this feat was accomplished again and again by rebels against established authorities, by pretenders to thrones and by impostors claiming a false identity to win power is the subject of this book. What we are after are the fig-leaves of dissimulation and deception, with which these characters covered the uncertainty of their sovereign claims or, if successful, their usually violent usurpation of the sovereign position, in order to mask their novelty and preserve the semblance of continuity which the world of tradition demanded. The kind of deception involved was, more often than not, self-deception rather than what we would class under the heading of propaganda, that is, a cynical message pumped out by a knowing élite for the consumption of a gullible populace. For in the world of tradition almost everyone was a believer. Critical distance from the entire system of thought represented by tradition, as opposed to certain specific aspects of it, was achieved by very few, *especially* among the ruling classes. Tradition, after all, was what endowed them with their exalted position. They needed it implicitly, and so trusted it wholeheartedly. Certainly they used tradition for their own ends and reinvented it for their own uses. But remaking is not necessarily manipulation. They were the children, not the masters, of the tradition and were incapable of standing apart from it. If they justified themselves with falsehoods, it was mostly because they believed them to be true.

In such a world, where tradition was malleable precisely because it promised to ensure stability, where events were constantly being retrospectively reinterpreted in order to conserve the reputation of the established order, how are we to distinguish between the genuine and the inauthentic, between the legitimate sovereign and the rebel, the pretender or the impostor? We might adopt the criteria applied at the time which, again, were mostly retrospective. If the rebel or pretender won the victory, he became the king and no pretender. If an imposture gained conviction, it became the truth. Failures, on the other hand, were condemned to the status of rebellious traitors. To this extent, there is little difference between the pretender and the king other than the crude fact of success. Both reigning and aspirant dynasties indulged widely in historical fictions to embroider the fame of their past and present members. No royal family has been royal forever; all arrived at their sovereign position either through war or marriage. Nevertheless, there is merit and interest in looking at the ways in which this transformation occurs, what conditions have to be met in order for legitimacy to be attained by the victorious rebel who has just overthrown his sovereign to become king himself.

Pretenders present a slightly different set of issues, and draw our attention to another aspect of the manufacturing of monarchies. It might be worth pointing out at the start that the verb 'pretend' has at least two different senses, both of which are relevant to our subject. 'To pretend *to* something' means 'to lay claim to something', a usage which is now almost obsolete; the second, nowadays much more familiar, sense, 'to pretend *that* something is the case', means 'to claim falsely'. The word 'pretender' relates to the first of these two meanings. A pretender will probably make many false claims in justification of his actions, but what qualifies him to be a pretender is the public expression of his claim to something, usually a throne, which he does not possess.

Not everyone can be a pretender. Who exactly could stake such a claim depended very much on the nature of the monarchy and state concerned. Some kingdoms were utterly dynastic in character, sovereignty descending by a fixed convention within a particular family or kinship group. The Ottoman Empire is perhaps the paradigm of the dynastic state, its ruling sultan of necessity belonging to the group of descendants of Osman (1258–1326), recognized as the founder of the family's imperial fortunes. Pretenders to the throne within states of this sort had to belong to that charmed group. It was to prevent the occurrence of such dynastic pretenders that new Ottoman sultans habitually ordered the murder of their male relatives upon accession.[1] This did not preclude local magnates unconnected with the imperial family from attempting to establish quasi-autonomous realms within the provinces of the empire, and even indulging in outright rebellion. Other empires had different conventions with no, or much looser, attachments to royal dynasties – the Roman Empire, for instance, investigated in chapter 1. In such states the field for pretenders was much more open and dynastic connections, though often useful, rarely decisive.

Most monarchies lie somewhere in between the Ottoman and Roman Empires with respect to the regard they show for the dynastic principle of succession, and they may also vacillate between them through time. The history of the English monarchy is a typical example, consisting as it does of a series of dynasties, each in some way related genealogically to its predecessor, such that the ancestry of Queen Elizabeth II can be plausibly traced back through the sequence of ruling houses to Cerdic, a sixth-century Saxon king of Wessex. But the change from one dynasty to the next also clearly represents a rupture in the regular succession of son to father on which monarchies often purport to rely for their legitimacy.

The danger in these dynastic transitions is that they tend to leave behind at least one member of the previous ruling family, and this can lead to the rise of a rival succession of pretenders over several generations. This

Medal by Bertoldo di Giovanni of Ottoman Sultan Mehmed II (1451–81), conqueror of Constantinople in 1453. The legend calls him 'Emperor of Asia and Trebizond and Great Greece'.

happens especially in those circumstances where the dynastic principle may be absolutely and not just pragmatically invoked, as it was by many after the ejection of King James II from Britain in 1688. His descendants, who attracted many supporters in England and Scotland, maintained their dynastic claim to the throne of Great Britain and continued to style themselves as kings until the death of James' younger grandson, 'King Henry IX', in 1807 (see chapter 2 for more on the Stuarts and the Jacobite cause). As time went on, the claim was increasingly unrealistic, but true dynasticism pays no heed to any source of legitimacy or authority other than itself, so much so that it reaches its purest manifestation precisely when wholly disconnected from political realities and shorn of every prospect of achieving

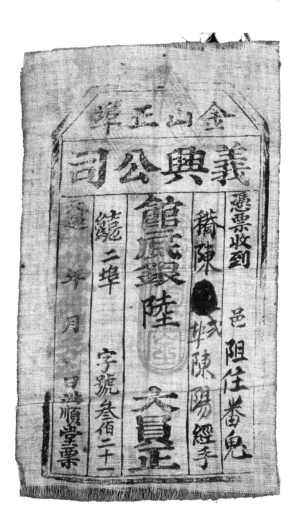

Secret society membership certificate, Patriotic Rising Society (*Yixing Gongsi*), San Francisco Chapter (founded 1860s). The society belonged to the Heaven and Earth Society (*Tiandihui*), dedicated to the overthrow of the Manchu Qing dynasty and the restoration of Chinese rule. Such societies spread to America with Chinese emigration in the mid-19th century.

its stated claim. Here we encounter a curious, modern sub-class of the tribe of pretenders, who appropriately combine both senses of the word. For the republican twentieth century witnessed a bizarre efflorescence of what we might call pretend pretenders. Now that most of the world's ancient monarchies and empires have bitten the dust, there is any number of loose ends to which would-be pretenders can attach themselves, by falsely alleging that they are the true descendants of the ruling house of some long-gone realm – Byzantium is a particular favourite. The object of their claims is not usually to attain to real political sovereignty over the territories of the state in question, but merely to gain recognition for the inflated titles to which they pretend, recognition which as often as not is hoped to lead to financial reward. The proper home for these insubstantial beings with their shadowy claims is the virtual world of the Internet, as we shall discover.

One might call these characters dynastic impostors. Yet they do not exhaust the contents of our third category, for the regal impostor, who falsely pretends that he is some royal personage, whether living, dead or invented, has a long and noble tradition. Put quite simply, before newspapers penetrated to mass audiences and photography allowed the images of the powerful to be disseminated to every order of society, it was a lot easier for an ambitious individual to pass himself off to ignorant populations as a prince of the blood royal, or even as a deceased king returned to life – so, for instance, the crop of false Neros after that Roman emperor's suicide in AD 68 (see further in chapter 3), or the three different false Dmitris who claimed to be the (dead) son of Tsar Ivan the Terrible and caused Russia endless troubles in the early years of the seventeenth century. A charismatic king who dies young, or a prince who dies mysteriously in infancy, may come to represent the unfulfilled hopes and frustrated aspirations of many. The fact of his death may be doubted in the absence of first-hand knowledge, which is anyway impossible for most people in pre-modern societies, thus opening the way for belief in the possibility of his return to save his people from the rule of the new, and probably rather unloved, king. The impostor is in this respect often a rather messianic figure, a feature he has in common with many a rebel and pretender.

After the beginning of the age of revolutions in the late eighteenth century, the long supremacy of tradition was overthrown by the new republics in America and France, and in Great Britain by the Industrial Revolution. Monarchies, pretenders and dynasties declined in significance. But other dreams arose to fill the vacuum they left behind, dreams of nations, of entire peoples stretching back uninterrupted into the unimaginably

$500 note of the Confederate States of America (1864). During the American Civil War (1861–5), the Confederacy used an image of the first US President, George Washington, both on banknotes (vignette on the left) and as its official seal, as a symbol of legitimacy. Washington was from Virginia, one of the Confederate States.

distant past, pretending to whole stretches of past history and even pre-history, represented only by the mute, and therefore highly manipulable, evidence of archaeology. They are in many ways the successors to the royal rebels and pretenders of the world of tradition.

What distinguishes this book from most other works of history is that it pays due attention to the significance of material culture for all of our three groups, the rebels, the pretenders and the impostors, and particularly to the coins and banknotes they produced. Since the invention of coinage in Lydia (western Turkey) and China in about 650 BC, the material forms of money have often been resorted to by the objects of our present interest as an expression or validation of their sovereign claims. This is for two fairly simple reasons. First, since coins have from a very early period been issued by a political authority, whether an individual or a community, with that authority's name inscribed on them, the issuing of coins has come to be regarded as a characteristic and prerogative of legitimate sovereigns. Hence, for those claiming to be or aiming

From AD 9 to 23, Wang Mang, a powerful courtier, usurped the throne of China, overthrowing the ruling Han dynasty. Tracing his descent from the legendary Yellow Emperor, he made knife-shaped coins recalling those of the ancient pre-Han kings of the Zhou dynasty.

to be one, the minting of coins and the printing of banknotes is understandably an attractive kind of activity in which to become involved. Furthermore, the coins will usually be inscribed with the name and sometimes the image of the rebel or the pretender, making him already look the part which he wishes to play in the future. Second, rebels and pretenders usually have to attract people to their banner to fight for them. Loyal devotion and hope of future reward upon attainment of success may work for a while, but nothing is as effective as cash in hand. Payment in coin bearing the name and image of the rebel is an extraordinarily persuasive argument in favour of sticking with him through thick and thin, especially if taken together with a strong personal attachment to the individual and his cause.

One of the pretenders we shall be looking at in chapter 1 is Postumus, a Roman governor who in AD 260 proclaimed himself emperor within the western provinces of the Roman Empire – Spain, Gaul, Britain and Germany. During his nine years' hold on power, until his overthrow and murder in 269, he issued an extensive coinage for both the reasons outlined above. Just how pressing was the need to get his image and likeness in circulation among his followers, especially the armies under his command, is demonstrated by the fact that he reused the coins of earlier emperors to manufacture his own. Plate 2 shows a detail from a splendid example of this phenomenon.[2] Postumus' profile, with its crown of sun's rays and long beard, is superimposed on the clearly recognizable bust of the emperor Hadrian (AD 117–38) with his close-cropped beard. The latter's coins were still in circulation 120 years after his death and available for recycling by Postumus the pretender in his efforts, rather successful as it turned out, to pass himself off as the genuine article.

This book is written in the conviction that there is a valid distinction to be drawn between the legitimate and the false, in historical argument as in claims to sovereignty. The universal acid of demythologizing approaches to the past and the present has, in Britain as in many other places, laid bare the invented nature of many of our most cherished communal myths about monarchy and nationality, and stripped tradition of its sacred untouchability.[3] Notions about the past, however attractive or convenient, based on falsehood are of course wrong and must be set aside. But the debunking, or the setting in context, of myths told about an institution's or a community's history is not necessarily the same thing as depriving the institution itself of legitimacy, unless it can be shown to be founded on a palpable untruth. Much of our faith in the comforting and awesome power of tradition may well be revealed thereby to be based on gullibility, wishful

The Coronation Chair, Westminster Abbey. Made in 1307 for King Edward I of England to contain the Stone of Scone (seen below), as a symbol of Scotland's subjection. The so-called 'Stone of Destiny', on which Scots kings had been enthroned, was identified with Jacob's Pillow. It was moved to Edinburgh in 1996.

thinking and a selective historical memory – a salutary, if often unwelcome, lesson. But there is a difference between the quality of the historical claim to legitimacy which can be made, say, for the present British Queen and those proffered by the current aspirants to various thrones around the world, vacant or otherwise, including that of Scotland where a self-styled HRH Prince Michael of Albany bases his claim on a dubious descent from the House of Stuart. We will meet him again in chapter 4. This is a position that can be maintained regardless of one's views on monarchy *per se*, which is quite a different matter. The British royal family, however they are regarded as an institution or as individuals, are quite clearly descended from those whom they claim as their forebears and, whatever one makes of the ceremonial mythologizing of those claims, they are not in themselves false. This may make no difference to our opinions on monarchy as a way of running states, but it should make some difference to the seriousness we accord to the claim being made. Conversely, even if we are in principle opposed to monarchy, it would still be wrong for that reason alone to suspend our historical judgement and lump kings, queens, pretenders and impostors together into one indiscriminately fraudulent and illegitimate basket. Uncritical scepticism is as self-defeating as naive credulity.

This book, then, is offered as a diverting and, we hope, illuminating investigation into one strand of the invention of historical tradition, and as an exposition, not to say in some cases an exposé, of some of the more engaging individuals – dastardly hoaxers, heroic failures and victorious insurgents – who have aimed at supreme power and laid claim to lofty-sounding titles. If thereby it also makes some modest contribution towards generating an appreciation of the value of the study of history, and of the disinterested regard for truth which that requires, it will have been more than worth the writing.

Chapter 1

The Rebel in Antiquity

For the modern observer, dynastic inheritance and monarchies seem to go hand in hand. From the standpoint of meritocratic republicanism, perhaps the characteristic mode of most current political discourse, monarchies represent the quintessence of hereditary power. In more recent European history, monarchies have indeed laid great emphasis on dynastic succession within the ruling family in determining who the legitimate heir to the throne should be, and particularly on the inheritance of power by the eldest son, the system known as male primogeniture which still operates in the British monarchy. But if we look further into the past and beyond the borders of Europe, it becomes apparent that crowns have not always passed from father to son, let alone to members of the extended royal family, and that dynasties and monarchies have not been constant or inseparable bedfellows.

Divine Election, Human Intervention

If family connections have not always been the primary determinant of who should succeed to a crown, what, or who, else has? One important voice, which is perhaps not heard quite so loudly nowadays as it once was, is that of Heaven, whether peopled by a multiplicity of gods or a monotheistic unity. For most of human history in most cultures, the will of God, or the gods, has been regarded as of far greater importance than the mere wishes of mankind in the business of choosing rulers. In many ways God used to play the same role as the ultimate source of legitimate political power for kings and queens as is now fulfilled by the electorate in modern democracies. His opinions, like theirs, were often obscure and hard to gauge, but were always sought and deferred to in public by human authority. God it was who chose and anointed monarchs, they ruled in His name and with His blessing, in Christian language by His grace. This ancient concept still appears in the titulature of Queen Elizabeth II, and on her coins as the abbreviation D.G. (for the Latin *Dei Gratia*, '[Queen] by the Grace of God'). But God, a being with preferences and the free power of choice, had the right to withdraw His support and transfer it elsewhere, if He so desired. Usually this happened for some good reason, at least in retrospect, mostly because the monarch had sinned against his Lord. But not always. The depths of divine judgement have as frequently been feared to be wilful and arbitrary as they have been trusted as good and righteous. Either way, it was the fact that God's vote was potentially open to change that left a door open for the usurpers of antiquity. They only had to succeed, and their very success would immediately qualify them for the position as God's elected monarch.

Some ancient mythologies taught that the gods themselves were usurpers, that the prevailing divine powers had only reached their position of sovereign pre-eminence by violently overthrowing a previous régime in heaven. The Greek high god Zeus overthrew his father Kronos, who had himself castrated his father Uranus. This is dynastic succession of a sort, but not of an ideally peaceful sort. Furthermore, there was no virtuous higher power guiding the course of events to which the kingship of Zeus, as of many others among mankind's great gods, could be referred. There was no obvious reason for Zeus' ultimate victory other than his more effective use of brute force in leading the Olympian gods against Kronos' team, the Titans. This pagan version of 'war in heaven' was, not surprisingly, widely exploited by Greek rulers as a symbol and justification of their earthly victories, achieved or desired, over their enemies. Zeus gave victory to men, and his support was regularly mobilized by ruling dynasties in their own support. But Zeus could not undo his own example. The potential legitimacy of supreme power gained by nothing other than dynastic dispute, usurpation and violence was part of the lesson of his career. The Greeks attempted to characterize the power he employed as civilized, in contrast to the animal barbarity of his

Silver tetradrachm of Diodotus I, first Greek king of Bactria (north Afghanistan). Diodotus was governor within the Seleucid Empire. He declared himself an independent king *c.*256 BC. The image of Zeus suggests his kingly power and the legitimacy of his usurpation.

Silver decadrachm, probably showing Alexander the Great (336–323 BC) with the divine attribute of Zeus' thunderbolt, being crowned by Victory and attacking an Indian war elephant, perhaps a reference to his campaigns in India of 327–325 BC.

opponents, the Titans and the monstrous Giants. There were similar stories told about the divine kings of many different pantheons in the ancient world, in Europe and beyond. Marduk, the great god of Babylon, whom we will meet again later in this chapter, came to power by slaying Tiamat, the monster of primeval chaos. Every year his deeds were recited in the epic poem called the *Enuma Elish* in the Babylonian New Year festival.[1]

Other gods left very different examples of sovereign behaviour to humanity. The God of ancient Israel was pure justice and invincible power, the great and eternal I AM, who ruled His people with fatherly tenderness and judicial severity. There was no standard mythological account of how the God of Israel gained power over heaven and earth. He was himself the creator and ruler of all, without ancestors or rivals. Various monsters are mentioned in ancient Jewish tradition as His unavailing opponents, Belial, Behemoth and Leviathan among them, together with Satan (meaning 'Adversary' in Hebrew), who in the later Christian tradition came to the fore as the fallen angel cast out of heaven for rebellion against God.

The history of ancient Israel was at least equivocal about God's views on the dynastic principle and indeed on monarchy itself. For God was the real king of Israel. Its kings were His stewards and retained the throne on condition that they remained obedient to Him. About 1020 BC Saul, the first king of Israel, was chosen by God and anointed as king by Samuel the Prophet (1 Samuel 10.1). But he sinned and God rejected him (1 Samuel 15.10). God transferred His support to David, a young boy unrelated to Saul. He eventually became a successful warrior and leader of men, and he succeeded to the kingship of Israel in about 1000 BC upon the death of Saul. The house of David ruled first over all Israel and then over the southern kingdom of Judah for four hundred years with God's blessing. Nonetheless, God was not slow to remove members of the family from the throne if they failed to walk in His ways. Perhaps in the early eighth century BC He smote King Uzziah of Judah for failing to expel the pagan worship of Baal from Jerusalem, 'so that he was a leper to the day of his death, and he dwelt in a separate house' (2 Kings 15.5). Within the northern Hebrew kingdom of Israel the situation was somewhat different. Usurpation of the throne and the overthrow of the ruling dynasty was tolerated by God so long as it was done in His name against a disobedient royal family: for instance, the general Jehu's righteous rebellion against the house of Ahab in Israel in about 843 BC, which resulted in the execution of the priests of Baal and ensured the restoration of the worship, and therefore the divine kingship, of God (2 Kings 9–10).

King David of Israel founded a dynasty chosen by God which continued to rule in the kingdom of Judah after the separation of the kingdoms upon the death of King Solomon in about 925 BC. But David's royal right, though divinely sourced, was not absolute. His accession to the kingship was accompanied by a covenant with the elders of Israel in return for their recognition that David was the charismatic individual elected by God to rule over them: 'So all the elders of Israel came to the king at Hebron; and King David made a covenant with them at Hebron before the Lord, and they anointed David king over Israel' (2 Samuel 5.3).[2] The kingship of David was held in tension between divine blessing and human acceptance, neither of which was an unqualified gift. Indeed most kings in antiquity held power within the context of a class of powerful noble families whose rights and privileges abutted and limited their own. No ancient monarchies were openly elective in the modern sense of the word, but aristocratic élites often played an important part in choosing, or acclaiming, a king from a new dynasty, usually one of themselves of course, when the need arose. As for the mass of the people, whether in the form of the populations of capital cities like Rome where their rulers resided or in the guise of the army, on whose loyalty the power of kings ultimately rested, they might perform an important walk-on part in deposing a reigning king and seeing a usurper on to the throne. More often than not they were perhaps merely the instruments of the designs of rival magnates seeking to position themselves in the race for power at the fall of a king or dynasty. But the people could be a powerful tool in the hands of anyone who attracted their support. So their more obvious interests, if not their views, were to varying degrees consulted both by ruling and aspirant kings.

Rome's Republican Monarchs

If Israel is the type of the divinely elected monarchy, the Roman emperors might be regarded as the paradigm of the civil monarchy.[3] The former was embedded in a theocratic society in which God and His law was sovereign, so much so that the Lord himself expressed considerable doubts when His people importuned Him to be given a king like other nations, on the grounds that He, and no man, was the king of Israel (1 Samuel 8.5). The Roman monarchy was established by Augustus in the 20s BC after his eventual victory in a twenty-year civil war which had begun when Julius Caesar invaded Italy in 49 BC. It was founded on the ashes of a ruined republican constitution in which sovereignty had been vested in the citizen adult male

Gold *aureus* of Octavian, the
future emperor Augustus, made in
28 BC. The reverse legend reads:
'He has restored to the Roman
People their laws and rights'. In
fact, he was establishing himself
as a monarch. (×1.5)

population and its elected magistracies, in the authority of the Senate, the
aristocratic council of ex-magistrates, and in the laws. Divine approval was
sought for all the major decisions of the Roman Commonwealth through
the science of augury, the observation of the flight of birds interpreted as
an indication of the will of the gods. But the kingship of the great god
Jupiter in Rome was not so thorough-going as that of the God of Israel. As a
consequence, the crucial constituencies for Roman emperors were not so
much the powers of heaven as those of earth: the powerful generals in
command of the great armies of the frontiers of the empire, the captains of
their own bodyguard the Praetorians, the Senate, and the million-strong
population of the city of Rome where during the first three centuries AD the
emperors tended to reside when not on campaign. Because of the republican
background to the rise of monarchy at Rome, dynastic connections were not
an essential qualification for imperial office. In Israel the king had to be
seen to be reigning because he was the Lord's choice, whereas at Rome the
emperor had to appear to be the choice of the Senate and people. In both
cases this might well mean that the succession fell on the son of the ruling
monarch, but dynastic proximity alone was not a sufficient reason for
inheriting the throne. What made an emperor legally an emperor was a vote
of the Senate.[4] This might in most instances have been a formality, but like
many formalities it was important.

Though the realities of power meant that sons did tend to succeed fathers
in Rome's post-republican monarchy, the necessity for all emperors, even
those who inherited power, to lay claim to a senatorial mandate as the
ostensible justification of their exalted position meant that the way was
potentially open for usurpers and pretenders to dispute the succession and
make good their own claim. If they succeeded, and this usually meant in
warfare, they too could become a legitimate emperor with the approval of the
Senate and people, no matter whose son they were. Sometimes the Senate
misinterpreted the actual nature of their role in negotiating the succession of

Base-silver 'radiate' of Pupienus, one of
the two co-emperors of AD 238 elected by the
Senate. The reverse legend reads 'The Fathers
of the Senate'.

emperors, as in AD 238 when, in opposition to the existing but unloved
emperor Maximinus, they elected two of their senior members, Balbinus and
Pupienus, to be co-emperors. This pair, though possessing the formal
qualification for legitimate power courtesy of the Senate, lacked any support
among the Praetorian Guard or the people and, though they saw off
Maximinus who was murdered by his troops, they lasted only three months
before they themselves were murdered by the Praetorians. They were
replaced by a thirteen-year-old boy, Gordian III, raised to the purple again
by the Praetorians. The senators wisely refrained from withholding approval
from their nominee. They had perhaps learnt their lesson, having
mistaken their power of formal validation for the power of real political
initiative which as a body they had lost early in the history of the empire.

Just how early this happened is shown in the first real succession crisis
which the Roman Empire faced in AD 41 after the murder of the mad, bad
emperor Gaius, better known to history by his nickname Caligula ('Little
Boot'). Gaius died without a designated heir. There were no precedents for
this event. Tiberius had succeeded Augustus in AD 14 and Gaius succeeded
Tiberius in 37, both by prearrangement. What should happen now? On the
very day of Gaius' murder the Senate met and, as reported by the late first-
century AD Jewish historian Josephus, the consuls declared their intention to
assume executive power themselves and return Rome to republican forms of
government after seventy years of monarchy (*Jewish Antiquities* 19.1–4). But
fine words counted for little against the will of the real power-brokers of
imperial Rome. And they were not the noble senators but the Praetorians,
stationed in their barracks in the city of Rome itself, twelve thousand or so

Gold *aureus* of Roman emperor
Claudius (AD 43–54) showing him
with a member of the Praetorian
Guard. The reverse legend reads
'Received by the Praetorians'. (×1.5)

troops whose loyalties were not to Senate or people but to the emperor who paid their wages and guaranteed their not inconsiderable privileges. Gaius himself had increased their numbers. This significant force in Roman politics had no interest in returning to the aristocratic republic and every reason to look for a new emperor. They found one in the person of Claudius, Gaius' uncle and a grandson of Augustus' wife Livia on one side and Augustus' sister on the other. His first act as emperor, once the Senate had come to its senses and acknowledged both him and political realities, was to order the execution of Gaius' murderers. In the following year, AD 42, the commander of the legions in Dalmatia, Scribonianus, and other senators declared against Claudius and for liberty. But the soldiers of the frontier armies were no more willing to fight for the old republic than were the Praetorians. They deserted their officers, and a savage witch-hunt was instigated against those involved in the conspiracy, whence Claudius' reputation for brutality in later historical tradition. To his existing names, Tiberius Claudius Nero Germanicus, the new emperor significantly added both Augustus and Caesar. They had been taken by all three previous emperors. By now they had become all but indispensable titles.[5]

Rebellion in the name of liberty stirred the breasts of some of the more romantic senators, but meant little to the common soldiery whose allegiances the emperors had wisely ensured were focused exclusively on themselves and their families. This was already clear in AD 41 at the fall of Gaius, but the banner of the Commonwealth, the *Res Publica,* and the Senate was briefly raised one final time in the course of two extraordinary years, 68 and 69, in which four individuals became emperor in quick and violent succession.[6] Claudius' designated successor, Nero, who became emperor, or *princeps,* in AD 54 had grown very unpopular with the senators because of a series of judicial executions of a number of prominent members of their order, which to them smacked of tyranny. Though the Senate as a body was weak, its members did command the great armies that defended the provinces and frontiers of the empire. An emperor who alienated the senators risked provoking a military uprising, which is precisely what happened to Nero. The general who eventually made the running was one Servius Sulpicius Galba, a distinguished member of an old senatorial family and the

Bronze *sestertius* of Roman emperor Galba (AD 68–9). (×1.5)

governor of Hispania Tarraconensis, one of the Roman provinces of the Iberian peninsula. He was invited to declare himself emperor in opposition to Nero by Julius Vindex, governor of the province of Gallia Lugdunensis, who had himself rebelled against Nero early in 68. At first, Galba had himself proclaimed not the new Caesar or Augustus, but the Legate of the Senate and People of Rome, at Nova Carthago (Cartagena) in April 68. This was a clear gesture towards old-fashioned notions of free republican government and senatorial sovereignty, appropriate enough in the light of the reasons for the fall of Nero the tyrant. But this could not last. The armies wanted a Caesar, and they wanted Galba to be their man, not the Senate's. In May, Vindex's rebellion was crushed by the legions from Germany, but crucially the Praetorians and their commander Nymphidius Sabinus, who reportedly had his own designs on supreme power, declared their support for Galba as emperor after Nero's suicide in June, and this was how the Senate recognized him as well. In a speech put into Galba's mouth by the historian Tacitus in his great work the *Histories* which began with Galba's reign, he summed up the practical and political dilemma he faced: 'If the mighty fabric of this great empire could stand and be stable without a single ruler, I would have the glory of being the man who restored the Commonwealth. But things have already come to such a strait that in my old age [Galba was seventy-one years old] I cannot give the people of Rome anything more than a worthy successor.' (*Histories* 1.16). In other words, 'I would if I could, but I can't.' As a senator and a member of the old nobility which had governed Rome before the emperors, Galba's republican sentiments were certainly more than merely superficial. But he was also a general, and clear-sighted enough to see that even the considerable dignity and authority of the Senate was no match for the unstoppable enthusiasm of the soldiers for a monarchy. Having taken the step towards filling Nero's place, he could not then change the job description. It was in any case no longer in his, or the Senate's, power to rewrite it.

Though astute enough to see that the old republic could never return, Galba did not quite understand what he had to do in order to remain emperor. Such indeed was Tacitus' famous epitaph: 'By general agreement, he was a man with the capacity for imperial power, had he never exercised it' (*Histories* 1.49). He quickly alienated the troops during his short reign in Rome itself which lasted only three months, from October 68 to January 69. He snubbed his ambitious ally, Marcus Salvius Otho, by adopting another as his designated heir, a promising young man called Lucius Calpurnius Piso Frugi Licinianus, whose appointment he hoped would bring round both people and army to support his cause. But he failed to pay the promised cash handouts, or donatives, to his soldiers, a big mistake. He was not making the friends in the army that he needed to secure his régime. A revolt broke out among the legions on the Rhine frontier led by their general, Lucius Vitellius, in January 69 and at the same time a conspiracy among the Praetorians, again, led by Otho plotted the overthrow of Galba. He was assaulted and hacked to death in the Forum Romanum, the civic heart of the city of Rome, whereupon the Senate duly recognized Otho as their new master.

In a speech given to Otho by Tacitus just before the death of Galba, he meditates to his troops upon the state of being a rebel. 'In what manner I should now address you I cannot say. I am not able to call myself a private citizen because you have hailed me as emperor (*princeps*), nor emperor when another still holds power. And how you yourselves are to be called is also an uncertain matter so long as it is in doubt whether you have the emperor of the Roman people in your camp or a public enemy. Have you heard how they cry for vengeance against me and punishment upon you at the same time? It is so far clear that whether we live or die, we will only do so together' (*Histories* 1.37). The significance of this speech is not whether it literally represents the sentiments of Otho on a particular occasion, or even in general. Greek and Roman historians regularly put speeches into the mouths of characters in their works. Its importance lies in the penetrating insight which it gives us into the nature of high-level power struggles among the members of the Roman political classes. Tacitus himself belonged to them – he was a consul in AD 97. Otho's words reveal the fundamentals of imperial usurpation in Rome. Everything depended on the personal charisma and prestige of the contender, and on his capacity to distract a significant proportion of the soldiers away from their settled loyalties to the reigning emperor and towards himself. He had then to hold their attention through the period of waiting until the final battle by binding them emotionally to his cause as closely as possible. This is what Otho is attempting to do in this speech, by arguing that, since they had gambled all on him as their candidate, they had no choice but to follow him through thick and thin.

The uncertainties inherent in making the choice to follow a usurper were legion. Even the most fervent supporters could turn into fair-weather friends overnight. Soldiers in one province tempted to follow a general into rebellion would for the most part have been in complete ignorance of what was going on elsewhere in the empire, and therefore unaware whether they represented the vanguard of a new movement or an isolated and futile lunge for power. Galba had not made his move before he was certain that he had support elsewhere in the western empire. Otho had no such support initially, but he had Rome and the Praetorians, and possessing the capital was still a *sine qua non* for the aspirant emperor. In and of itself this endowed him with the aura of legitimacy and was a persuasive factor encouraging others to declare in his favour, as many of them did. But some armies, including those in Germany under Vitellius, knew nothing of Otho's usurpation and looked to their own commanders for leadership against the loathed Galba.

There was little that Otho could do about this rival rebellion other than wait for the inevitable forthcoming battle. But in the meantime he attempted to conciliate the people to their new emperor, to embed his presence in their minds and discourage them from switching their loyalties once again. The problem always faced by usurpers is that they cannot abolish their own example. What they have done, so can others similarly minded. They have to move quickly to establish their rule in the hearts of the people, the army and the other important players on the political scene. Force can be part of the answer, but you cannot kill all your opponents, potential or actual. Though personal charisma is vital for the usurper, it is not enough to take him beyond the initial stages of success. To soothe the consciences of those unsettled by the experience of regicide and discourage others from becoming habituated to the opportunities offered by continuing civil war, the usurper emperor had to be able to broaden the basis of his support beyond his immediate following.

The way in which intelligent Roman usurpers tended to do this was first to secure the formal approval of the Senate and people and pay large donatives to the Praetorians and the legions. But this was only a start. Usurped power could always be legalized and fidelity bought, but to acquire an enduring hold on the Romans' imagination, the person of the emperor had to be able to represent something more than just his own personal interests. That something was usually the restoration of the Roman past and Roman tradition, as defined in a variety of different ways by successive contenders. Galba claimed to be the Legate of the Senate and People, adverting to Rome's pre-monarchical republican tradition and suggesting, though not explicitly promising, that he might be about to revive it. Otho took a different, perhaps rather unexpected path. He looked back not to the republic but to Nero, whose close associate he had once been before transferring his allegiance to Galba. This was not such an extraordinary tactic as might first appear. Nero had been deeply unpopular with many senators but not with the army, or the people. Like Nero who was only thirty when he died, and unlike the aged

Galba, at thirty-six Otho possessed the attraction of youth which, since Alexander the Great, had been recognized as a desirable quality in a new ruler. According to Suetonius, the biographer of the early Caesars, Otho was hailed as Nero upon coming to power and was reported to have signed his name as Nero on documents (Suetonius, *Life of Otho* 7). In chapter 3 we will encounter the posthumous personality cult which grew up around Nero's memory, prompting the appearance of a number of impostor Neros. This is presumably the context into which Otho's rehabilitation of Nero's reputation fits. Otho had Nero's public statues and images re-erected, and paid for the completion of his notorious palace, the Golden House, constructed on the ruins of the great fire of Rome of AD 64. He also reportedly intended to marry Statilia Messalina, Nero's widow. All of this might simply be attributed to a deep streak of misguided megalomania in Otho, not perhaps unexpected in one who aspired to be Roman emperor. But there is good reason to believe that much of this Neronian revivalism was designed and conscious, aimed at appealing to those sections of the urban populace and the army that still held Nero's name in high regard. Like Claudius, and Galba eventually, Otho too adopted the names Caesar and Augustus which no emperor could do without. His own name was not to be entirely without honour. It appears on his coins in the slogan 'The Victory of Otho' (*Victoria Othonis*). This was the first time that any emperor had used his personal name rather than the imperial name Augustus as a complement to one or other of the divine personifications that decorated Roman coins, Victory, Peace, Concord and so on.

Almost at the same time as Otho overthrew Galba in January 69, Aulus Vitellius, commander of the legions in the province of Lower Germany, was acclaimed *imperator* (emperor) by his troops in Cologne. That two revolts should have broken out simultaneously is a clear reflection of the widespread unpopularity which Galba had quickly won for himself. Tacitus reports the stages by which the revolt on the Rhine took place, and they are very revealing. The troops heartily disliked Galba and, on New Year's Day 69, instead of repeating their oath of loyalty to him, they smashed his images that were affixed to their standards and swore an oath to the Senate and people of Rome: an interesting step this, reminiscent

Silver *denarius* of Roman emperor Otho (AD 69). The reverse legend reads 'The Victory of Otho'. (×1.5)

of Galba's initial republican reticence about calling himself emperor. But once Vitellius had been saluted as emperor by another senior commander, Fabius Valens, the legions quickly abandoned their former oath and swore in the name of Vitellius, all of this within a week. Taking oaths, attaching images to military standards and erecting statues of the emperor were crucial signs and symbols of loyalty. Conversely, the breaking of all three was the essential mark of rebellion.

Initially Vitellius seems to have avoided the imperial names Augustus and Caesar, taking instead the name Germanicus. This was a choice with complex connotations. On the one hand it was a traditional title of a sort taken by triumphant generals, meaning 'victor over the Germans', and was as such desirable enough. But it was also the name of one of the most beloved princes of Augustus' family, who had once been intended by Augustus to succeed Tiberius, but predeceased him in AD 19. Germanicus had campaigned extensively in Germany and his memory was no doubt cultivated by Vitellius' German legions even fifty years after his death. This, in other words, was a name with evocative imperial resonances. Pretenders to thrones are often astute manipulators of such intangible assets as names. They cost nothing, but can be extraordinarily effective in motivating support by evoking past celebrities or lost dynasties to which the otherwise historically rootless usurper can be assimilated in the willing minds and hearts of his following.

On 14 April 69, Vitellius' armies met those of Otho near the town of Bedriacum in northern Italy and were victorious. Otho killed himself. Five days later the Senate recognized Vitellius, betraying its essentially secondary role in conferring the status of emperor when the issue was in doubt. Though all the major competitors for power were senators, as a body the Senate commanded the loyalty of no troops whatsoever, as the swift desertion of their quasi-republican oath by the German legions between transferring allegiance from Galba to Vitellius amply demonstrated. All it could realistically do was wait until one of the rivals for power came out on top and then enthusiastically rubber-stamp the *fait accompli*.

Vitellius' hold on power was brief and inglorious. Yet he attempted to establish a dynasty during this period. He, like Galba, recognized the need for a son and heir, always popular with the troops who liked to attach themselves to a whole family over several generations, as they had to the Julian line for ninety years from Julius Caesar to Gaius. Though there was nothing inherently dynastic about the Roman monarchy, dynasty was often used by emperors as an instrument to encourage affection and loyalty, and

Gold *aureus* of Roman
emperor Vitellius (AD 69)
showing his two children.
(×1.5)

Brass *sestertius* of
Roman emperor Vespasian
(AD 69–79).

as a means of attempting to control the succession. Both Vitellius' children
and his father, Lucius Vitellius, a great general and public figure of the reign
of Claudius, appeared on his coins, while his mother was awarded the
imperial name Augusta, recalling Augustus' formidable wife Livia. She
outlived him – some said she had killed him – and was granted that titular
name in his will. Once in Rome, Vitellius took the name Augustus but
delayed taking the name Caesar until November 69, shortly before his own
downfall at the hands of Vespasian, commander of the armies of the east. In
July, immediately after recognizing Vitellius, Vespasian's armies had sworn
an oath to him, since when disaffection had spread to the Danube legions
and a battle lost by Vitellius' forces at Cremona in northern Italy. Rome was
finally taken by Vespasian's troops in December and Vitellius killed by the
mob. Vespasian was a more successful architect of a dynasty. He and his sons
Titus and Domitian together reigned for the next twenty-six years.

Although each of the three short-lived emperors of AD 68 and 69 came
to power as a violent pretender and usurper whose legitimacy depended
first upon securing the defeat and death of his predecessor and only then on
legal acknowledgement from the Senate, they all ended up as undeniably
authentic and legitimate, their status never questioned by later historians,
whatever opprobrium may otherwise have been heaped upon them. In the
absence of a strong sense of the dynastic principle, and of the idea that
the emperor should be really, not just formally, chosen by a council of state,
armed rebellion was a perfectly reasonable way of setting about becoming
emperor. Birth was no bar, and the Senate had only a reactive role to play.
Ultimate victory ensured legitimacy, but legitimacy did not in and of itself
ensure either a secure hold on power or loyalty. The emperor had to work at
that, to keep the eyes of his legions, the urban populace and the Senate fixed

on him and his family alone, and their minds off other potential attractions. And there were in principle as many of these as there were commanders of major armies on the frontiers. The events of 68 and 69 showed all the major army groups across the empire lining up behind one or other of the prospective emperors: Spain and Gaul for Galba, Germany for Vitellius, the Praetorians for Otho, Danube and the east for Vespasian. Even the armies of Roman Africa (modern Tunisia) had a go with Clodius Macer, a minor player in the story who nevertheless managed to issue some coins in 68. There was considerable competition between the different provincial armies over which could get their man into power next, no doubt in the hope of receiving special treatment from him once he was installed. This was an important dynamic underlying the quick turnover from one emperor to the next, until Vespasian managed to stop the wheel turning late in 69.[7]

An important issue facing would-be usurpers in the Roman world was how to differentiate themselves from their opponents and competitors. What was in it for their supporters, why should they transfer their allegiance to them? Government in the Roman world was not about politics or policies, emperors had no manifestos or concerted propaganda programmes. Ruling in Rome was not about producing new ideas, so much as enacting a more authentic and effective realization of the old ones. Emperors were not meant to be innovators, but renovators. Novelty was understood only as revival, a New Age as the cyclical recommencement of the Golden Age, the *saeculum aureum*, the Roman functional equivalent of the Garden of Eden, a distant time of peace and plenty when the gods lived with men. This was a potent and enduring myth in the Roman mind, one to which Roman emperors, and particularly would-be usurpers, had frequent recourse. An interesting case in point is that of Carausius, who assumed the title of emperor, or Augustus, in Britain, probably in AD 286.

Carausius, Roman Emperor of Britain

The late third century AD was a very uncertain time for the Roman Empire. Internal strife, constant attempts at usurpation by a series of generals, and the lack of a figure such as Vespasian who could unite the empire for any length of time, coupled with invasions of the northern and eastern frontiers by Germans and Sasanians, had destabilized matters considerably. In the reign of Gallienus (AD 253–68) two peripheral empires had emerged within the Roman frontiers, as either rivals or complements to the so-called 'central empire' based on Rome. The first was located in the western provinces of

Base-silver coin showing the image of Zenobia,
mistress of the eastern Roman Empire, AD 271–4,
in the guise of a legitimate Roman empress. (×1.5)

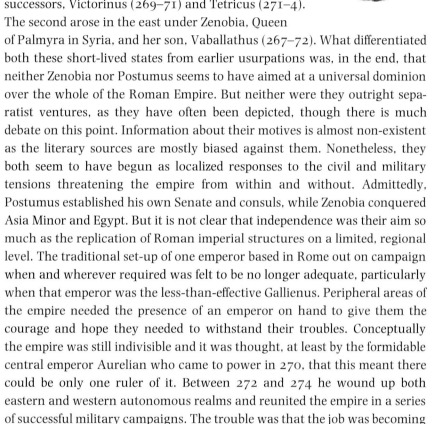

Germany, Gaul, Britain and Spain, ruled by a
powerful general named Postumus (260–9) and his
successors, Victorinus (269–71) and Tetricus (271–4).
The second arose in the east under Zenobia, Queen
of Palmyra in Syria, and her son, Vaballathus (267–72). What differentiated
both these short-lived states from earlier usurpations was, in the end, that
neither Zenobia nor Postumus seems to have aimed at a universal dominion
over the whole of the Roman Empire. But neither were they outright separatist ventures, as they have often been depicted, though there is much
debate on this point. Information about their motives is almost non-existent
as the literary sources are mostly biased against them. Nonetheless, they
both seem to have begun as localized responses to the civil and military
tensions threatening the empire from within and without. Admittedly,
Postumus established his own Senate and consuls, while Zenobia conquered
Asia Minor and Egypt. But it is not clear that independence was their aim so
much as the replication of Roman imperial structures on a limited, regional
level. The traditional set-up of one emperor based in Rome out on campaign
when and wherever required was felt to be no longer adequate, particularly
when that emperor was the less-than-effective Gallienus. Peripheral areas of
the empire needed the presence of an emperor on hand to give them the
courage and hope they needed to withstand their troubles. Conceptually
the empire was still indivisible and it was thought, at least by the formidable
central emperor Aurelian who came to power in 270, that this meant there
could be only one ruler of it. Between 272 and 274 he wound up both
eastern and western autonomous realms and reunited the empire in a series
of successful military campaigns. The trouble was that the job was becoming
too much for one individual, unless he was of exceptional talent, charisma,
determination and good fortune. Aurelian possessed all except the last. He
was assassinated by a conspiracy in 275.[8]

But not everyone was against the idea of having more than one emperor
at one time. There were precedents for the notion of co-emperors. The idea of
collegiate chief magistracies had a long tradition in Rome. From the foundation of the republic in 510 BC there had always been two consuls every year
of equal standing. At the very inception of the principate, the term often
given to the Roman monarchy in its earlier stages, Marcus Agrippa had been

the colleague of the emperor Augustus in holding the constitutional powers of a tribune (a republican magistracy which formed the legal channel through which the emperors exercised much of their authority). Marcus Aurelius (161–180) had reigned together with his adoptive brother, the ineffectual Lucius Verus, until his early but fortunate death in 169, and later, in 177, Marcus unwisely elevated his wayward son Commodus to the rank of emperor, or Augustus. Similarly, Septimius Severus (193–211) had raised his sons to be his colleagues as emperors before his death, Caracalla in 198 and Geta in 209. These were of course examples of the dynastic designation of successors rather than genuine power-sharing, but Severus clearly meant his sons to be joint rulers. Caracalla had other ideas and, the year after his father's death at York in 211 while on campaign, he did away with his younger brother. The precedents for co-emperors may not all have been terribly encouraging, but they were there. Unlike most other imperial monarchies, the Roman emperorship was not necessarily a unitary institution, even if up to the late third century AD most collegiate reigns had consisted of fathers and sons ruling together as a means of securing the succession.

In 284, nine years after Aurelian's death, Diocles, commander of the then emperor Numerian's imperial guard, was declared emperor by the troops upon his master's murder. He went on to defeat Carinus, Numerian's brother, in battle, thus becoming the sole emperor by the now time-honoured right of conquest, and changed his name to Diocletianus, by which he is better known to history. Sensibly drawing the conclusion that the dynastic principle was not necessarily the best means of securing a stable succession or a good ruler, he appointed his capable and loyal comrade in arms Maximian to be his fellow emperor. This was a significant innovation, and an important answer to the hydra-like problems faced by an empire which required that more than one emperor be available at any one time to meet the military challenges on the frontiers.

If then two emperors, why not three? So, it seems, thought Carausius, a powerful naval commander in the English Channel from the Low Countries, who either declared himself or was declared emperor probably in 286, the year after Maximian's appointment. Under his sway fell Britain and much of northern Gaul. No doubt Carausius' proclamation as emperor was at least partly a regional response to the external problems faced by the province of Britain as well as an audacious move by an ambitious individual. The motivation underlying many of these proclamations of imperial status on behalf of one general or another was that only an emperor could save the

Romans from catastrophe and restore their fortunes. The crisis, perceived or real, demanded the quality of charismatic leadership which only an emperor could provide, and the armies got what they wanted.

The difference between Carausius and Maximian was, of course, that Diocletian had not co-opted him. The rank of emperor need not be restricted to one man, but neither could there be an infinite number of incumbents. To assert the point Maximian attempted to dislodge Carausius from his island realm in 289 or 290 – even the outlines of these events are extremely unclear – but he seems to have failed disastrously. Despite Carausius' success, his position was no doubt vulnerable to internal as well as further external assault, because of his obvious failure to gain recognition of his position from the two emperors on the continent. There is some suggestion that they may have agreed to leave him alone for the moment, on the grounds that he was at least successfully defending Britain from barbarian assault. But there was never any public acknowledgement from them of Carausius' imperial claim. He eventually fell foul of this persistent insecurity in 293 when, probably after the loss of his continental possessions which were centred on Boulogne, he was murdered and succeeded by his financial minister, Allectus, who perhaps thought himself, or was thought by others, more capable of either withstanding or reaching an accommodation with Diocletian and Maximian. The apparent coincidence of Carausius' demise with a further reorganization of the imperial office by Diocletian in 293 may also be significant. In that year he divided the whole empire in two halves under an Augustus, Maximian in the west and himself in the east, each assisted by a deputy with the title Caesar. Two talented commanders called Constantius and Galerius were appointed and adopted by their respective seniors. This was a clearly articulated system, known to historians as the Tetrarchy, which met the need for a sharing of the imperial burden but which also excluded Carausius. His luck had run out. Allectus' own would not last much longer. In 296 Constantius invaded, reannexed Britain and secured the death of Allectus.[9]

We know precious little about Carausius himself, or the events of his reign. The historical sources are poor and thoroughly biased against him. But the designs on his coins, which have been found in some numbers in Britain and France, give us clues as to how he attempted to turn himself into a convincing emperor in the eyes of his subjects and his would-be colleagues on the continent. Ancient coin types should probably not be interpreted as the ancient equivalent of propaganda, on the uncertain assumption that they were designed primarily to convey a persuasive message about the

Base-silver 'radiate' of Carausius, Roman usurper
emperor in Britain and Gaul (*c.* AD 286–93), showing his
bust together with those of his reluctant colleagues on
the continent, Diocletian and Maximian. (× 1.5)

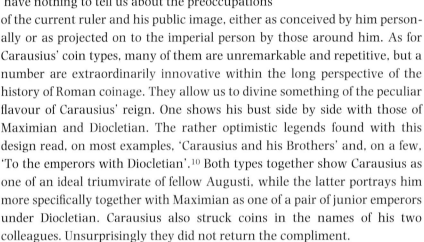

emperor depicted on the front to the mass of the
coin-using population. But that is not to say that they
have nothing to tell us about the preoccupations
of the current ruler and his public image, either as conceived by him person-
ally or as projected on to the imperial person by those around him. As for
Carausius' coin types, many of them are unremarkable and repetitive, but a
number are extraordinarily innovative within the long perspective of the
history of Roman coinage. They allow us to divine something of the peculiar
flavour of Carausius' reign. One shows his bust side by side with those of
Maximian and Diocletian. The rather optimistic legends found with this
design read, on most examples, 'Carausius and his Brothers' and, on a few,
'To the emperors with Diocletian'.[10] Both types together show Carausius as
one of an ideal triumvirate of fellow Augusti, while the latter portrays him
more specifically together with Maximian as one of a pair of junior emperors
under Diocletian. Carausius also struck coins in the names of his two
colleagues. Unsurprisingly they did not return the compliment.

If legitimate colleagueship was one important context in which Carausius'
image was promoted – understandable given the uncertainty of his actual
position – another, equally significant, was that of Roman revivalism. This
northern European who ruled a restricted realm on the far peripheries of the

Bronze medallion of Carausius with
the enigmatic inscription INPCDA legible
beneath the chariot.

Silver *denarius* of Carausius
showing the emperor
(right) being greeted by the
personification of the
province of Britannia.
The legend reads 'Come, O
long-expected one'. (× 1.5)

empire was proclaimed on his coins as saviour and conqueror not just of Britain, but of the whole empire. In part this is just run-of-the-mill stuff for Roman emperors. They had to be world-conquerors almost by virtue of their station. But Carausius' coins and medallions are out of the ordinary. One famous, and unique, example shows the goddess Victory in a chariot with, below, an enigmatic legend unparalleled on Roman coins elsewhere: INPCDA. Archaeologist Guy de la Bédoyère has only recently deciphered it as representing the initial letters of the words from a line of one of the poet Virgil's most famous pieces, his fourth *Eclogue.* The theme of this remarkable poem is the predicted birth of a wonder-child who will bring back peace and justice to the world. In Latin the line reads *Iam Nova Progenies Caelo Demittitur Alto* ('Now a new child is sent down from high heaven'). The implication is that the child from on high is Carausius, who through his beneficent rule will restore the blessings of the Golden Age to the world. A similar suggestion is made by an equally unusual coin design which shows Carausius being greeted by a personified figure of Britannia, with the legend *Expectate Veni* ('Come, O long-expected one'). These words are also taken from Virgil, this time from his great epic the *Aeneid,* slightly modified to suit the messianic tone of Carausius' style. Another shows the wolf and twins, Romulus and Remus, the legendary founders of Rome being suckled by a she-wolf, a visual reference to the very foundation of the city and community of the Romans. The accompanying legend reads 'The Restoration of the Romans'.[11] Its clear meaning is that Carausius will take the Romans back to the Golden Age of the beginnings of Rome itself. Many great Romans before Carausius had been hailed as the refounders of Rome, Cicero and Augustus among them. That Carausius was, in an innovative fashion, following in a solid Roman tradition demonstrates how incontrovertibly Roman he was. There was no sense in which his was a breakaway British

Silver *denarius* of Carausius showing Romulus and Remus being suckled by the wolf, one of the most potent of Roman national symbols. The legend reads 'The Restoration of the Romans'. (×1.5)

Silver *denarius* of Carausius showing Oceanus, god of the outer sea. The legend reads 'The bliss of [i.e. caused by] Carausius the emperor'. (×1.5)

Empire, as believed by a former generation of historians. Under him Britain remained Roman and, if the coin types give us any insight, it may even have reasserted its Romanness as a means to resolve its besetting difficulties and cope with the insecurities of the times. One final silver coin design bears a unique image of the sea-god Oceanus. His associations were twofold: he was the benign protector of the seas and of sea-traffic, and therefore of sea-borne trade and commerce, both important features of the universal state of peace characteristic of the Golden Age; he was also, of course, the protector of Carausius' island realm in Britain, the one province of the Roman Empire situated beyond the waters of Ocean.

The range of Carausius' coin-types, many of which are genuinely imaginative within the often rather repetitious stock of Roman coin designs, enables us to form some idea of how his rule and his image were represented, and they present us with a case-study in the manufacture of monarchy under the Roman Empire. Messianism is an important theme. It is not one that we might instinctively associate with the pagan Romans, but the salvation and restoration of the empire and its inhabitants were among the most vital functions of the emperor. He was the crucial figure on whom the stability of the heavens and the cosmos, not merely the earthly empire, depended. If this was a regular aspect of the imperial persona, it was all the more vividly emphasized by usurper emperors such as Carausius whose claim on power was disputed or insecure.

Dynasties, Real and Imagined

What of other tactics adopted by the Roman usurper? Though the emperorship was not completely dynastic, a good pedigree could help. Augustus had the best ancestry of all through Julius Caesar, his adoptive father, whose clan, the Julii, claimed descent from Aeneas the Trojan and his mother, the goddess Venus. Both Caesar and Augustus took this quite seriously. Caesar dedicated a temple to Venus *Genetrix* (the Mother), while Augustus accepted as the crowning celebration of his monarchical rule Virgil's epic poem, the *Aeneid*, which recounted the achievements of his mythical forebear. Others were more circumspect about the value of invented progenitors. The hard-headed Vespasian laughed at those who attempted to trace the origins of his clan, the Flavii, back to a companion of Heracles the demigod. 'It is true, his house was,' as his biographer, Suetonius, frankly admitted, 'obscure and without family portraits, yet it was one of which the Commonwealth had no reason whatsoever to be ashamed' (Suetonius, *Life of Vespasian* I). Here is the characteristic Roman tension between an instinctive respect for noble genealogy and a republican reluctance to exalt it into an all-sufficient merit. Following in Vespasian's footsteps, several individuals rose to the imperial office from very ordinary backgrounds, usually through the army. However, while many of them regarded their humble origins as an irrelevance, others tried to conceal them with invented ancestries produced for them by obliging antiquarians, fawning courtiers or credulous followers. Marius, a briefly-reigning usurper who, according to the collection of (mostly fictional) biographies of the later Roman emperors, the *Historia Augusta*, was a blacksmith elevated to the purple for all of three days before his overthrow in 269, was said to have been descended from Gaius Marius, a famous general and politician of the late republic (Aurelius Victor, *On the Emperors* 33.11), while the mere coincidence of names allowed Tacitus, elected emperor by the Senate in 275 after the death of Aurelian, to be linked with the great Latin historian of the early imperial period (*Historia Augusta, Life of Tacitus* 10).[12] Even Constantine the Great (306–37) manufactured a family relationship with Claudius II Gothicus (268–70), a short-lived but successful emperor of a previous generation, in order to emphasize his hereditary right to the imperial position at a time in the early fourth century when competition for it was particularly intense, this despite the fact that he was anyway the son of the emperor Constantius I Chlorus. An interesting variation on this theme is represented by Zenobia who, probably in 271, assumed the female form of the imperial title, Augusta, while she usurped the imperial position itself for her son Vaballathus. She declared a probably invented descent from Queen Cleopatra of Egypt, her great predecessor as would-be dominatrix of the Orient, as well as from the Seleucid royal dynasty of Hellenistic Syria, both famous enemies from Rome's past. These historical choices were politically significant. Though the titles to which Zenobia laid claim were Roman ones, and the images which appeared on her coins were standard Roman productions, as were the coins themselves, the dynastic heritage to which she resorted was unequivocally eastern and non- if not anti-Roman.

Invented genealogies may often have been little more than a *post eventum* stylistic reflex in the relatively undynastic Roman Empire where less hung on them. But their persistent recurrence suggests that they were useful, if not essential. In other ancient monarchies, genealogical legitimacy was an important prerequisite for inheritance. The kingdoms established by the various Greek successors of Alexander the Great in the different parts of his trans-continental empire in the late fourth century BC were thorough-going dynastic states. The Seleucid dynasty, descended from Seleucus, one of

Alexander's associates who founded a kingdom based on Syria and Babylonia which at its greatest extent stretched from Asia Minor to northern India, continued to reign over an ever-diminishing realm until 64 BC when the two last feuding Seleucids, Antiochus XIII and Philip II, succumbed to the power of Rome in the shape of the all-conquering armies of Pompey the Great. The Seleucids' kingdom had no independent existence apart from the dynasty. It was coterminous with the sway of its current representative, and lasted only as long as the dynasty itself. The Roman Empire by contrast had a life independent of its rulers. Many of its free inhabitants, and all of them from AD 212 onwards, were Roman citizens who continued to identify with such republican, civic notions as *Res Publica Populi Romani* (the Commonwealth of the Roman People), even under the emperors. Hence the relative unimportance of dynasticism among the Romans. In the dynastic kingdoms of the Hellenistic East, individual cities and communities had their own local identities, civic, ethnic and religious. But these tended not to be transformed into stable, empire-wide identities. In consequence, the kingdoms which arose from the empire of Alexander depended much more than the Roman Empire on the continuity and security offered by the dynastic principle, in the absence of other focuses for identity.

The Ptolemaic dynasty which ruled Egypt continuously from 305 to 31 BC is so called because all its male sovereigns took the name Ptolemy (*Ptolemaios* in Greek). The name itself became part of the royal titulature, as would the name Augustus at Rome. Its last representative, Cleopatra VII, attempted to prolong the dynasty, and thereby the autonomy of its kingdom, by contracting unions with the two most prominent Romans of the 40s and 30s BC. Through her son, Ptolemy XV Caesarion ('Little Caesar'), who she alleged was the son of Julius Caesar, and her three children by Mark Antony, she planned a revived Ptolemaic Empire, or even a new empire of Alexander. The great man himself was after all buried in Alexandria, her capital. But it all came to nothing in the waters off Actium in 31 BC, a battle which was as much a clash of dynastic claims as of arms. Octavian, who had been adopted by Julius Caesar in his will, made good his filial rights as the new Caesar, secured the defeat and eventual suicides of Antony and Cleopatra, did away with his potential rival, Caesarion, and added Egypt to the Roman Empire. The ascendancy of the Julian family, itself a characteristically Roman legal fiction rather than a real dynasty, was thus founded on the ruins of the last of the Hellenistic dynastic kingdoms.[13]

One important reason why the Hellenistic kingdoms of the Macedonian Greek empire of Alexander the Great were so strongly dynastic in character lies in the fact of their usurpatory origins. For all of them had begun by violently displacing indigenous ruling houses from their realms, above all the Iranian Achaemenid dynasty which ruled most of Western Asia and Egypt. None of the founding kings of these new territories could claim any dynastic relationship with Alexander himself. So in a sense they were doubly usurpers, pretending to be the successors to Alexander and also the legitimate kings (*basileis* in Greek) of their respective portions of his empire. The *Suda*, a Byzantine lexicon, reveals the truth about the foundation of the Hellenistic successor monarchies in its entry on kingship (*basileia*):

> It is neither descent (*physis*) nor legitimacy (*dikē*) which gives kingship to men, but the ability to command an army and handle affairs competently. Such was the case with Philip and the successors of Alexander. For Alexander's natural son was in no way helped by his kinship with him because of his weakness of spirit. While those who had no connection with Alexander became kings of almost the whole inhabited world.

This is a good description of how Alexander's generals transformed themselves from governors, or satraps, of particular provinces within his empire into autonomous monarchs after his death. But it is not quite the whole story. While military and political competence were certainly what enabled the successors to take and keep power in the first generation, it was precisely descent and the legitimacy which it granted to the kings' designated successors that became the critical factors in determining who should inherit in the second generation and thereafter. These new kingdoms had been founded by charismatic individuals who identified in dynasticism a mechanism to prevent another candidate from following their example. In Rome too, Vespasian and other emperors attempted to pass the succession on to their children for very much the same reasons. But while Roman dynasties usually lasted little more than a couple of generations at most, the two great Hellenistic dynasties, the Seleucids and the Ptolemies, endured a good two and a half centuries. The reason for this success might be sought in their Macedonian roots and in the royal traditions of the areas over which they came to rule, in Egypt, Mesopotamia, Iran and Asia Minor. For in all these cultural contexts, dynastic monarchies had been the norm before the establishment of the successor kingdoms. This was emphatically not the case in Republican Rome before Augustus, which made a difference.

In the successor kingdoms, then, the successful implementation of violence was the necessary preliminary to the usurpation of monarchy, as the *Suda* makes clear, but the dynastic principle was essential to its effective maintenance. Dynasties operate to cover up the secret of their own, usually

(*Right*) Silver tetradrachm of Seleucus I, showing the goddess Athena in a chariot drawn by four elephants, with an anchor, symbol of Seleucus' divine paternity, above. (×1.5)

(*Far right*) Silver tetradrachm of Ptolemy I, king of Egypt and founder of the Ptolemaic dynasty (305–282 BC).

violent, rise to power by projecting an image of divinely guided changeless-ness and stability from one generation to the next, in order to transform kingship from the rule of an arbitrary succession of monarchical strongmen into a settled family business. To deal with the potentially problematic issue of their own seizure of power, first-generation usurpers will often pretend to some sort of royal connection, in order to minimize the psychological rupture among their subjects entailed by the necessary transfer of loyalties from the old dynasty to the new. Legend turned Ptolemy into the half-brother of Alexander. Better yet, divine paternity. An inscription from the reign of his descendant Ptolemy III (246–221 BC) proclaims his descent from Zeus on both sides of the family via the gods Heracles and Dionysus.[14] It was widely claimed that Seleucus was the son of Apollo, as proof of which he and his descendants all bore a birthmark in the shape of an anchor, a motif that duly appeared on Seleucid coins.

Ritual and ceremonial also played their part in cementing the idea of the new king in the minds of his people. They were doubly important for the Macedonian successor kings, who had not merely supplanted a former imperial dynasty, the Persian Achaemenids, but were also ruling over alien peoples with whom they had little in common. Hellenistic royal patronage of indigenous religious cults and rituals opened up an important channel of communication with these subject populations, who were thus able to come to terms with the possibly rather unattractive idea of the new dynasty as their rightful rulers, and comfort themselves with the notion that they must have been the gods' choice. Among a previous generation of historians it was generally thought that the Hellenistic Greeks held themselves rather aloof from their barbarian subjects in Western Asia and Egypt, and from their cultures and religions. More recent investigations have revealed that this was far from the case. Perhaps the most famous surviving inscription from the ancient world, the Rosetta Stone, as well as being the key to the decipherment of Egyptian scripts, is also an important record of the crowning of Ptolemy V (204–180 BC) at the traditional Egyptian religious centre of Memphis by the priests of the native Egyptian god Ptah. This seems

The Rosetta Stone, dated to 196 BC, written in Greek and two Egyptian scripts, hieroglyphic and demotic. It details the increased patronage by King Ptolemy V Epiphanes of the Egyptian religious centre of Memphis. This was a means of legitimating his foreign rule in the face of prolonged native revolts.

The Cyrus Cylinder, a clay foundation inscription which emphasizes the support given to King Cyrus of Persia by Marduk, the great god of Babylon, in his conquest of the city in 539 BC.

to be the first time that a member of the Greek Ptolemaic dynasty had participated in indigenous coronation rituals in this way. It appears to have been an attempt to cultivate native sentiment during a prolonged period of rebellion involving the proclamation of two ethnically Egyptian pretender-pharaohs, Haronnophris and Chaonnophris.[15] Inscriptions on clay tablets surviving from Babylon reveal that the successors of Seleucus participated in its religious ceremonies, including the New Year festival which celebrated the cosmic victory of the god Marduk over primeval chaos. They also restored the god's great temple in Babylon, Esagila. In this they were merely following in the footsteps of any number of Babylonian kings in previous centuries, those who succeeded by inheritance as well as usurpers and invaders, including Alexander the Great himself. The performance of these actions was in and of itself a persuasive indication of legitimate kingship.

In Babylonia, Seleucus' son and successor Antiochus I patronized the cults of the ancient cities of the region. In a building inscription from Borsippa near Babylon dated to 268 BC, Antiochus prays to the god Nabu, son of Marduk, that he will 'regard me joyfully and, at your lofty command, which is unchanging, may the overthrow of the countries of my enemies, the achievement of my battle-wishes against my enemies, permanent victories, just kingship, a happy reign, years of joy, children in satiety, be your gift for the kingship of Antiochus and Seleucus, the king, his son, for ever'. Antiochus associated himself closely with the gods of his new kingdom, as had another foreign conqueror of Babylonia before him, Cyrus the Great, founder of the Persian Empire of the Achaemenid dynasty. On the famous 'Cyrus Cylinder' in the British Museum, Cyrus identified the divine protection of Marduk as the reason for his successful conquest of Babylon in 539 BC.

Like Cyrus before them, the Seleucids knew how to use the ritual language of religion to help them transcend cultural, ethnic and historical barriers and win recognition as the rightful and divinely blessed successors of the ancient kings of Babylon, who stretched back into the third millennium BC. The unlucky victim of Cyrus' conquest was King Nabonidus, who had himself usurped the kingship in a violent coup in 556 BC. A clutch of inscriptions from his reign reveal how he too exploited the power of religion and antiquity, restoring ancient temples and the statues of past kings, including one of Sargon I (2340–2284 BC), the famous king of Agade who, according to the stories told about his rise to power, was also a usurper and one of the greatest kings in Mesopotamian history. This history was already unimaginably long by the time of Alexander's conquest. Sargon was after

Relief showing Nabonidus, usurper king of Babylon (556–539 BC), presenting him as the true and pious successor of the ancient kings of Babylon.

all two thousand years his predecessor. So by the time of Seleucus' takeover in the late fourth century BC, there was a fairly well-established procedure for budding usurpers to follow, such that they merely added another layer to the constantly reworked, and renewed, palimpsest that was the local tradition of kingship.[16]

All these kings naturally had the willing co-operation of the priests of the great god Marduk, in whose interests it certainly was to guarantee a smooth transfer of power from one king to another, despite the political difficulties of the moment. Kings came and went, but the god and his great temple complex of Esagila in the city of Babylon remained, growing ever richer on the largesse bestowed upon them by each successive monarch, usurpers above all, in return for the ritual orchestration of the god's blessing. And if the king turned out not to be the god's favourite, the priests would of course collaborate in the ritual damnation of his memory by the new ruler. The god and his priests in Babylon played the pivotal role of validating royal power which in Rome was performed by the Senate and people. They were not themselves able to propel into power individuals who did not have the support of other important constituencies within the community, nor could they long withhold their blessing from a candidate of whatever background who did. Nevertheless, these enduring institutions provided the stability which underpinned their respective communities' political identity and, in a sense, created a safe space within which violent civil war between rival pretenders to the throne and bloody usurpation could take place without shaking the whole framework to its foundations. Rome, Babylon, and Egypt for that matter, survived any number of rebels and pretenders for, though their monarchies were to varying degrees dynastic in character, Rome less, Babylon and Egypt perhaps more, they were not dependent on dynasties for their existence. The Seleucid realm, by contrast, was nothing without the royal family that brought it into being. The god Marduk could be enlisted by the Seleucids in their capacity as kings of Babylon, as doubtless were other local gods in other parts of their empire, but over its whole sprawling expanse there was no single political or religious institution that could provide the kind of universal validation offered by the Senate within the Roman Empire. The Seleucid Empire was thus faced with the awkward challenge of having no other source of sustenance available to it than its ruling dynasty, hence perhaps its very durability. Yet the inevitable consequence was that as the Seleucids' military fortunes waned against rival empires over the last two centuries BC, Rome in the west and Parthia in the east, so did the borders of their realm contract like a deflated balloon. There was little that Marduk could do about it. By the time of the fall of the last Seleucids in 64 BC, he had other matters to attend to. Babylon had passed out of their control in the mid-second century BC, and into that of the Parthians.

The nature of rebellion, pretendership and usurpation in the ancient world was determined very much by the historical character of the monarchy and community within which it took place. For not all monarchies are alike or develop in the same ways, even ones sprung from the same root. The northern Hebrew kingdom of Israel changed its dynasties, underwent rebellions and accepted usurpers as kings, while the southern kingdom of Judah, though it experienced periodic upheavals, remained wedded to the succession of the House of David throughout its existence, from the separation of the kingdoms in about 924 BC to the destruction of Jerusalem by King Nebuchadnezzar of Babylon in 587 BC. Where the dynastic idea is the principle determining succession to the throne and guaranteeing the existence of the state, usurpers and pretenders, or would-be revivalists, must either belong to, or be insinuated into, the dominant family tree. So in ancient Israel again, the hope of the restoration of the line of David never left the Jewish imagination and, for some at least, it found fulfilment in the person of Jesus, whose birth in Bethlehem, the city of David, and descent from David are carefully rehearsed in the Gospels.[17] In a later generation the rebel Jewish leader Simon Bar Kokhba also probably had Davidic descent attributed to him. A self-declared prince (*nasi*) of Israel, he was recognized as the Anointed One, the messiah, by the great Rabbi Akiva, and as such led his people in a disastrous revolt against the Romans (AD 132–5).[18] Where the dynastic idea is less dominant, as at Rome, flattering genealogies may be manufactured after the event by the new monarch's entourage, but they are not essential to his position. Pretenders must simply make good their claim by force, which will usually be enough to ensure that the necessary traditional forms of legitimation, political and religious, are ascribed to them.

It is all at bottom a question of different kinds of communal identity: whether the identity of a state or a community is so closely bound up with the ruling family that it cannot conceive of itself governed by a different one, or whether there are other salient focuses of attention and loyalty within its mental horizons. If the latter, the pretender has greater scope to establish himself within the minds of the population, or at least of those that matter, as the best, and therefore the rightful, defender of its sacred and civic traditions. Let us now test the historical validity of these general laws of monarchical pretendership in antiquity by looking at later worlds and other contexts, in medieval Europe and beyond.

Chapter 2

Kings and Pretenders

In AD 476 Rome fell to Odoacer, who ruled Italy not as emperor, or in any imperial post, but as king, the position he already held in relation to his own Germanic followers. In 493 Odoacer was defeated by the Ostrogothic leader Theoderic, who was likewise a king.[1] Neither ruler had any desire to destroy the civic traditions and governmental structure of Rome, and both had a working relationship with the eastern half of the Roman empire at Constantinople. Thus while allowing their noble Roman subjects to carry on serving as consuls, they recognized that many still regarded a Roman emperor as the only source of legitimacy for this office and permitted the consuls to seek recognition each year from the eastern emperor. Yet Odoacer and Theoderic were not vassals of the eastern emperor and their own position could not be fitted anywhere in the existing hierarchy.

The importance of their advent to power was that it put an end to the formal unity of the world centred on Rome. It had long been only a *formal* unity, of course. The empire had been divided in two for nearly two centuries, a division that had begun as a merely administrative separation of the still unitary imperial authority, but had gradually widened to create two distinct empires. Furthermore, the area covered by the two empires had diminished, making it ever less possible to ignore the world beyond. But the theory of an empire that was both united and all-encompassing remained; it was a world-monarchy, in which the name of the inhabitants, Romans, no longer referred to Italians or Greeks or any other ethnic group, but to the citizens of the empire.

After 476 Odoacer, Theoderic and their successors prevented Rome from continuing to belong to this world-monarchy, though in cultural terms the nobles clearly still regarded themselves as its citizens. The kingdom of Italy was merely one of many Germanic kingdoms being carved out of the western

Proclaimed king by his army on 23 August 476, Odoacer (seen here bareheaded on a silver half *siliqua* of the 470s) did not bother to replace the emperor he had ousted, and initially sought authority from the eastern emperor to govern Italy on his behalf. (×2)

half of the empire. It could not possibly be seen as, and made no claims to be, a successor state to Rome. What was the source of authority in this post-imperial world, and what distinguished the true sovereign from the false?

Universal Emperors and Subordinate Kings

One response to the defeat or loss of a unifying authority is to look around for its replacement. The notion of successive dominant monarchies was an old one even by the time of Rome's advent on the world stage, let alone by her departure from it; we have already touched on it in the first chapter. In Daniel 2.31–45 the prophet Daniel interpreted Nebuchadnezzar's dream of the metal statue as a vision of the four great monarchies, of which the first was Babylon. Rome, far from being one of the monarchies represented in the body of the statue, was taken by some as being the vast and everlasting rock by which it was destroyed. Other powers were able to incorporate themselves into the series: Achaemenid Persia, which captured Babylon; the Macedonian-led empire of Alexander, which brought Persia to an end; Hellenistic Syria and Egypt, which divided up much of Alexander's empire between them. There is a messianic flavour to many of these beliefs, for central to the notion of a world-monarchy is world peace, though frequently it is represented as being arrived at only after a period of great destruction and carnage.

Rome was received naturally and easily into this view of history. Hellenistic monarchs, beset by internecine strife and disputes over succession, even saw her as a saviour, and between 155 and 74 BC five kings bequeathed or tried to bequeath their kingdoms (or parts thereof) to the Roman people. The reign of Augustus, with its rhetoric of imposing world-wide peace, brought the doctrine of *translatio imperii*, the successive transfer of unitary power, to the forefront.[2]

The fall of Rome in 476 did not impinge on the ability of the eastern half of the empire to continue to fill this rôle for centuries to come. In fact many would argue that Constantinople, refounded by Constantine as 'Nea Roma' or New Rome in 324, had already been filling it for some time. But it was hard for the eastern empire to fulfil the spiritual dimension that the Christian vision of its founder required of it; not only was the Pope, head of the church, firmly established in Rome but, increasingly, much of Christendom lay beyond the eastern emperor's control. Nor could the Pope carry the burden of a temporal ruler, as shown by the fact that when the Lombards threatened Rome in the late eighth century Adrian I had to turn to the Franks under

Charlemagne for help. This did not prevent the papacy from claiming temporal power – the forged 'Donation of Constantine', purporting to bestow territorial rule on the Popes, probably dates from this period – but the difficulty of achieving it drove Adrian's successor, Leo III, to an extraordinary act: on Christmas day, 800, he crowned Charlemagne emperor in Rome. The meaning of this event has of course been subject to interminable discussion, since it is essentially obscure, but it is highly likely that Leo wished in some way to reunite universal temporal and spiritual authority, if not in one person, then at least in two closely associated ones, with the temporal ruler acting by authority of the spiritual one.

The unity was not to last. The later Carolingians failed to maintain the idea that their authority derived from the Pope, and in the first half of the tenth century a series of Italian nobles were crowned emperors instead. Thus began the long tug of war between Pope and emperor that lasted until

The arms of the emperor (left) and the Pope, from a 15th-century German manuscript. Medieval and Renaissance heraldry expresses well the imagined continuity of the ancient and contemporary empires, ascribing the double-headed eagle to the timeless figure of 'the emperor', whether Julius Caesar or Maximilian of Habsburg.

the start of the nineteenth century. One of the lowest points was the dispute between the popes and the Hohenstaufen emperors, resulting in a series of anti-popes, sponsored by the latter, in the mid-twelfth century; but there were many other conflicts, and even the denomination of the western empire as the 'Holy Roman Empire' can be seen as a counterblast to the claims of the Holy Church.[3]

The ideal of a single focus for both spiritual and temporal unity was not unique to the west. In the Islamic east the caliphs, temporal and spiritual rulers, were the designated 'successors' of the Prophet Muhammad, and at first it was clear that there could only be one, who from 750 was a member of the 'Abbasid dynasty based in Baghdad. The tenth century, however, saw this unity strongly challenged. First, in 909, the Fatimids of North Africa began to call themselves caliphs. Then, twenty years later, a similar move was made by the Umayyad dynasty of al-Andalus in Spain. The Umayyads had been ousted from Baghdad and the caliphate by the 'Abbasids in 750 and for almost two centuries, while refusing to acknowledge the 'Abbasids as caliphs, they abstained from assuming the title themselves. This changed in 929 when 'Abd al-Rahman III issued an edict that he be recognized as caliph in traditional style. This western caliphate did not itself last beyond the early eleventh century, but it opened the door to many other such claims. By the early modern period the unity of the institution had fragmented beyond repair, and eventually the word *khalifa* came to be applied not only to the great Islamic sovereigns, but also to relatively lowly religious leaders. Its last and most original usage in this context was in the course of the Mahdist revolt in the Sudan in the 1880s, when it was bestowed both on the Mahdi's prominent adjutants and on local leaders, prompting in turn a wave of still more humble pretenders to the title.[4]

By the Middle Ages the appropriate title in the west for the holder of over-arching temporal power was, where there was a linguistic distinction, that of emperor. For the Greeks the King of Persia had been 'the Great King' or, more simply, 'the King'; in his own language he had been 'King of Kings'. Alexander and his Hellenistic successors had just been kings. But Rome had no taste for kingship; kings were minor potentates, usually barbarians and with something ridiculous about them. Augustus had needed to find another title, that of *princeps*, or first citizen, though his names of Augustus and Caesar soon overshadowed this less resonant invention. The *princeps* ruled over an *imperium* or unitary block of authority, which might encompass within it vassal kings and other subordinates, and in accordance with this his military title of *imperator* or commander came to be used for the supreme position. From *imperium* and *imperator* derive 'empire' and 'emperor'.

'Emperor' was not the only appropriate title. In the Greek-speaking parts of the world the Greek *basileus* (king) had been widely used for the Roman emperor, and so it continued under Byzantine power, a situation that could give rise to confusion when it came to talking about barbarian kings in the west.[5] But even in the west itself the phraseology was far from rigid. Some early Holy Roman Emperors (described in their titulature as Augustus or Caesar) could be referred to as kings of the Romans, a title which later was applied only to the designated heir.

By the ninth century, however, if not before, a clear hierarchy had been settled, with emperors senior to kings. This was an arrangement that seems to fit admirably with the theory of the feudal system as it developed in the high and later Middle Ages, whereby many kings actually held their lands from higher authorities, or at any rate acknowledged greater authority than their own. As if to emphasize the point, kings who held two or more distinct kingdoms, or claimed that they were no one's vassal (and particularly not that of the Holy Roman Emperor or the Pope), sometimes called themselves emperors: thus Alfonso VII of Galicia and Castile is said to have adopted the imperial crown and title in the twelfth century; and the Act of Supremacy of 1534, whereby Henry VIII became head of the Church of England, refers to that realm as an empire and to its crown as an imperial one, meaning no more and no less than that it was a sovereign state at the summit of its own feudal system, rather than held from some higher ruler.[6]

In claims of this nature as much pretence and imposture could be exercised as lower down the scale. It cannot be doubted that the long-term effect of the notion that an empire was just a fully independent sovereign state contributed to a general inflation of titles, by which their circulation

Bronze medal of Agustín, emperor of Mexico from May 1822 to December 1823, and his wife Ana. Of partly native descent, Agustín Iturbide resembles somewhat the local, rebel emperors of the late Roman world, save for the vital fact that as emperor of Mexico he was instituting a new empire.

increased and their worth diminished. The application of the imperial title to the more fabulously powerful non-European rulers encountered, such as those in China, northern India or (while they lasted) central America, no doubt pegged its value quite high for a while. But it is interesting that the nineteenth century saw the title gain currency both in Europe (where the end of the Holy Roman Empire in 1806 gave birth to two new empires, that of Napoleon and the empire of Austria) and as a designation for the large overseas possessions of the colonial powers, whether ruled by the colonizing country's monarch (as in the case of India) or separately by a member of the same family (as in Brazil). No doubt some sense of sympathy with both these trends, combined with more than a glance towards the indigenous history of the region, made Agustín Iturbide, leader of the successful 'Army of the Three Guarantees' which wrested independence for bourgeois Mexico, style himself emperor (and the 'New Montezuma') shortly after gaining power in 1822. Iturbide's empire was short-lived, but it did mean that Napoleon III had more than the Brazilian precedent and his own when installing Maximilian of Austria at the head of Mexico's second empire in 1864. In Europe the continued usage afforded the title was seen by the creation of the last new empire in the west, that of Germany, established on the basis of the Prussian monarchy after the Franco-Prussian War in 1870.[7]

The fluidity of a world in which empires can be created so easily and with regard to such different circumstances as has been the case contrasts notably with the ancient approach. The proliferation of the supreme designation has, furthermore, gone hand in hand with uncertainty in the application of the lesser ones. It is a fact that seems obvious to us, but which would have struck antiquity as odd, that a sovereign power can use what designation it chooses for its ruler. Without a unitary, over-arching empire,

Silver scudo of Teodoro, King of Corsica (Theodore von Neuhoff: see frontispiece), 1736. Theodore's crudely struck coinage, showing a distorted version of the arms of Corsica, was widely counterfeited in Italy, the forgeries frequently being better than the true pieces.

even notionally, there can be no superior arbiter in these matters. Certainly some cases, such as that of Theodore von Neuhoff, the adventuring 'King of Corsica', strike the hind-sighted observer as straining the definition of regal status somewhat. But had he been – implausible as it may seem – a success, he would have been neither the first nor the last king to originate as a rebel leader.[8]

Feudal Fragments

Whereas maps of modern Europe show large, distinct blocks of unalloyed nationhood, the medieval political map is a variegated patchwork, attempting to encode by means of colour, hatching, intricate fractal lines and broad, all-encompassing borders a confusing system of allegiances and diverse degrees of autonomy. This dichotomy is of course enhanced by the nature of the political map, a creature of the modern age, to which it is therefore better suited. Recent historical atlases have to a certain extent given up trying to plot the Middle Ages in terms of national units, drawing instead the larger and more uniform patterns of cultural, religious and political influence. This undoubtedly has its benefits, but it is also a loss, and not only because of the fascinating beauty of political maps of Germany under Frederick Barbarossa, for instance, or France and the Holy Roman Empire in the late fifteenth century. By using a modern idiom to describe a pre-modern age, however inarticulately, they made the differences between our world and the one described plainly visible.

In this world kings stood towards, but not necessarily at, the summit of a pyramid of power. Below them were many local lords of varying rank, some of whom might stand at a different relative position in respect of different parts of their land. Developed feudalism, both in England and on the continent, seems to present a continuum of authority from the lowest feudatory to the highest landgrave or margrave, duke or even prince. Church lands, often ruled over like mini-states with bishops or abbots taking the part of the prince, and free cities owning the authority of the empire and no intermediate lord, complicate the picture further. Where, in such a world, does mere land ownership merge into sovereignty? How can one spot the upstart nobleman or feudal baron who usurps a sovereign position when the world is full of subject kings?

Distinctions were in fact preserved in many ways, preventing the feudal system from looking entirely like a set of Russian dolls, with nested elements identical in all but scale. In England, for example, the theory is that all land was ultimately held of the king. In certain clearly demarcated areas – the Palatine counties of Chester, Lancaster and Durham – the king devolved certain regal powers and attributes to the local landowner: the Earl of Chester, the Duke of Lancaster, the Bishop of Durham. In these areas, for instance, landowners who held directly of the local devolved authority were feudal 'barons', in the same way that in the rest of England a feudal baron was one who held of the king. The palatine counties were, therefore, to some extent like little kingdoms, one of the reasons that the duchy of Lancaster became such a contested title in the Middle Ages and was ultimately kept by the sovereign for himself. But these were clearly marked-out exceptions. In the main the king's functions in a feudal society made him not just paramount, but qualitatively unique. 'Regalian' right over the church, for instance, whereby in the vacancy of a bishopric the king took over certain ecclesiastical functions and – more willingly, perhaps – the see's income, was specific to the king and in England at least did not apply to lesser lords: the bishops derived from the king not only their lands but their episcopal status. Even before the Reformation one of the features of the sovereign was that he was a meeting-point between church and state.[9]

Even so, the power and autonomy of many medieval lordships – in essence no more than landownership received from the Crown, bolstered by Crown-granted privileges – would strike modern Europeans as sitting uncomfortably with the sovereignty of the nation state. Those few great lordships that did survive into the early modern world were in the main reformed or reclaimed by the sovereign, while those that continue to exist do so very much on sufferance. The Isle of Man, for instance, was a sovereign lordship held directly of the Crown and not constituting part of the realm

Isle of Man penny, 1733, showing the badge of the island on the obverse (the *triskeles* or three conjoined legs) and the crest of the Stanleys, Earls of Derby, on the reverse (the eagle and child).

Modern Manx coins are identical in form and value to their mainland British counterparts. Though their reverse designs are distinctive (this one-pound coin seems to show a mobile telephone), they owe nothing to the island's feudal past.

The Stanleys were not the only claimants to the sovereignty of Man. Seen here, an 18th-century print of Anna Quarl, a 'poor mad woman of Douglas Isle of Man who fancies herself queen of the island'.

of England or Great Britain until 1765, when it was purchased from the last lord (the Duchess of Atholl) for £70,000 and a life annuity. It remains outside the United Kingdom and thus all bodies (such as the European Community) of which the UK is a member, but its allegiance is not questioned now that it shares the UK's sovereign: it might have been very different if the lordship had remained as it was, as the subordination of one minor sovereign to a major one is something with which modern international law would have had a hard time coping.[10]

As it is there are many hazards left by the feudal period for modern Europeans to get to grips with, many anomalies to delight and entertain. One of these arises from the nature of landownership. The importance of real property in the English common law, deriving from the feudal system of tenure, is reflected in the popular maxim that 'an Englishman's home is his castle'. If this relates to anything in the law at all, it means little more than that a property holder can exclude all-comers from it, thus giving him the semblance of sovereignty over his holding.

It is, of course, only the *semblance* of sovereignty. Behaving as if it were the real thing, in the modern world, is a definite error. Many small and remote geographical entities have toyed with ideas of independence, investing their local functionaries with grandiloquent titles. The island of Bardsey off North Wales, for instance, has a curious and not entirely clear history of electing kings; but the island's owners, the Lords Newborough, were never part of the game and it thus never escalated beyond a fierce and slightly unfriendly attitude to outsiders. When a landowner joins in, or initiates the claim, things can get out of hand. The best case from the British Isles is that of Lundy. Between 1883 and 1916 this small island off the north coast of Devon belonged to a clergyman called Hudson Grossett Heaven, who argued that it did not form part of England, to which it accordingly owed no taxes and from which it derived no political obligations or benefits. The basis for his claims, which inevitably led to the island being referred to as the Kingdom of Heaven, appears to have been no more than the fact that it was uncertain which mainland county, poor-law union and parliamentary constituency it belonged to.

In 1920, however, Lundy was acquired by one Martin Coles Harman; he had big plans for the island, which he hoped to regenerate agriculturally and economically, and indeed for himself. These gradually inflated, and in 1929 he declared his property an independent state within the British Empire, with himself as its ruler. Postage stamps and coins were issued, both denominated in 'puffins' (the island's main sea-bird). This was a mistake. The 1870 Coinage Act, a re-enactment of earlier measures

Brass coin (denominated 'one puffin') produced by Martin Coles Harman of Lundy, 1929.

(*Right*) Lundy postage stamp produced by Harman, 1929.

(*Far right*) Lundy postage stamp, 1992.

all embodying a common-law rule, forbade the minting of coinage other than on the sovereign's behalf and with the sovereign's effigy. He was tried at Bideford Petty Sessions, found guilty and fined £5. It was a salutary lesson.[11]

The production of stamps, however, went ahead, and has from time to time been taken up again. Postage stamps are not currency; they are merely labels to show that postage has been paid and ensure safe carriage. They can of course be used in a quasi-monetary fashion, rather like the tradesmen's tokens that the law has always allowed, but their production has never been considered part and parcel of sovereign rights in the same way as coinage. So tourists visiting Lundy today may still affix a local stamp to their postcard home; this will ensure its safe passage to the mainland. If they want it to travel further, they must add a stamp with the Queen's head.

A slightly different example of the misunderstanding of feudal tenure is provided by the so-called principality of Seborga. Seborga is a village of between 350 and 400 inhabitants in the province of Imperia, in the northern Italian region of Liguria. In 1963 it elected a prince, one Giorgio Carbone, and declared independence from Italy. This was not an entirely arbitrary act: Carbone had persuaded the villagers, on the basis of research he had done, that Seborga had been an independent principality within the Holy Roman Empire, and that its independence had never been lawfully surrendered at any stage thereafter, though it had been overlooked. Prince Giorgio I still rules, and though his principality has yet to receive recognition from the Italian republic or any other significant nation, it has in recent years achieved a higher profile than ever before in his reign. Prince Giorgio's account of Seborgan history as related in the press and on the inevitable national website is on first perusal somewhat suspect – to say the least. Seborga was apparently a fief of the Counts of Ventimiglia granted in 954 to the Benedictine (later Cistercian) monastery at Lérins. In 1079 it became, as aforesaid, a 'principality' within the empire, with an abbot-prince. Later, like Lérins, it adopted the stricter rule of the White Friars, and

One 'luigino' coin minted for the 'principality' of Seborga, with the distinguished profile of Prince Giorgio on the obverse. The arms consist of a white cross on a blue shield, better known as those of the kingdom of Greece.

remained a 'Cistercian state' until 1729, when it was sold to Vittorio Amedeo II of Savoy, King of Sardinia. Prince Giorgio contests the validity of this sale, and argues that Seborga was accordingly never incorporated into the kingdom of Sardinia, the unified kingdom of Italy, or the latter's modern successor state.[12]

As told the story bears considerable similarities to the 1949 Ealing film comedy *Passport to Pimlico*, in which the researches of a resident of Pimlico in Westminster reveal that the area was ceded to the duchy of Burgundy in the Middle Ages. It is then argued that since Burgundy no longer exists, Pimlico must be independent. A declaration of independence, or at any rate secession, from the United Kingdom, is met by the latter taking the equally logical step of cutting off provision of all supplies, on the grounds that services of that sort are not provided for foreign countries.

The residents of Pimlico might have had a leg to stand on if the document they had found really showed that the area had been ceded to the Duke of Burgundy to form part of his duchy. This is admittedly an unlikely thing to imagine. A far more probable reconstruction – to continue the game for a moment – is that the manor of Pimlico was ceded to the duke, to hold of the English king, in the same way as anyone else might hold it. The film crystal-lizes a classic instance of the modern misunderstanding whereby medieval tenure is confused with sovereignty, particularly frequent when the tenant is a sovereign.

In fact the Duke of Burgundy was only arguably a sovereign; he was actually a vassal of the King of France. But one can easily posit another case. From 1124 to 1136 and from 1157 to 1174 the King of Scotland was also Earl of Huntingdon in England, holding large estates in baronial tenure from the English king. This does not mean that those estates were part of Scotland, though Scotland was undoubtedly a sovereign power. To return to the case of Seborga, it is likely that the sale of the village to the King of Sardinia had nothing to do with any claimed independence of the village, but was merely part of the general selling-off of monastic estates which occurred in Italy in the eighteenth century. The 'independence' itself was probably no more than the recognition of certain immunities and privileges by the feudal overlord, as appropriate for monastic property. Seborga's national allegiance doubtless followed that of the region in which it stood.

It is easy to see why the idea of an autonomous Seborga has struck some as plausible. Italy has at least two small independent countries within its borders – San Marino and the Holy See – and arguably a third, the head-quarters of the Military Order of Malta in Rome. Not far into France is the principality of Monaco. The histories of some of these entities may not bear that close a scrutiny; whether San Marino was truly independent of papal and seigneurial authority at all times in the last eight hundred years is questionable, and its national myth of perpetual liberty from the year 301 is certainly impossible to maintain.[13] It might therefore be argued that, even if Seborga is founded on a misunderstanding or a deliberate fudge, it nevertheless has as much right to recognition as some of the other mini-states of Europe.

This is a relativist argument, suggesting that sovereign states are no more and no less than those entities that are treated as sovereign states by the world. It is neither a true picture nor a particularly hopeful one from Seborga's point of view. It makes recognition of sovereignty a circular concept, difficult and unnecessary to account for where it exists; but also – and this is fatal for Seborga – impossible to call into being where it does not. If one argues that there is no logic to its incidence, one cannot complain if it is not forthcoming in any particular case. San Marino, for all the exaggeration and romanticism of its official history, is now treated as an independent state and has been since the end of the Napoleonic era; Seborga does not receive this treatment, and it is hard to see how it could obtain it. If it did, it would probably be as unwelcome to the inhabitants as it was to those of Pimlico.

In fact of course the recognition of sovereignty is not as capricious as this, and – however misguided and imperfect their attempts may be – people still try to adjudicate these matters on the basis of empirical evidence such as the historical legal rights of the entity, or the wishes of the populace. An international commission assessing Seborga's claim to independence would probably seek information on two questions: whether the claim had any historical basis in fact, and whether the inhabitants wanted independence. The decision might be taken entirely on the basis of the latter point, and if in seeking to do so the commission were misinformed about the popular desire, it would make perfect sense to say that the decision was made on the basis of a mistake. The same logically applies to the question of the claim's historical basis: if they were misled or romanced into falsely believing that the village had been independent for centuries in earlier ages, it would be perfectly legitimate to say that their decision was mistaken.

If a mistaken decision were to be made and a state such as Seborga were awarded sovereign status that it had never held before, and the decision were respected, there would certainly be no point in arguing that it was not in fact a sovereign entity. But in advance of that decision there is no reason not to object to a historical argument that strikes one as phoney; particularly not the reason that arguments of similar phoneyness have worked in the past.

The 'relativist' argument, with its dismissal of the legalities of history as pedantic technicalities, is in fact considerably at variance with the character of the position taken up, explicitly at least, by supporters or proponents of 'states' like Seborga. Whoever came up with the idea that this small village was independent on the basis of medieval land grants and the politics of the gradual unification of Italy was by definition of a pedantic and technical turn of mind; nothing could be more wrong than to dismiss the details as irrelevant.

Another example, from a common-law region, is the so-called Hutt River Province Principality, a large farm in Western Australia ruled over since 1970 by the jovial Prince Leonard. The principality's origins lie in a dispute over a low wheat quota imposed on the 18,500-acre farm in 1969, against which a strong but ineffectual appeal was lodged. The threat of sequestration for non-compliance was raised. In reaction, the owners of the farm, the Casley family, took the unusual step of declaring independence, initially as a province with a board of administrators. This was something that the government of Australia had to be careful about, even while categorically refusing to recognize the new state. The spectre of sequestration diminished, while the state and dominion authorities wondered how best to go about things, and the Casleys argued that the decision whether to recognize them was purely a matter for the Royal Prerogative, which was unchallengeable in law, and that the delay over a decision, coupled with the fact that letters from the Australian governor-general had been addressed to Leonard Casley as 'administrator' of the province, meant that the Prerogative had in effect been applied in their favour. To make doubly certain of their position the family made Leonard Casley their prince, on the basis that in English law interference with a prince's fulfilment of his princely duties is treason. In fact in this context 'prince' merely means 'sovereign authority' and would equally well have applied to the board of administration; but it is in any case clear that the correct forum for enforcement of this principle would be Hutt River's own courts, if it had any. Australia is unlikely to try its own sovereign authority for treason against a foreign prince.[14]

Thirty years after the momentous events that led to its secession, the Hutt River Province Principality seemingly thrives. The sale of postage stamps, coins and banknotes, not to mention 'citizenship' (conveniently tenable with that of other nations) and titles, and its status as a minor tourist attraction

Fifty-cent coin of the Hutt River Province
Principality, with 'Prince Leonard of Hutt'
on the obverse, 1977.

have doubtless more than made up for the low wheat quota. The size of
the farm makes it quite large in comparison with other micro-states; it is,
for example, fifty-eight times larger than Monaco. This means that grand
gestures such as setting aside 5,000 acres as a 'floral reserve' can be comfortably made, while also allowing the Casleys to diversify into the lucrative
sale of blooms.

If there ever really was a flurry of political alarm at the secession of Hutt
River in 1970 (the account given above being that of the Casleys themselves), it has long since receded. That is not to say that an accord has been
reached in regard to the claim to sovereignty, or indeed the other activities
that the principality pursues. The sale of purported titles and coats of arms in
particular is something that in other cases than Hutt River's has justly
caused concern, as it often involves persuading uninformed people to part
with money for something that in no way measures up to what is claimed: a
confidence trick, in other words.

Recent years have seen quite a few enterprises similar to the Hutt River
phenomenon. Some are even bolder – or more comical. In January 1972
an American entrepreneur called Mike Oliver, a devotee of 'radical liberal
capitalism', led a small expedition to take over and occupy the uninhabited
Minerva reefs 400 miles south of Fiji. A republic was declared, with an
administration based upon the founder's principles of complete freedom from
taxation and open settlement for the very rich, and the nations of the world
were alerted to the existence of the new state.
The only attention received, however, was
of the most unwelcome kind: on 21 June a tiny
expeditionary force from Tonga took over the
reefs and sent Oliver and his companions
into exile, whence for a while he continued to
push the claims of his short-lived state.[15]

Silver coin (face value $35) offered in the name of
Mike Oliver's 'Republic of Minerva', 1973.

Two of a set of stamps commemorating
great explorers produced by Sealand,
1969. The principality can be seen in
the right half of each stamp.

Of slightly greater duration was the principality of Sealand, a decommissioned radar platform in the North Sea which was 'occupied' by two individuals called Roy Bates and Ronan O'Rohilly in the late 1960s. Their intentions, it seems, were to use the platform for any or all of a number of money-making schemes: pirate radio, gambling resort, tax haven for companies. None of these came to pass, and they do not seem to have spent much time there, but in 1967, after a disagreement with O'Rohilly, Bates declared the platform an independent principality (it stood just outside the limit of the then accepted British territorial claim) and himself took on the mantle of sovereignty, with his wife Joan as consort. The production of stamps and coins followed; but unfortunately the principality seems to have been defunct by the early 1980s and so was unable to make the natural progression to a website.[16]

Mention of the Internet is opportune, for it has had a considerable impact on the world of fantasy states like those described above. To list and discuss here all the recent instances of property-passed-off-as-sovereignty would have been a mammoth task, and a largely repetitive and uninformative one at that. To do so with all the 'virtual' states that are proclaimed on the Internet would be impossible. For Seborga and Hutt River the web is a useful medium, a welcome new addition to the apparatus of pseudo-statehood, albeit one that in fact proclaims their slender and ephemeral nature, by implying that they can be encapsulated in a single website. There is now, however, an array of imaginary kingdoms and principalities for which the

Internet itself is not merely a medium, a vehicle for publicity, but the only sphere of existence.

Another point can be made. Sealand and Minerva demonstrate for pseudo-statebuilders an *arcanum imperii*, a secret of rule, that it is not necessary to dwell physically in the place whose claims one is pushing. The virtual states of the Internet show that it is not necessary for there to be any physical place at all. While their less virtual predecessors make play of and bend the rules of property holding and territorial sovereignty, these new entities happily ignore more basic distinctions between imagination and reality. Unfortunately or otherwise, they locate themselves beyond the mundane purview that this book must adopt.

Usurper Kings

Sovereign powers that do not derive their status from a central, over-arching authority usually create some unchanging standards or rules by which to abide, criteria for judging legitimate from false in internal constitutional matters. Thus in a kingdom power is naturally, though far from always, hereditary. The kingdoms that divided up the Roman world between them were largely hereditary in one of several straightforward manners, with fathers being succeeded by sons or brothers by brothers, though other systems also existed. Certainly firm rules about succession did not in some places come into existence until quite late on in the medieval period, but this did not mean that there was no concept of usurpation. Nor should the frequency of usurpation among medieval kings lead one to believe that the express rules of succession, if there were any, must be revised or treated as a sham: the ingenuity of the usurpers should be given closer attention, and not dismissed as meaningless lip-service to the legitimists. For the usurper was rare who did not care if he seemed to take a throne by force; if he could do so by bending, or reinterpreting the rules of succession, or better still by bending or reinterpreting the facts so that the rules, rigidly applied, made him king, then he would. This was of course easiest for those starting within a reasonable distance of the object; they had to be within the set of individuals who might benefit from the rules of succession in the first place. That is why so many usurpers were undoubtedly royal.

The English monarchy of the fourteenth and fifteenth centuries is as good an example to choose as any. No one can doubt that by the 1200s a relatively clear and in principle uncontested law of succession had developed, tempered only in the way that all laws were tempered, namely by the king's

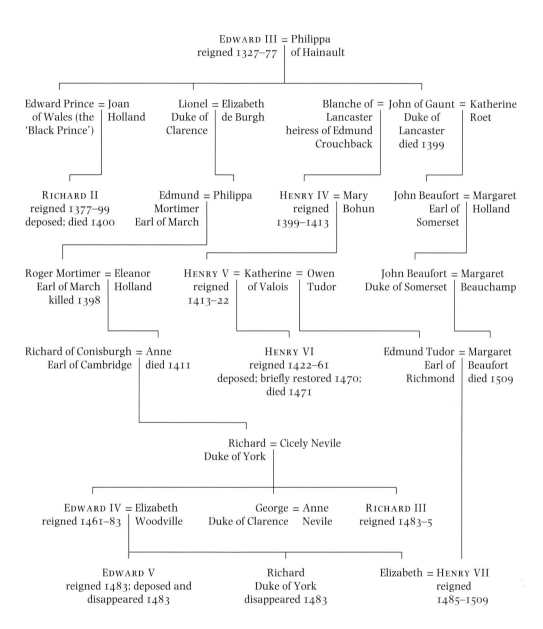

The main lines of descent from Edward III, showing the houses of Lancaster and York and the relationships of Henry VII.

own prerogative. Thus the king might nominate a successor who was not heir at law. At any rate, for two full centuries from 1199, when the Crown passed to John rather than his elder brother's son Prince Arthur (whom he held prisoner and later had killed), succession to the English monarchy can be entirely explained with reference to the system we know today, namely male primogeniture. Thus Henry III was John's eldest son, Edward I his in turn, and so forth. In 1399, however, a usurpation undoubtedly took place. The long-standing dispute between Richard II and his first cousin Henry, Earl of Derby and Hertford, reached a head. Henry deposed Richard and took the Crown for himself as Henry IV, arguing in part that Richard (certainly not one of England's better kings) was mad, incapable and tyrannical. The action was widely perceived as unjust, and – thanks in part to Shakespeare's treatment of the subject – remembered so today. The taint of usurpation stained even the otherwise bright reign of the usurper's son Henry V and was to resurface as grounds for deposing his son in turn.

What is interesting is that though the disagreement between Richard and Henry was well known, and the usurpation looks obvious to us now, considerable effort was expended at the time on a justifying account of Henry's actions. Part of this, as already stated, was the argument that Richard simply had to go; but this did not account for Henry's becoming king himself. As reference to the pedigree will show, Henry was not next in line to the throne, as his father John of Gaunt had not been the next youngest brother to Richard's father, the Black Prince. This had been Prince Lionel, Duke of Clarence, whose grandson Roger Mortimer, Earl of March, would be recognized as heir to Richard II by modern laws of succession and was, in fact, nominated by Richard as heir in 1394. Roger was killed in an ambush in 1398, leaving a young daughter, but by then Henry's ambition for the Crown was in the open, and the principles of succession remained the same.

The nomination of Roger Mortimer in 1394 had been made in response to a forceful petition from John of Gaunt that his son Henry be declared heir to the throne. This was not, it should perhaps be explained, out of the question. As stated above, it was clearly accepted that it was in the king's prerogative to nominate the heir. Furthermore, there was perhaps some opposition to the idea of the throne passing through the female line, out of a house that had held it for more than two and a half centuries and into the hands of a relatively humble earl. Any objection to the passage of the throne in the female line was illogical and unhistorical, for it was by such means that the Plantagenets had inherited it in the first place; but many states in Europe (those operating by the custom known as the 'Salic' law) did not recognize any such mode of kingly inheritance.

However, it was not on these grounds but rather according to the basic rules of primogeniture that John of Gaunt argued that his son was the rightful heir to the throne. Henry's mother, John's first wife, had been the heiress of a junior line of the royal house, descending from Edmund Crouchback, Earl of Lancaster, younger brother of Edward I. Ingeniously, Gaunt claimed that Crouchback had in fact been Edward's elder brother, but had resigned his rights to the kingship in favour of Edward on account of his disability (plain to all from his name, which obviously meant 'hunchback'). This was a reasonably sound argument, looked at in terms of rights and customs. There was a perfect response, of course: why had Edmund's brother inherited the Crown after his resignation, rather than his son? If Gaunt's story was that Edmund had resigned his own rights *and those of his descendants* in Edward's favour, it was in fact of no use to him, for it disqualified Henry too.

The imperfection of the tale does not outweigh the fact that it was produced, or the thought that went into it. That it was a fiction is certain: the sobriquet 'Crouchback' refers not to a crooked back but rather a back with a cross on it, just as the Crutched Friars of London were those whose habits were marked with crosses. Edmund had been a crusader rather than a cripple. Gaunt's story, which interestingly shows how swiftly the language and usages of the recent past could become obscure even in the Middle Ages, would not have withstood close examination (though one source relates that in an attempt to give it as much chance of success as possible, Gaunt had a chronicle forged in its support and copies placed in libraries around the country). But the story's ingenuity does not mean it was an exercise in legalistic pedantry; in the context of a debate about Henry's right to the throne it was precisely to the point.[17]

Later, in fact, the dubious tale was to resurface, this time at Henry's own instigation. According to the chronicler Adam of Usk, Henry convened a council of learned men (including Adam himself) to come up with ideas for justifying his deposition of Richard and assumption of the Crown. They soon produced the Crouchback story; but on investigating the records they found it would not stand up. They were spin-doctors rather than forgers, and the story could go no further. The episode is intriguing, however: not only did Henry bother to convene such a body, but the Crouchback story appears to have been precisely the sort of thing it was convened to come up with – until it was found to be false. This sheds important light on the nature of these justifying tales: they were not, ideally at any rate, cynical falsehoods. Even if a less scrupulous think-tank might have been prepared to fabricate the evidence as John of Gaunt was said to have done, the account presented to the public still needed to be believable, to stand up to some basic form of test. That is, if a cynical falsehood *were* to be presented to the public, it could not be obvious that it was so. This, after all, is common sense: there is nothing more pointless than an obviously false falsehood. Where the cynicism and falsehood in the council's operation lie is of course in the logical direction which their task implies: the conclusion (that Richard should be deposed) was their starting point, the premises the objective.

Drawing a reluctant blank with the Crouchback story, the council turned to simpler, general-purpose stand-bys, such as Richard's poor personal and kingly qualities. It is probable that they also raised the matter of his legitimacy, which Adam of Usk certainly questioned in his chronicle, and which could easily be linked with his poor qualities as ruler: inadequate kingship showed he was of mean birth.

These strategies were to be common currency in the fifteenth century. Most of them were wheeled out again in the reign of Henry VI, grandson of the usurper of 1399. This time the stories were produced by the Yorkist camp: Henry was weak and feeble; he was guilty of offences against his subjects; prophecy said his time had come; and, most tellingly of all, he was on the throne only because of his grandfather's usurpation. Despite the passage of three eventful decades since the aftermath of Richard II's deposition and death, and sustained and calculated efforts by Henry V to shed the blemish on his title by honouring Richard's memory and appropriating it as much as possible to the house of Lancaster, it was easy to resuscitate popular awareness of what had happened. It was particularly relevant, furthermore, because the house of York, though in the male line the junior surviving branch of Edward III's progeny, was descended in the female line from Roger Mortimer, Earl of March. Indeed the Duke of York, who acted as Protector when the young king was adjudged out of his wits for a period in the 1450s, was heir at law to Lionel, Duke of Clarence: had Roger Mortimer succeeded as Richard II intended, the Duke of York would now be king. The wars between the red rose of Lancaster and the white rose of York, which now commenced, were thus in part built upon a dynastic dispute of more than half a century earlier.

In 1461 the unfortunate Henry VI was ousted and replaced by Edward IV, son of the Duke of York (who had been killed the previous year in battle). At once the Lancastrian onslaught on the Yorkist king began, paying close

Gold 'angel' of Edward IV, 1473, showing the Archangel Michael on the obverse and the ship of state on the reverse, a pairing of designs that was to last for more than three centuries.

attention, for instance, to the fact that he was born abroad and thus in all likelihood a changeling. Of particular interest this time was the claim that Edward was shown not to be a true king by his inability to heal the 'King's Evil' or scrofula. The Kings of England and France had for centuries 'touched' for this disease in a ceremony from which descends the modern Maundy celebration, the sufferer being given a gold coin to mark the occasion. These coins, by a natural thought process, were themselves considered endowed with healing or at least protective powers, and were worn as charms or amulets. Though coins were not especially minted for the occasion (unlike Maundy money), the gold piece that was bestowed from 1461 onwards was the angel, a new coin distinguished by a fine image of the Archangel Michael on the obverse. St Michael's associations with healing have led to the suggestion that this design was chosen specifically to emphasize the Yorkist sovereign's possession of thaumaturgical abilities: it was, at any rate, a particularly appropriate design.[18]

Despite the reappearance on the throne of Henry VI for a few months in 1470–1, the house of York just managed to hold on to the Crown long enough for its own cause to be split by faction. The first dissent came from the king's middle brother George, Duke of Clarence, part of whose explicit cause for complaint centred on Edward's marriage to a relatively low-born widow Elizabeth Woodville, and the advancement of her family at the expense of his own wife's. Clarence was condemned for treason and, in 1478, put to death (by being drowned, famously, in a barrel of wine). This brought about only a temporary respite. In 1483 Edward IV died, leaving two sons, aged thirteen and ten (the elder of whom succeeded as Edward V), and two daughters. Perhaps acting in part to guard against the consequences of a young and inexperienced king, but certainly full of personal ambition, the dead king's younger brother Richard had the two boys arrested and imprisoned in the Tower of London, from where they are not known ever to have emerged. On 26 June 1483 he ascended the throne himself as Richard III.

According to an interesting contemporary account by the Italian Angelo

Cato, *On Richard III's usurpation of the kingdom of England*, the arguments adduced by Richard to justify his right to the Crown closely resemble those we have already seen deployed in similar circumstances. Edward IV's marriage was invalid, as kings of England were anciently prohibited from marrying any but virgins, and because Edward himself had been contractually betrothed to another at the time; thus Edward's children (including the princes in the Tower) were illegitimate. Edward IV himself, furthermore, had been illegitimate, as he had been conceived in adultery and was not really the son of the late Duke of York. As for the Earl of Warwick (the young son of George, Duke of Clarence, whom Richard had also imprisoned), he was attainted as a result of his father's felony. This feat of argumentation left Richard the next heir to the throne.[19]

Whether these arguments convinced is not a matter we can guess. Certainly they were as cynically conceived and as conclusion-led as anything produced in the previous hundred years. But it seems a far from trivial point to make that, had they been true, they would indeed have established Richard's right to the throne. Were anyone to be convinced by them, that person would not regard Richard as a usurper. That would not be a negligible achievement, and, given the regularity with which arguments of this sort were produced in the Middle Ages, it is natural to conclude that they were thought to serve their purpose.

As stated above, arguments to justify usurpation in this fashion were of best use to those starting within the charmed circle of people who might conceivably inherit the Crown anyway. Such usurpers have the further luxury that, if all else fails, they can dispose of all the individuals standing between themselves and the throne and thus, incontrovertibly, become the next in line. This approach was in fact always present in some degree: thus whether or not the Princes in the Tower were legitimate, they were undoubtedly dead, and only the Earl of Warwick remained to argue around. If they can avoid retribution for their sins, usurpers of this sort still satisfy the legitimists, and if they do not they still die as rightful kings. To draw on lesser dignities for a parallel, Louis Mazzini, who in the 1949 film *Kind Hearts and Coronets* murders his way to the title of Duke of Chalfont, is no less Duke of Chalfont for that.

When the claimant was not within the charmed circle, neither approach was sufficient. The arrival of Henry VII on the throne is remarkable for the extent that he did not belong to this group by birth: though by the 1480s the nearest thing the Lancastrian party had to a senior representative, by virtue of his descent from John of Gaunt and from Henry V's queen, he was barely a member of the 'royal family' (to use a modern concept). Though it was by faction, invasion and popular persuasion that he took the throne, it is not clear that he stands in the same category at all as the examples discussed so far. Neither elimination of every one higher up the order of succession than himself, nor construction of a precise legitimist argument to show that he was the rightful king, were options for him.

Nonetheless a case of sorts was constructed, if largely after the event. Lord Chancellor Bacon, writing a history of Henry's rule many years afterwards, identified three 'titles to reign'. One of these was the title 'of the sword or conquest', in short the fact that he had won the Crown in battle. The other two, however, were vaguely legitimist. First, there was the 'ancient and long disputed' title of the house of Lancaster. To argue this precisely meant claiming that all the Yorkist kings were usurpers, perhaps not an onerous or unwelcome conclusion for Henry in itself, but inconsistent with Bacon's third 'title', deriving from Henry's marriage with Elizabeth of York, one of Edward IV's two daughters.

Despite its inconsistency, Bacon was quite right to formulate this title: Henry's relationship with the house of York, his uniting of the red and white roses, was an essential part of his presentation. Even his demonization of Richard III was not necessarily anti-Yorkist; Richard himself was a usurper within the house of York, who had put to death a young Yorkist king and his younger brother to take the crown. But in reality, from Buckingham's rebellion early in Richard's reign onwards, anti-Ricardian feeling had been pro-Tudor. The fact was that Henry's main genealogical claim to the throne was through his descent from the house of Lancaster, and his position was weakened if there were too many descendants of the opposing faction in existence.[20]

By killing Edward V and his brother the Duke of York (the Princes in the Tower), Richard III had partly resolved Henry's problem for him. He also declared the issue of his elder brother George, Duke of Clarence, to be unable to succeed on account of their father's treason. This dealt with Clarence's son Edward, Earl of Warwick, who was still alive and a potential claimant to the throne. But in his thoroughness Richard had created other problems. He had declared the Princes in the Tower and their sisters illegitimate; one of these sisters was Elizabeth, Henry's queen. Henry could scarcely cancel the statute by which this was achieved while maintaining the decree by which the young Earl of Warwick was disinherited. More importantly, perhaps, a decree made by the usurper Richard to justify his claim was simply not creditworthy any more. So, though Henry was married to the daughter and heir of Edward IV, a fact which ought by rights to have brought the Crown if not to him then at any rate to his son, there was at least one Plantagenet prince still alive. And since Richard III had diverted the succession away from the heirs of Edward IV, however usurpatory the manner in which he had done it, it would have been difficult to argue that this prince and the other remaining Plantagenet descendants were technically further away from the throne than Henry's queen. They were not further away from it than Henry himself; they were members of or closely allied to the dynasty that had ruled England for three hundred years; they were not upstarts from Wales; and they had suffered injustice, which Henry seemed intent on continuing.

These points may not have been actively persuasive to those who were not already opposed to the advent of Henry Tudor, but they were undoubtedly points that could be made in favour of the remaining descendants of the house of York. The only way Henry could deal with them was to try to control matters and give people no reason to wish for the return of the Plantagenets. To this end the Earl of Warwick, already held in house arrest by order of Richard, was seized soon after Bosworth and placed in prison. But memories would not be swiftly erased, and even the death or imprisonment of a Plantagenet prince did not remove him from the scene. As we shall see in the next chapter, usurpation is frequently followed by imposture, and it was not long before impostors appeared in the guise, first of the Earl of Warwick and then of Richard, Duke of York, the younger of the Princes in the Tower. There was no guarantee that this might not carry on, or that one of the other descendants of the house of York might not decide to make a challenge in person. Nothing could be done about those that were already dead, but the living descendants of the house of York who presented a risk were gradually dealt with. Warwick was executed on trumped-up charges in 1499; by the end of Henry VIII's reign in 1547 a further eight prominent descendants of the last Plantagenet kings had been put to death.[21]

This, however, was a process that never neared completion in Henry VII's own reign, and can now arguably never be completed, as the descendants of the Duke of York (Edward IV's father) continue to this day. The fact is that, because of Henry Tudor's more distant starting position, the legitimist case made on his behalf had to be more vaguely defined, which meant not only broader in scope but more practical in implementation. There were far too many people higher up the order of succession for them all to be killed or argued around: only the obvious ones, the serious contenders, needed to be dealt with; but they were to be dealt with forcefully. Henry VII's spin-doctors,

An 18th-century engraving of Henry VII, quoting the lines of the Gallo-Roman poet Ausonius on the Emperor Severus: 'Your might did not seize command; it received it.'

Titulum ne horresce novantis,
Non rapit Imperium vis tua, sed recipit .
Ausonius de Seuero .

unlike those of Henry IV, were put on to other matters, questions which had not been neglected by earlier kings, usurpers and inheritors alike, but which now received more attention, sponsored at a higher level, than before. This was the broader, antiquarian-inspired form of genealogical presentation by which the claimant was shown as descended not only from the long line of English rulers, but also from the pre-conquest kings of the Anglo-Saxons and ancient Britons, among whom Arthur was of course pre-eminent. Once this far back, there was no reason to stop, and many genealogies rose as far as Brutus, the mythical founder of Britain, the Trojans, Noah, and Adam and Eve. Lines of descent like this had frequently been produced in the Yorkist period – one done for Edward IV is seen in Plate I – but with Henry VII they acquired a new and slightly more specific significance by presenting the new king as embodying the prophesied resumption by the British of their ancient kingdom, the return of the red dragon. Though no one in that day regarded this matter as any less capable of treatment in terms of truth and falsehood, evidence and fabrication, the purpose of such a presentation was altogether different from what we have been discussing, for it did not rest on the sparse facts of recent genealogy and succession law, and could never identify the claimant quite so precisely as that approach did. Which is why, in the restricted, internecine disputes of the Plantagenet era, the latter was consistently resorted to.[22]

The Pretenders

In 1900 there were eighteen separate kingdoms or empires in Europe (United Kingdom, Sweden, Denmark, Netherlands, Belgium, Spain, Portugal, Russia, the German Empire, with Saxony, Württemberg and Bavaria within it, Austria-Hungary, Serbia, Roumania, Bulgaria, Greece and Italy), with a nineteenth (Norway) added in 1905, a twentieth (Montenegro) in 1910 and a twenty-first (Albania) in 1914. Of these only the first six and Norway survive today. The nineteenth century had already seen an empire brought to an end by political changes (France) and a kingdom subsumed in a larger entity (Sicily). Two European-founded empires in Latin America had also been toppled, in Brazil and Mexico. Add to these the large number of principalities and duchies, chiefly in Germany, that have ceased to exist in the last two centuries, and a high total of defunct monarchies is arrived at. In almost all these cases, where the last ruler does not himself survive, descendants of the last or penultimate ruler do, and it is usually easy to identify the individual family member who would be the monarch had history run a different course.[23]

So Europe and the Europeanized world are now quite heavily populated with ex-kings and their near descendants, many of whom are pretenders in the sense of maintaining an absolute or hypothetical claim to the throne they were deprived of. By an absolute claim is meant the claim that the throne in question is rightfully theirs; that the means by which they were dispossessed or prevented from inheriting it were unlawful. They may, as we shall see below, claim not merely that they *should be*, but that in fact they *are* kings. A hypothetical claim is less strong, and in some cases amounts to little more than the claim to be head of a family; it is in essence the claim that, *if* the crown had not been taken away, it would now be vested in the claimant. This can be uncontroversial enough, and often the heads of families are not really pretenders or claimants at all, though there may be others who make the claim for them. In popular usage the word 'pretender' tends to be applied to both sorts. They both derive from the logical pursuit of the idea of legitimacy discussed in the last section.

Pretendership was well known in the ancient and medieval worlds. The habit of certain Hellenistic monarchs to will their kingdoms to the people of Rome tended to leave disinherited and disgruntled relations who refused to accept the situation. Thus when Ptolemy Alexander so bequeathed his kingdom of Egypt in 80 BC, two nephews of his predecessor Euergetes travelled to Rome to maintain their rights, and another member of the family, Ptolemy Auletes, had himself crowned, and later purchased recognition from Rome for the vast price of 6,000 talents, recognition which Rome – uncertain of the wisdom of annexing so large and distinct a kingdom – was relieved to give. It was left to Auletes' daughter Cleopatra to change Rome's mind.

Some of the longest-lasting examples of pretendership were in fact perpetrated by individuals who were undoubtedly rulers. Thus from the mid-fifteenth to the seventeenth century the Dukes of Savoy (later Kings of Sardinia and then all Italy) held out a claim to be Kings of Cyprus, Jerusalem and Armenia. The kingdom of Jerusalem was also claimed (along with the Duchy of Lorraine) by the Emperors of Austria until their loss of the crown in 1919. From 1340 until 1801 the kings of England and Great Britain held out an initially serious but increasingly meaningless claim to be rightful kings of France, indicating the fact in their titulature and their heraldry. Pretenderships like this are perhaps less striking to the observer – and even to the claimant – because they take their place in the midst of a panoply of titles, some significant, others less so; they are often referred to as 'titular' kingships, which seems to diminish the extent of the claim. But 'titular' kingship could be deadly serious. Thus from 1290 to his death in 1295 Charles Martel, son of the King of Naples and nephew of the last King of Hungary, claimed the latter crown in opposition to the wishes of the Magyars themselves, but with the Pope's support. The claim was given concrete form in his free usage of the title, and it was as King of Hungary that his son Charles Robert fought a bloody war to turn it into reality.

More tenuous still than this were the claims deriving from the Frankish tenure of the throne of Constantinople between 1204 and 1261. By means of express assignment and inheritance, the titular claim to the Empire of the East passed from the Courtenay family to a junior line of the French royal house before terminating with Jacques de Baux who died in 1382. Claims to the short-lived Frankish kingdom of Thessalonika in the northern Aegean were likewise maintained long after they had lost any substance, again on the basis of inheritance and by the disposition of Baldwin de Courtenay, Emperor of Constantinople. It has been argued that the titular afterlife of these Frankish realms was much more significant than their brief *de facto* existence, being used as bargaining tools among western princes and nobles, and between west and east.[24] This was only possible because these claims, though empty in themselves, were transmitted by strict rules in which people believed. Though the substance had long since disappeared, the hypothetical legitimacy of the claim remained.

For many the archetype of this sort of pretendership is provided by the Stuarts. The episode is certainly one of the most intriguing and important in the history of European monarchy, and many aspects of it are relevant to this book. In fact, however, though it well illustrates the long, slow progression from a serious, politically viable claim with a military dimension to a flimsy and insubstantial piece of nostalgia, it displays another element: ideology. If ever an unrealized claim shed light on the ideology of a monarchy, it was this one.

In late December 1688 James II and VII, the last Stuart King of England and Scotland, sailed for France, leaving his kingdoms to decide their own fate. He had been ousted by the arrival, under arms, of his son-in-law William of Orange, the hope and saviour of all who loathed James' overt pro-Catholic stance and disregard for Parliament. William made no explicit bid for the Crown; he would depart when Parliament had been summoned. Though it was scarcely an invasion in the full sense, William's expedition threatened violence and James' supporters got the message. By the end of November most had gone. In February the following year Parliament offered the Crown jointly to William and his wife, James' elder daughter Mary. The constitutional interpretation of the events is and was hard to assess. Various constructions were placed on what had happened, none entirely satisfactory.[25]

On 5 February 1689 Parliament declared the throne to be vacant on account of James's breach of the 'original contract' between king and people, and offered it to William and Mary. This formulation, the work of the House of Commons, did not find favour in the Lords where – apart from Tory and Jacobite sympathy – there were objections to this contractual interpretation of kingship and indeed to the idea that the throne was vacant. An interregnum implied elective monarchy, whereas it was a basic tenet of the English and Scottish approach to the Crown that its destination was pre-ordained, and no election or selection – whosoever might carry it out – played any part.

These objections did not force a rewording of the resolution, but thereafter the contractual theory is notable by its absence from all but the most extreme Whig versions, and certainly did not figure at all in the official accounts of how the Hanoverians came to power. The fact that it was a central part of John Locke's theory of sovereign power did not guarantee it immediate acceptance, and many people were still content with Hobbes' notion of a 'covenant', under which the burden of obedience fell largely on the governed rather than the governor.

Instead the notion that James had abdicated by fleeing the country gained some ground. The word 'abdicate' had also appeared in the resolution of 5 February, though its rôle there is far from clear, and the Lords had objected to this too, claiming that abdication was a concept unknown to English law, and that in any case the word implied a voluntary departure. However, the idea had some popular success over time and, embellished by the story that James threw the Great Seal of England into the Thames as he escaped (a clear act of abdication), it later became part of the orthodoxy.

Whigs of a later date could comfortably admit that there had been no pre-existing constitutional rhyme or reason in the events. With this in mind, the notion of the 1688 'Glorious Revolution' (a phrase first recorded in November 1689) came in useful. This was fitted into the idea of a great and irresistible march of rationalization and modernization in the late seventeenth and eighteenth centuries, part of the 'Whig interpretation' of English history. Sovereignty had passed from the Crown alone to a new composite body called the Crown-in-Parliament, an idea that was slowly worked out in the eighteenth and nineteenth centuries, given great prominence at the start of the twentieth by the constitutionalist A. V. Dicey, and is still in place. The concept of a revolution of some sort, with or without the radical associations deriving from the modern usage of the same word, has retained its appeal for a wide variety of commentators ranging from the left-wing historian to the right-wing parliamentarian. In reality of course to call the events of 1688–9 a revolution is merely to give them a name; it is not to give them a constitutional explanation, an explanation which many sorely felt the lack of.

The fact remains, however, that at the time the question of how the Crown came to be in the hands of William and Mary was not resolved in an official sense. The presentation of the Crown and declaration of rights passed on 13 February made no mention of breach of contract, abdication or revolution. It merely stated that ancient rights had been violated, and that Parliament was certain that William and Mary would instead safeguard them. The resolution can be read as an offer of the Crown or as a declaration of the fact that the Crown had already automatically been vested in the addressees, according to one's inclinations.

What made this ambiguity possible – indeed, what made the whole enterprise of 1688–9 possible – was the fact that William and Mary were within the ambit of the possible destination of the Crown. Mary was James's elder daughter, and William his nephew as well as son-in-law, his mother being the departing king's sister. Admittedly the Crown could not by straightforward succession have come to him ahead of Mary's younger sister Anne; but Anne had advised Parliament on 6 February that she waived her superior rights in William's favour for his lifetime. Furthermore, there was the possibility of William becoming not just consort but joint ruler *jure uxoris*, in right of his wife, though the most recent precedent was perhaps not auspicious: Philip of Spain, who as husband of 'Bloody' Mary had been King of England. The practice recurred quite frequently in Spain and Portugal.

James had of course by now fathered a son, a boy certain to be brought up a Roman Catholic: he preceded William, Mary and Anne in the natural order of succession. This presented a major problem to those who wished to explain the events of 1688–9 as far as possible in customary terms. The 1701 Act of Settlement, resettling the throne on the Protestant descendants of the Electress Sophia of Hanover, resolved matters for the future more formally than the cruder measure of twelve years earlier, by which James' Catholic descendants were barred; but both these acts were made under the new régime, thereby leaving a gap which might seem to call their own validity into doubt. It is not perhaps surprising that the logical shortfall was to be bridged (temporarily at least) by rumour and falsehood, as we shall see. For most Whigs and those Tories who were not Jacobites, the problem was resolved simply and without recourse to scheming or sophistry, by invoking the occasional, exceptional rôle of Providence in the disposition of the Crown; a kind of extraordinary intrusion of the abnormal into the normal scheme of passive obedience and non-resistance, a scheme which it was not necessary to alter.

For the genealogically and legalistically inclined this was doubtless an unsatisfactory position. For many it remained important to show the current monarch to be not merely within the group of possible monarchs by right of birth, but the *only* possible monarch by birth. Curiously, the accession of George I on Anne's death in 1714 (which followed automatically from the Act of Settlement, though if one disregards that act George was only fifty-eighth in line to succeed) was more open to this interpretation than William's or Anne's had been. George was descended in the direct male line from Henry the Lion, Duke of Saxony and Bavaria (died 1195), and his wife Matilda, elder sister of King John of England. In 1200 John divorced his first wife and married Isabella of Angoulême, a marriage from which all the later Kings and Queens of England derived. The divorce, argued some, was invalid, and thus the later marriage illegal. This made John's children by Isabella illegitimate and rendered void their descendants' right to the throne, which instead passed to the offspring of Henry the Lion, currently represented by George I.[26]

This reconstruction, it need hardly be pointed out, was an extreme one, signifying as it did that all English monarchs between 1216 and 1714 were usurpers. It did gain support in surprising quarters – John Wesley was one who toyed with it – but it was not likely to convince many. Its importance is merely in showing the continuing need to seek purely hereditary explanations for the succession to the Crown.

As stated above, the departing King James had recently fathered a son. On 10 June 1688, to some popular disbelief, a son James had been born, fifteen years after his parents' marriage (though his mother was still only thirty) and six years after the last child, a daughter who had died young. The existence of this new heir, immediately nominated Prince of Wales, created the possibility of a Catholic succession, which had not previously been a danger: James' two daughters Mary and Anne, born by a previous marriage, were Protestant. To many the event seemed rather too convenient for the king, and rumours that the birth was a fabrication soon began to circulate, being voiced even by Mary and Anne. There was really no more basis for mistrusting the news of this particular royal birth than that of any other, but the impossibility of establishing its genuineness with certainty, and the existence of the rumours, allowed the unscrupulous to take advantage. This was the origin of the story of the 'warming-pan plot'.

William Fuller, the great publicizer of this chimera, was by his own confession a man of great deceptive ability, and it is clear from his work that he was also conceited, ambitious and plausible. Having worked first as an agent for the exiled Jacobite court at St Germain in France, and then as a double agent for the régime in London, Fuller was by 1692 thoroughly discredited by both sides. After some years in the wilderness and, indeed, in prison, he decided to join in the still hotly contested debate on the Prince of Wales' birth. In 1696 he published *A Brief discovery of the True Mother of the Pretended Prince of Wales, known by the name of Mary Grey*. The book, like two pamphlets Fuller produced later the same year, claimed that the supposed prince had been born to a gentlewoman in the service of the Countess of

Tyrconnel, who had then been spirited away to France and kept there for two years before being murdered on the orders of the French king. Fuller stated, furthermore, that the truth of the matter had been imparted in some letters sent to Lord Nottingham, William of Orange's secretary of state, in 1690, but nothing had been done about it. Before long one of the purported letters was published – perhaps by Fuller himself, perhaps by someone else stepping in to provide confirmation. Finally, towards the end of 1696, *A Compleat History of the Pretended Prince of Wales* came out. Again anonymous, again perhaps by Fuller, this book argued that the substitute prince might have been brought in to the queen's bedchamber in a warming-pan.[27]

William Fuller (1670–1733) aged about thirty, as depicted in the frontispiece to several of his controversial books.

The story made an immediate sensation and brought Fuller – already a notorious figure – much publicity, both favourable and hostile. This was of little concern to him in itself: he was by now a hardened confidence trickster and knew that all publicity has its uses. Other schemes proving fruitless, he returned to the topic in 1700, with his *Plain Proof of the true Father and Mother of the Pretended Prince of Wales*, a still more specific account of the claimed imposture, citing and even quoting at length written evidence from most of the major players, all of it fabricated by Fuller himself. He had over-egged the pudding for the public palate, however; his notoriety and fixation on the one subject began to backfire, as the following ditty declared:[28]

> When to His Majesty there ran
> An ape with visage furious
> And said My Liege, here's ten to one
> The Lion has no living son,
> I'll prove his birth is spurious;
>
> Hold! said the sovereign beast, thou sot,
> And straightaway withdraw thy phiz,
> Should such a rascal say he's not
> Legitimate and true begot,
> The world will think he is.

As forceful as the contention that when someone like Fuller makes a claim, people instinctively conclude the opposite to be true, is the simple characterization of the participants: King James might be deposed and in exile, but he is still a lion; Fuller is an ape.

Fuller's reaction was to increase the flow of pamphlets. Broadening his scope once more, he indicted the current administration for failing to react to his revelations; the reason was obviously that it was riddled with Jacobites and crypto-Catholics, and those in their pay. He was arraigned before the bar of the Commons and told to produce the evidence for these charges, which he miserably failed to do, and in June 1702 he was convicted of criminal libel and sentenced to stand in the pillory at three places, be whipped at Bridewell, serve six months' hard labour and pay a fine of 1,000 marks. On his release he published a confession of his fabrications concerning Mary Grey, imputing the scheme to his association with that other great false witness Titus Oates (who had sent many supposed Catholic conspirators to the scaffold in the reign of Charles II). Fuller was to live a long while yet and spin many more yarns, but his famous warming-pan was set on one side. Though occasionally brandished from time to time by anti-Jacobites, it was generally used only to add a little heat to the debate. It was now a symbol; few if any believed there was anything in it.

Anti-Jacobitism did not die, however, because Jacobitism itself did not. For many years there has been a marked difference in approach to this matter between academic and popular writers. Historians, no doubt under the influence of the Whig interpretation of history mentioned above, have treated Jacobitism, much like Toryism, as an increasing irrelevance in the eighteenth century and therefore bestowed little attention on it. Only in the last twenty or thirty years have academics emerged who, frequently with an unsparing use of vitriol, have tried hard to set the picture straight, pointing out how long-lasting, how influential and indeed in many ways how respectable Jacobite sympathies were. Much of this is plainly justified. On the other hand, their protestations at the neglect of Jacobitism until their own arrival must be read strictly in relation to the historical profession. There has in fact been no shortage of sentimental attention lavished on the unfortunate Stuarts, their romantic lost cause and the cruel treatment they suffered at the hands of the Hanoverians. Few English children, let alone Scottish ones, can have grown up in the twentieth century without being made to sing *My Bonny lies over the Ocean* and inculcated with a vision of the wicked pursuit of the highlanders after Culloden by 'Butcher' Cumberland. Nor have the sustained covert activities of secret Jacobite sympathizers in London society and elsewhere been neglected by the writers of popular fiction: it is Britain's answer to the intrigues of the French Revolution, after all, and too exciting a story to overlook. It may be that this sympathetic picture – turning Jacobitism from a rigorous application of legitimist principles into a brave, romantic 'cause' – derives from the Victorian affection for Scotland, when it was no longer a live issue. Alternatively, as the revisionist historians would perhaps argue, it is merely evidence of the phenomenon they describe: the continuation, albeit in a debased form, of Jacobite sympathies; all the more remiss, they would say, of their professional opponents to ignore the topic.

At any rate there is certainly much evidence for the duration of the Jacobite interest within English society until the middle of the eighteenth century, and there can be no justification for treating it as unimportant merely because it did not reflect 'the way things were going' as historians might interpret it. That is surely an absolute principle; but in any case it can be shown that certain aspects of the way things went in the eighteenth century were not in fact that foreign to the principles used to justify Jacobitism.

Engraving by T. Scott of the Young Pretender, about the time of the 1745 rebellion. The Latin motto ('Much storm-tossed out on the deep, he at last reaches Latium') is a paraphrase of the opening of Virgil's *Aeneid*.

This has already been hinted at above. The absence of contractual theory and revolutionary principles from the general justifying account of the events of 1688–9 means that to a large extent Tories and Whigs coincided over the nature of the monarchy. More positively, there is the question of the theory of divine right. It used to be generally accepted that the notion of the divine right of kings had ceased to be seriously entertained in Britain after the Glorious Revolution, maintained doggedly only by the Stuart pretenders in exile. This view cannot now be held. It might be argued that God wanted a Stuart on the throne; the state of affairs showed otherwise. As time wore on and attempts to subvert the settlement failed, it became ever easier to hold simply that it must have been divine providence that dispossessed the Stuarts in 1688 and bestowed the Crown on another line. There was no visible diminution in the emphasis on the monarch's God-given authority after the Revolution or after 1714; indeed, if one has regard to the coronation ceremony of 1953, the theory is still prominent in monarchic ideology. The sovereign as *persona mixta*, part priest and part king, was just as firmly delineated in the eighteenth century as before.

It was not divine right that the Stuart pretenders clung to as necessarily supporting their claim to the Crown (though they certainly maintained it), but the theory of indefeasible hereditary right, according to which the Crown, once bestowed, could only and did only pass by the unadulterated rules of succession. Obviously there are certain problems with this theory, both empirical and cultural. English and Scottish history both showed many instances of hereditary right being defeated by other considerations: it would be hard for the Stuarts to show that they had obtained the two crowns by means of the right they now invoked. Secondly, what rules of succession? Different countries, even within Europe, had adopted quite different systems, and it would be difficult to argue that one was more favoured by God than the others. If there was a model for the right, it was perhaps the succession to lesser dignities such as peerages. In that field no one presumed to argue that a younger son might be invested as a peer in preference to his elder brother. In cases where succession to a peerage was uncertain, the search for the heir was in the nature of an inquest, trying to find out where the title (which knew its own destination) had gone. If the wrong person was recognized as heir and treated as the peer, it did not defeat or extinguish the true heir's right to the original title; indeed he was already possessed of it. However, this model only shows up the difficulties of applying the same approach to the Crown. Peerages have patents of creation, in which their limitation is expressly spelled out, or else are governed by simple common-law rules that leave no room for doubt.

Nevertheless it was argued strongly by Jacobites that there was a hereditary right pertaining to the Crown and that it favoured the Stuarts. According to this theory, James II did not cease to be king in 1688, his son the Prince of Wales inherited the Crown in 1701, his elder grandson Charles in 1766 (after the longest reign in British history), and his younger grandson

'Touchpiece' of Cardinal Henry Stuart as Henry IX of England and Scotland, showing the basic design of the late medieval 'angel': St Michael on the reverse and a ship on the obverse (see p. 67).

Henry in 1788. In their behaviour the first three of these and to a large extent the fourth acted in accordance with the theory. Angels were minted with each pretender's full pretended titulature, and handed out as touch-pieces in an explicit confirmation of his kingly power to heal. Titles were bestowed on deserving supporters as a sign of the pretender's status as *fons honorum*, the fount of honour. As long as resources allowed and willing hosts were available, a court was maintained in exile, with regular appointments by warrant and commission.[29] Even Henry Stuart, the cardinal of the Roman church, who had been created Duke of York by his father the Old Pretender, though many years had passed since the 'cause' had a hope of success, did not refrain from calling himself Henry IX.

But from the middle of the eighteenth century the cause was in retreat. The Young Pretender correctly noted that if his claim to the throne were to be realized, it would require military action. While the campaign of 1715 had failed and led to no real diminution of support, that of 1745 very nearly succeeded but prompted a general decline.[30] The disastrous defeat at Culloden was romanticized, and the ferocity of the twenty-five-year-old Duke of Cumberland (George II's younger son) in pursuing the rebels widely deplored; but anti-Jacobite Cumberland Societies sprang up all over the country, Scotland included, and it was clear that many were disinclined to assist providence in inflicting the trauma of another dynastic change. Even the grounds for sentimental support slowly evaporated, as Charles grew old and became a rather unattractive and pitiful character, and the British crown passed (in 1760) to the young George III, the first king of his line not to seem a foreigner.

By the time of the last Stuart claimant, pretendership had indeed become pretence. Henry was on good terms with his Hanoverian cousins and even received a pension from George III. To George IV he sold some of his Stuart crown jewels. These transactions reveal his straitened circumstances and it is possible that,

A pleasantly gory anti-Jacobite medal from the time of the '45, commemorating the Duke of Cumberland on the obverse. The reverse shows the recommended treatment for the 'more rebels a-coming'.

if better-off, the cardinal would have been less willing to build bridges. But it was doubtless felt on both sides that the crisis was long past, the problem nearly resolved. After Henry's death in 1807 the representation of the dispossessed line passed to foreign princes, the dukes of Modena and thence the Kings of Bavaria. Though the arguments deployed early on in support of the Stuart claim were in theory no less valid in relation to these more distant claimants, few felt inclined to resurrect them. As George III's second daughter Augusta said, 'after the death of Cardinal York, I felt myself to be really Princess Augusta'.[31]

Bronze medal of Cardinal Henry Stuart by G. Hamerani, 1788, according the pretender the full regal titulature that he in fact only fitfully claimed.

Chapter 3

Impostors and Slave Kings

The most brazen sort of usurpation is achieved not by fabricating or manip-
ulating the rules of succession or one's own family history, but by falsely
assuming someone else's identity. The classic examples from English history
are Lambert Simnel and Perkin Warbeck, who impersonated sons of the last
Plantagenets. In some ways this form of imposture is quite straightforward:
it needs involve no subtle constitutional argument, no questioning of the
current régime, no military support; it can be carried out (and perhaps is best
carried out) by one person acting alone, the impostor himself. Reciprocally,
it is easily dealt with, by showing that the claimant is not the person he
pretends to be. But despite this basic simplicity, the phenomenon is
frequently part of a much wider and much more interesting context, in
which the régime might well be questioned, the constitution hotly debated
and armed rebellion resorted to.

Pseudo-Neros and Richard Imitators

Near the start of his second book of *Histories*, writing of the year AD 69 and
the period of great unrest and uncertainty in the Roman world that followed
the suicide of the Emperor Nero, the Roman historian Tacitus relates a
strange tale:

At about this time Greece and Asia were stirred up by a false report that Nero was
about to arrive, and the different versions of his death which led many to pretend, and
believe, that he was still alive. We shall deal with other attempts and enterprises of
this sort in the course of this work; this episode concerned a slave from Pontus or –
according to another account – a freedman from Italy, an accomplished lyre-player
and singer, which fact along with his facial similarity made his suitability for the
imposture better still. He rounded up some deserters, resourceless vagrants whom he
waylaid with the promise of great things, and put out to sea. Driven by bad weather
to the island of Cythnus, he signed up some of the soldiers stopping there on their way
back from the East, and had those who refused to join him killed. He then proceeded
to rob the local businessmen and armed a few of their strongest slaves. A centurion
called Sisenna, who was escorting tokens of friendship to the Praetorians in the name
of the army of Syria, was harassed in various ways until he took fright and fled the
island, fearing attack. The terror spread far and wide, many being prompted to
respond to the famous name by their love of novelty and their hatred of the way
things were.

(Tacitus, *Histories* II. 8)

Nero (ruled AD 54–68) shown playing the lyre
on the reverse of a copper *as*. Nero's musical tours
of Greece were ridiculed by Roman historians but
brought him great popularity in the east. (×1.5)

Within the senatorial order in Rome and
the west, Nero had been despised. In the
east, however, he had made lavish attempts
to court popularity, inspired by an
apparently sincere feeling for Greek culture,
and had succeeded in earning love and admiration.
It is not surprising that in the political tumult of that year many in the east
turned to his memory for support, and that certain individuals were ready to
step into the breach, providing the public with what they wanted – and
themselves with a brazenly direct access to prominence and power.

This sort of event was far from uncommon in the ancient world. Indeed we
are told that at least two other individuals tried to pass themselves off as
Nero, one in AD 80 and yet another in 88. The former even gained support
from the King of Parthia, Rome's great eastern enemy. More than thirty
years earlier an ex-slave had pretended to be Drusus Caesar, Nero's uncle,
who was actually in prison at the time. Tacitus retold this episode in almost
precisely the same terms as the ones he used to describe the false Nero,
including the simple but perfect phrase he adopted for the state of mind of
each impostor's followers: *fingebant atque credebant* (they both pretended and
believed in the pretence) – a phrase which might be used of many of the
impostures and falsehoods detailed in this book.[1]

As for the wider reception of the imposture, Tacitus explains it in two
ways. The first is a deprecating judgement on the love of the general public
(and especially the Greek section of it) for sensational news; *nova et mira*,
literally 'new and amazing things', as good a title for a Latin-language
tabloid newspaper as could be imagined. This is a timeless explanation,
offered by the moralist in Tacitus rather than the historian.

The second explanation for the success of the imposture is kinder on those
who were taken in, and recognizes the perils of the contemporary political
situation; it is given at the end of the passage on the false Nero quoted above,
their 'hatred of the way things were'. Add to this the uncertainties about
Nero's death and the phenomenon is accounted for. Not that a functional
account like this rules out ascribing the instance in question to the nefarious
character of specific individuals.

These two explanations are of great interest, and this section will in some ways be an examination of their validity. Both have merits and can undoubtedly be expressed more subtly than the crude formulations given above. To take the first one, Tacitus' retelling of the appearance of the false Drusus and false Nero also implicitly puts them in the context of the marvels and omens that other, less sceptical historians used to mark moments of great tumult and significance; not just appearances but 'apparitions', *monstra* or *prodigia* in Latin. Tacitus did not hold much with the two-headed lambs and talking dogs that some Roman authors record, though he did report the sighting of the phoenix. However, even his dry account of imposture preserves something of the ominous and prodigious character of the phenomenon for believers and disbelievers alike. For the former the impostor's claims revealed or implied great intrigue or natural events: Drusus had escaped from gaol, Nero was not dead after all. For the latter, the imposture was itself the prodigy, a sign of a turbulent, uncontrolled time.

The association between imposture of this sort and myths, omens and prodigies has been made in the context of the Middle Ages and early modern period. In particular it has been correctly linked with messianic myths of the 'sleeping hero', the great, almost superhuman king from a former age who will one day return and resolve the problems of the present by returning things to a pristine state. King Arthur, the once and future king, is the best example of the phenomenon in western literature.[2] This association, however, needs to be kept fairly loose. Those impostures that have achieved most success have rarely taken as their subjects the 'sleeping heroes' themselves. Even in a more 'superstitious' era than the present, an individual presenting himself as King Arthur in person would not be entertained as a serious candidate for temporal power by many, or for long. The idiom of the claim would be correctly understood as lying firmly at the mystical or esoteric end of the religio-political spectrum.

This is because the classic sleeping hero is, in the phrase just used, a king 'from a former age'. Though the limits of popular gullibility are not fixed, and depend on the extent to which people have access to reliable information about political events, the sort of imposture we are dealing with is restricted by the fact that it must stand a chance of being credible. Therefore the subject of the imposture must be a recently deceased or defunct ruler, one who might well become, in later centuries, a 'sleeping hero', but one who for the present, and for some at any rate, remains fresh in the memory.

In addition, and perhaps more essential to the phenomenon than the point about sleeping heroes, is the fact that imposture frequently takes place when there is a sense of injustice or intrigue about the subject of the imposture. If he or she died in mysterious circumstances, or young and with much promise unfulfilled, or leaving a chaotic and traumatic situation behind, or was simply much loved, then imposture may follow. The chaos might result, for instance, from the fact that the deceased was the last of a line, and the succession is now in doubt. If he or she was murdered or assassinated (either provoking or resulting from a traumatic situation, or both), so much the better. Any element of mystery or uncertainty about his or her death obviously favours those who want to argue that it never happened; but, equally importantly, it will add to the general sense of grief and perhaps even panic, and thereby make a convincing stand-in more welcome.

Not that heroic figures cannot be the subject of imposture. A well known medieval case was Frederick II, the Hohenstaufen Holy Roman Emperor who died in 1250. Ruling not only the Frankish empire of the west but also, in right of his second wife, the crusader kingdom of Jerusalem, he was a mighty figure in European affairs for thirty years, and it was scarcely surprising that the millenary mythology of his day should adopt him as an iconic figure, the 'last emperor'. After his death pseudo-Fredericks sprang up in many parts of Germany, attracting wide popular support; two ended by being burnt at the stake.[3]

More to the point is Don Sebastiano, the young, fanatical King of Portugal who was lost in battle against the Moors at Alcacer Quibir in Morocco in 1578 and was gradually transformed into a sleeping hero. A devoutly religious ascetic, Sebastian dedicated his brief reign to the expansion of Portuguese power and the implantation of Christianity in north Africa. The manner of his death was certainly heroic and mysterious, his body not being found immediately, and the saintly but warlike nature of his rule inspired admiration and fear in equal parts. Both these factors, added to his youth, made him a prime candidate for imposture. The point that clinched it, however, was the fact that his death led to great political uncertainty; his only

Frederick II, Holy Roman Emperor and King of Sicily and Jerusalem, *immutator mundi* (the world's 'transformer' or saviour). Twice excommunicated, he was reported to have called Christ, Moses and Muhammad three impostors. After his death it was believed – among many other things – that he had been transported into Mount Etna.

heir was an aged, unmarried great-uncle, a cardinal in the Roman Catholic church, who died two years later. The inheritance was then adjudged to have passed to Philip II of Spain, who was related by descent and marriage to the last king. The matter was not, of course, simply resolved by cool consideration of the laws of inheritance, and there were many interests involved. Philip was said to have justified his title to Portugal with the words 'I inherited it, I bought it, I conquered it'.

Portugal now stood in relation to Spain as Scotland did to England between 1603 and 1707, and it is widely held that for the monied and powerful classes the loss of a separate monarchy brought more advantages than inconveniences. At a popular level things may have been different. From the outside, furthermore, the death of Sebastian could only seem to have led to the end of Portugal. It was a major event that attracted attention all over Europe and created a highly attractive opening for opportunists. Before the sixteenth century was out, four individuals had surfaced claiming to be Sebastian, two in the Iberian peninsula and two elsewhere in Europe.

With the passage of time, and the breakdown of the union between Spain and Portugal, the memory of Sebastian assumed a different character and the king himself became ever more a sleeping hero: a *rei encuberto* in Portuguese, or 'hidden king'. In this guise, 'Sebastianismo' was still reported in existence in Brazil in the mid-nineteenth century.[4]

Don Sebastiano, then, was or at any rate became a heroic figure, an Iberian Arthur. Far otherwise were certain subjects of imposture in the later English Middle Ages. What they share with the Portuguese case is not heroism but the fact that their deaths or disappearances were premature, mysterious and parts of larger, politically troubled contexts. The highly charged nature of these contexts will be familiar from the last chapter, as in each case the imposture was the direct result of a usurpation.

Chapter 2 examined the seizure of the throne by Henry IV and the mixture of arguments, pragmatic and historical, that were deployed to justify it. As stated there, the taint of usurpation remained with Henry throughout his reign and even clouded those of his son and grandson, eventually providing the rhetorical point of departure for the Wars of the Roses. Richard II had not been loved; his weakness was widely recognized, shown up particularly starkly by the heroic virtues of his father the Black Prince. However, the circumstances in which he was deposed and met his end were riven with intrigue, uncertainty, mystery and a wide sense of injustice. In the absence of firm proof of his death, it was scarcely surprising that false Richards should present themselves. One, an individual called Thomas Ward of Trumpington, was taken in by the King of Scots and maintained at his court as an alternative strategy to the more orthodox methods of involvement in English affairs. He remained there twelve years, possibly more, supported by payments from the exchequer.[5]

The two great names in late medieval imposture in England were Perkin Warbeck and Lambert Simnel. Immortalized as one of English history's 'waves of pretenders' by *1066 and All That*, this pair of impostors and the complex events surrounding their respective appearances in the early years of Henry VII's reign were until recently part of 'what every schoolboy knows' – or, as Sellar and Yeatman indicated, what every schoolboy had been taught but then had immense difficulty remembering clearly. This was perhaps because of the way the episodes were taught, as part and parcel of the intricate and confusing political intrigue and uncertainty surrounding the early years of Tudor rule. This is not surprising; it was their political significance that earned them their place in the school curriculum, after all. Both episodes were, indeed, of great importance to domestic affairs and relations with Ireland, and in the case of Perkin Warbeck – as a recent book on the subject has convincingly shown – to the whole European situation as well. Furthermore, unlike the pseudo-Fredericks, neither Simnel nor Warbeck managed to arouse large-scale popular, fanatic support; their political significance was on the level of pre-existing factions or parties. On this stage most of the other players were aristocrats, gentry or local potentates, drawing certainly on their own followers when necessary, but merely to strengthen a personal cause. However, it would be entirely wrong to overlook the dramatic context of the Simnel and Warbeck episodes, for they fit precisely with the phenomena we have been discussing.

Both Simnel and Warbeck impersonated scions of the Plantagenet dynasty, and more particularly of the house of York, with which Henry Tudor had – as described in chapter 2 – a very finely balanced relationship. The subject of Simnel's imposture in 1486–7 was Edward, Earl of Warwick, the eleven-year-old son of George, Duke of Clarence, who had been disinherited and held prisoner by Richard III. For him Bosworth had meant only a change of gaoler; his plight was widely known and pitied, and made him a focus for legitimist aspirations. Simnel, apparently tutored in deception by a wily priest named William Symonds, was the son of an Oxford tradesman. Whether there were any more exalted sponsors for the scheme is not known, though it has been suggested that the Queen Dowager (widow of Edward IV and Henry VII's mother-in-law) was involved. At any rate, others of lofty status soon took up the cause. Simnel's first apparition was in Ireland where

Silver groat or fourpenny-piece minted in
Dublin early in 1487 for a King Edward,
who can only have been Lambert Simnel,
the false Edward VI.

the Yorkist interest was strong, and the influence of the Earl of Kildare
induced many to join in hailing him as the disinherited prince. Whether
they believed is not a question we can now attempt to answer; they were
probably like the supporters of the false Drusus, *fingebant atque credebant*.
They were joined in May by two well-born rebels from England: Lord Lovell
(Richard III's great minister) and, more strikingly still, the Earl of Lincoln,
whose mother was Richard's elder sister. With the support of Lincoln, himself the next best thing to a Plantagenet prince, the movement gained in
military strength (he had brought 2,000 German mercenaries with him) and
in confidence. Simnel was crowned at Dublin as Edward VI, a coinage was
struck in his name and a parliament summoned to attend him. The only
logical step that remained was to invade England.

A mixed army of German and Irish accordingly landed in Lancashire in
early June and made progress south-east. They met with little local support,
however. At the first report of the apparition, Henry had exhibited the real
Earl of Warwick widely in London, allowing him to meet with those who
knew him. More importantly, perhaps, the invasion struck the wrong note
with the English; as Francis Bacon later wrote, they were not inspired by a
king 'brought in to them on the shoulders of Irish and Dutch'. On 16 June
the invading army was defeated by Henry at Stoke, the Earl of Lincoln
being killed with many others. Symonds and Simnel confessed (the former
being imprisoned for life, the latter set to work in the royal kitchens) and
Henry was able to taunt his captives, 'My masters of Ireland, you will crown
apes at last.'[6]

The failure of the Simnel imposture to inspire the English had been fatal.
The problem was not, perhaps, simple chauvinism; the apparition seemed to
come from the wrong quarter. To the Irish, it had been easy to imagine this
Earl of Warwick coming across the sea to them from England; the mechanics
need not be worked out in detail, for the concept made dramatic sense. The
return journey was not so easily explicable in dramatic terms to the English.
The *monstrum* had been revealed elsewhere, overseas, and had undergone
the crucial initial phase of winning support there. It was now presented to

them as a fully formed king, and it came not from London or any other seat of power, but rather from Ireland, a country of *monstra*, not to mention rebellion. The sense was not so much dramatic as, all too clearly, that appropriate to imposture.

This was inconvenient for the impostor and perhaps inconsistent of the English. Most tales of the secret survival of kings and princes had them biding their time abroad or in border regions. But this might be a structural paradox lying at the heart of tales of this nature: secret survivors must lie away from the centre of power, but by doing so they dissociate and distance themselves from the trappings of that power and risk seeming ramshackle parodies of the real thing. There was, after all, another common image in the popular mind, as we shall shortly see: the bandit prince, gypsy leader or slave king. A faltering impostor, hoping to emerge as the long-hoped-for hero of the hour, might fall instead into a category not far removed from these.

Perkin Warbeck managed, at least, to avoid this fate for longer. His imposture, as indicated above, was a real crisis in Henry VII's reign and an important episode in European politics; a full account cannot be attempted here. The son of a rich merchant of Tournai in Flanders, Warbeck related in a frank confession of 1497 that his adventure began around 1491 in Cork, where he had gone in the service of a Breton master. Seen by some of the townsmen dressed in his master's silk clothes, he was hailed by them as the young Earl of Warwick (the one impersonated by Simnel). In front of the mayor of the town he made oath that he was not; to no avail, however, as they now assured him that they knew he was the bastard son of Richard III and need not be scared of admitting it. He again swore it was not so and the conspirators (whose names he gives) now said he was Edward IV's younger son Richard, Duke of York – the younger of the Princes in the Tower. This time they gave Warbeck no chance to disagree: he was forced to dress, behave and speak like a prince, and exhibited to the Earls of Desmond and Kildare, in the hope of wider support.

Support, however, was not forthcoming in large quantities in Ireland, perhaps because of a long-lasting recoil from the Simnel episode, and the conspirators decided to seek it in France. At this point the tale ceases to be one of intrigue among the mercantile municipal classes of Ireland and becomes a matter of high politics. The original conspirators recede and it becomes clear that Warbeck was no longer an entirely passive party in the enterprise – though he may not have had full control of the headlong course he took. His passage to France was at the invitation of the king, Charles VIII, who saw in Warbeck a bargaining tool to use against the English; he could threaten to support the impostor if things went badly, or offer to repudiate him otherwise. This, however, placed a clear limit on the bogus Duke of York's utility. Sure enough, when the Treaty of Etaples was agreed between France and England in November 1492, Charles expelled Warbeck. He now went to the Netherlands where he was received by Margaret, Duchess of Burgundy, sister of Edward IV – his notional aunt – who maintained a Yorkist court in exile at Antwerp.

This was perhaps the most glorious period of Warbeck's success. Margaret (who had been married off in 1468, five years before her nephew was born) may or may not have believed in him herself, but she worked hard to have him accepted by others including the Pope and Maximilian of Austria, Holy Roman Emperor, whose daughter it was even rumoured that he would marry. Undoubtedly any agreement of that sort was dependent on his gaining the throne of England. Nonetheless the warmth of the reception he

The only known contemporary picture of Perkin Warbeck, a pencil drawing held at Arras, showing him in the guise of Richard, Duke of York.

was experiencing provoked Henry Tudor to impose a trade embargo against the Netherlands in summer 1493, which was reciprocated a year later. The situation was deleterious to both sides, of course, and it is not surprising that in 1495 the Dutch decided to rid themselves of Warbeck by mounting an expedition to place him on the English throne and sending him off to meet his fate: if he succeeded, all well and good; if not, they were shot of him.

The expedition was a fiasco and Warbeck realized promptly the time was not right for his advent; without even disembarking he sailed off to Ireland where he met up with the Earl of Desmond and the remnants of his earlier support, before proceeding thence to Scotland. Here he was received in state by James III, the King of Scots, given a pension and married to a daughter of the old nobility. But his position was again dependent on his host's relations with England. An abortive Scottish invasion in 1496, and a tin-miners' revolt in Cornwall, minded both kings to patch things up and Warbeck was once more a hindrance. James gave him a boat and thirty followers and sent him and his noble wife on their way.

The last chapter was a sorry tale. Warbeck sailed back to Ireland and gathered some more forces before embarking for Cornwall, where the miners' revolt seemed to offer some hope of success. Landing in September 1497, he did indeed gain support rapidly – at first. At Bodmin he proclaimed himself Richard IV and set off to take Exeter. This proved a disaster. His army was beaten back and soon took to its heels, while Warbeck and a few others sought sanctuary at Beaulieu Abbey, before surrendering in early October. Held prisoner for two years, in which time he made two confessions of his imposture and escaped once, he was at last reunited with those he had named as the original conspirators and, with them, executed. One other was hanged by their side: Edward, Earl of Warwick, the unfortunate true-born Plantagenet whose existence was such a thorn in Henry Tudor's side.[7]

The two impostures certainly read like episodes in domestic and international politics, rather than instances of widespread popular delusion or prophecy-led uprising. As stated above, the pathetic remnants of the house of York have little in common with Don Sebastian, and the straggling bands of Irish and Swiss mercenaries even less with the huge crowds that flocked to support the false Fredericks. The latter difference is really perhaps just a difference of character, rather than structure. Warbeck may have been sponsored by mighty individuals, but at certain points he did, fleetingly, inspire limited popular support, particularly during his last campaign in Cornwall. Popular delusions are by their nature fleeting and ephemeral: however briefly, Warbeck and Simnel do exemplify the phenomenon. The first difference can be resolved by a wider appreciation of what sort of royal individual might be the subject of imposture; not just 'heroes', but anyone associated with an unjustly or prematurely extinguished cause or lineage. Certainly any royal personage, no matter how uninspiring, can become the subject of myth and prophecy, as illustrated by the widely held beliefs about the survival and imminent return of Edward VI, the boy king of the Tudors. As late as the early seventeenth century it was still being reported that he was dwelling in some foreign clime – Africa was cited – and would come back to claim the throne. The latter sixteenth century had seen several instances of Edward impersonators. It might be asked why, since the Tudors were scarcely dispossessed on Edward's death but continued to reign until 1603. The answer is that the mood which gave rise to these beliefs and the resulting impostures was the mood of the 1550s, the immediate aftermath of Edward's unhappy and young death and the much dreaded arrival of the Catholic Mary, who was naturally rumoured to have done away with her brother. The traumatic effects of that period lasted well beyond Mary's death and replacement by a rule more congenial to the majority.[8]

The early seventeenth century in Europe was a time that was much aware of and much interested in imposture. Even an age that is likely to be taken in (and what age is not?) can be intrigued by the phenomenon itself, and experience a delightful frisson of horror as it learns of the brazen attempt of some scoundrel to pass himself off as a prince or king, and the gullibility of those who fell for the ruse. The saga of the False Dmitri in Russia was one distant case that received a large amount of attention in the west, with many books and pamphlets published containing first-hand accounts. The Dmitri episode was a classic case of imposture consequent upon usurpation and the extinction of an ancient line. In 1584 Ivan the Terrible died, leaving two sons of whom the elder, Fyodor, succeeded him as tsar. The much younger son, Dmitri, came to a mysterious end in 1591; some said he was killed on the orders of Fyodor's brother-in-law, a powerful and ambitious man in the state called Boris Godunov. At any rate, on Fyodor's death in 1598 Boris took the imperial crown and the house of Rurik came to an end.

Five years later the impostor appeared: the manservant to a Polish prince, claiming to be none other than Dmitri. Winning Polish support by adopting Catholicism, and help from the Don Cossacks whose hatred of Godunov was their main policy, he accrued a sufficient force to march on Moscow in 1604; the following year, after Godunov's death, he entered the city and was crowned tsar. Those who had opposed Godunov were happy to receive him. Then followed a turbulent reign of several months, but – as with Warbeck

Two of the tiny base silver coins
that are the only remains of the
brief reign of the false Tsar Dmitri.
(×2)

and Simnel – the support he had gained in exalted quarters dissolved when he became an embarrassment. His Polish and Catholic connections aroused popular opposition, and those who knew or suspected he was an impostor had no compunction about declaring him to be so. A mob stormed the palace and lynched the false tsar. His body was left lying in the courtyard for three days before being burnt. The ashes were loaded into a cannon and fired westwards towards Poland.[9]

At the root of these phenomena are certain widespread thought patterns about political intrigue that can be traced in imaginative literature and myth-making. One is the optimistic idea that evil designs – such as the intention to put an unwanted or inconvenient child to death – can be foiled. Ancient and modern literature bristles with tales of royal or significant babies whose deaths were ordered but who survived through the incompetence or mercy of the retainer entrusted with the task; Moses, Oedipus and Cyrus are merely the start of the story. The other recurrent element is the related, but distinct, *topos* of the heir to an ancient line brought up in obscurity and quite frequently in ignorance of his true status. The end of the house of Plantagenet has not infrequently given rise to tales of this sort, of which John Buchan's *The Blanket of the Dark* is a very readable twentieth-century example. At a non-royal level, the very occasional instance of titles of nobility passing to distant heirs who were humbly born and unaware of their ancestry has probably assisted the conviction that this was something that might happen with the Crown itself.

These fantasies have continued to hold attention in the modern age, meaning that the right circumstances for imposture continue to arise. There are new obstacles to overcome, of course. Illustrated newspapers and, more recently, newsreels and television have disseminated royal faces far more reliably and effectively than anything that was available in the Middle Ages, and thus require a higher standard of physical similarity from would-be impostors. Furthermore, the simple fact of modern methods of gathering and broadcasting news means that a standard (if not necessarily correct) version of the events surrounding a ruler's demise can be circulated widely and rapidly, leaving less room for that useful element of doubt in the public's

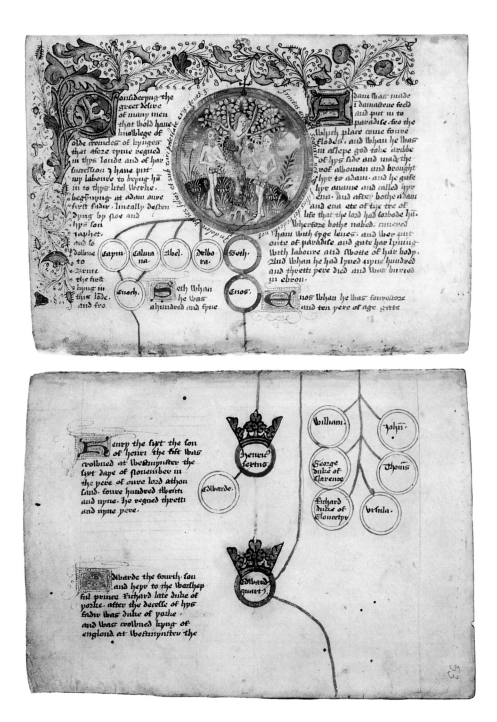

PLATE I The beginning and end of a folding manuscript pedigree of Edward IV, showing his descent from the Anglo-Saxon and pre-Roman kings of Britain (including Arthur), the rulers of classical antiquity and the Old Testament, and (perhaps least controversially of all) Adam and Eve. See p. 71.

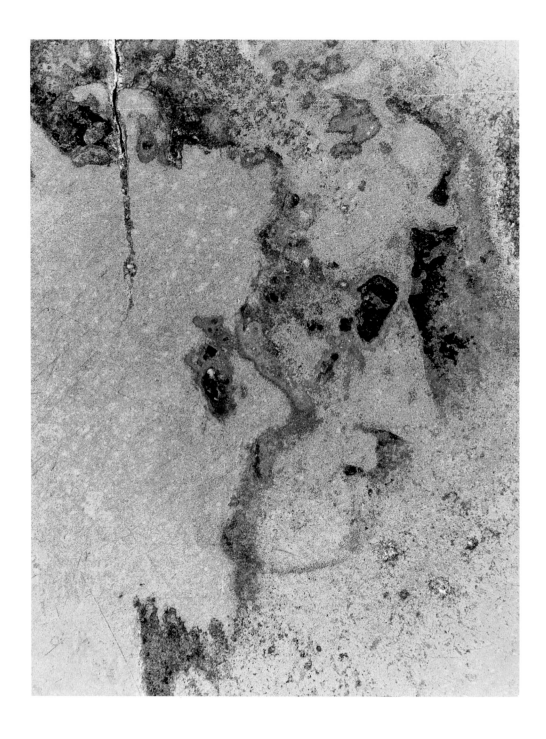

PLATE 2 Detail from a double *sestertius* of the Roman usurper emperor Postumus (AD 260–9) overstruck on a *sestertius* of Hadrian (AD 117–38). Postumus' profile is on the left, Hadrian's on the right. See p. 14.

PLATE 3 Four coats of arms from the *Armorial Général du Royaume de Hayti*, recording the heraldry of the newly created nobility of King Henry, 1811. See p. 115.

PLATE 4A
Set of tiles displaying the emblem of the kingdom of Araucania and Patagonia, fixed by French author Jean Raspail to a shed on the island of Minquiers in the English Channel in 1998. Raspail was claiming the island from Britain in recompense for the Falklands. See p. 146.

PLATE 4B (*Above*) Flag of the Soviet Socialist Republic of Byelorussia (until 1991).

PLATE 4C (*Above right*) Flag of the Republic of Belarus (1991–5).

PLATE 4D (*Right*) Flag of the Republic of Belarus (from 1995). See p. 172.

mind. On the other hand, conspiracy theories continue unabated, and they all plausibly suggest that the technology of those who would discover and make known the truth is, if anything, outstripped by new methods of intrigue and deception.

Shored up by these beliefs, then, imposture continued unabated into the nineteenth and even twentieth centuries. Revolution and popular disruption proved a particular boon. Thus Karl Wilhelm Naundorff (1785–1845) managed to convince quite a variety of people that he was the last Dauphin of France, the sickly and pathetic boy whose short life was largely spent in prison, and who had from the monarchist viewpoint reigned as Louis XVII after the execution of his father in 1793. According to the standard accounts the son, stricken by scrofula and rickets, had died in 1795 and been buried in an unmarked grave by the embarrassed and disorganized revolutionary government.

Naundorff, a watchmaker from Berlin and a convicted arsonist, claimed that the boy who died and was buried had been a poor nobody, a sickening lad intruded by the revolutionaries to cover up his escape, which had been effected by monarchist supporters. Why those supporters had then lost the initiative, and failed to broadcast their daring success, he did not explain. Instead of being fêted by royalists and anti-revolutionaries the world over the young, rightful King of France was left to make his own way in life, unknown and unrecognized.

Naundorff began his campaign in the 1820s. Letters to the Dauphin's surviving sister Marie Thérèse, and his uncle the new king Charles X, did not receive a response, but a visit to Paris in 1833 was more successful. Naundorff managed to persuade a surviving governess of the Dauphin that he was her charge. For others with the eyes to see, it seems he did in fact bear some resemblance to the family, and he satisfied some of those more detailed physical requirements – moles and scars in the right places – that seem in fact to be very inconclusive. But Marie Thérèse still refused to see him, and he turned to litigation and religious mysticism as both solace and as a means of attack. Neither approach working, he was deported from France in 1836. The rest of his life was spent in England and Holland, where he died; his gravestone at Delft reads 'Here lies Louis XVII'. His remains, however, recently subjected to DNA analysis, tell a different story.[10]

Bearing close similarities with Naundorff's case, but conducted in the face of a much more piercing media scrutiny, and much better known, is that of Anna Anderson, whose claim to be the last tsar's youngest daughter Anastasia has been the subject of countless articles, books, films and plays.

The duration of her claim, from 1921 to her apparent repudiation in the late 1970s, is probably without parallel, though as early as 1927 it was proposed that she was in reality Franziska Schanzkowska, a Pomeranian factory worker – a proposal that now seems confirmed by DNA analysis. Certainly that analysis seems to have scotched entirely the claim that she was the Grand Duchess Anastasia.[11]

Anna Anderson's tale is a remarkably successful one, even in the context of the whole history of imposture that we are considering. But it also shows the extent to which the art is hampered in the modern world. The princess she impersonated lived and died at the dawn of the era of all-pervasive media; only a few living people had a good memory of what she was like close up (though the ease of travel meant that it was easier to bring them into contact with the claimant than it would have been at any earlier date). These conditions will be ever rarer in the future. The public desire to believe that great and well-loved figures have not died continues, but it must now be content with less. This section began with the emperor Nero; it will end, not entirely frivolously, with Elvis Presley. Like Nero, Presley was a much-loved and charismatic figure who died prematurely in unexpected circumstances. It is not too far-fetched to discern certain physical similarities in their last years, and Nero considered himself a musician. Presley, however, though frequently impersonated, is too well recorded for full-scale imposture to be possible. The public love of *nova et mira* is gratified instead by a constant stream of brief, fugitive sightings, reported as sensations in the popular press. Presley thus lives on like the deathless Scholar Gypsy, who was seen by rare glimpses, pensive and tongue-tied: 'none has words he can report of thee.'

Elvis Presley, the King of Rock and Roll, whose 'immortality' is interpreted both metaphorically (in terms of his lasting influence) and in the concrete terms of his supposed physical survival.

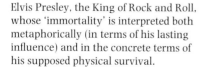

Kings, Slaves and Kings of the Slaves

The amount of work necessary to pull off an imposture is frequently not very great. If the circumstances are amenable, the impostor need make only the merest suggestion of his identity and others will draw all the conclusions necessary. In the ancient world another factor reinforced this point. There was in fact no need for firm claims of identity. To assume a resonant name and make a bid for power was enough. The name was a statement of policy.

Names, in the ancient Mediterranean world, were widely understood as significant. This can be easily misunderstood as a statement that esoteric beliefs in the 'power' of names were widely held; that a person given a certain name was endowed with a certain destiny. This idea was scouted in Plato's *Cratylus* and thereafter held no more and no less fascination for the ancients than for later ages. Likewise beliefs about the magical hold that knowing someone's name gave you over that person. There are signs of both these tendencies in the Roman and Greek world, but they are not relevant to the current question. More important, and certainly more widespread, was the idea that particular names were appropriate – either by virtue of their lexical sense or for their non-linguistic associations – for certain situations, trades, professions, or beliefs; and that this appropriateness could be read backwards, as it were, so that certain names, in certain circumstances, in effect became badges, expressing some characteristic of the bearer.[12]

This state of affairs was in part created by the simple fact that in the Greek world, though there were no automatically hereditary names akin to modern surnames, the same given names were repeatedly used by the same families, with the result that the names used by those families that had hereditary roles or functions naturally became associated with those functions. But it was also the case in the Greek world that people were readier to change their name to something that was appropriate to their circumstances.

These points can be examined at two widely diverse social levels. First, hereditary kingship was a means by which certain names – insignificant in themselves – became firmly associated with the monarchic function, in the minds of Greeks and later of Romans too. The two great Macedonian dynasties of the Hellenistic world were far from eclectic in their naming patterns: the descendants of Seleucus who ruled over Syria and the Middle East were all, without exception, called either Antiochus or Seleucus, while in Alexandria, the long, unbroken line of Ptolemies firmly associated what was in origin a fairly plain north Greek name with Egypt. When the Seleucids lost control of Parthia around 250 BC, the conquering king was called Arsaces, a name taken by practically all his descendants who ruled there until about AD 230.[13]

In other areas of the ancient world the same effect was achieved by different means. Thus in Ptolemaic Egypt the ruler or pharaoh was often known simply by that designation, the phrase *per-aa* ('great house'). The resulting impression, as in those cases where king after king had the same name, was of a single, unbroken rule.[14]

A connection can perhaps be made between this and at least one topic already mentioned, namely the messianic return of dead kings. There is possibly a closer parallel in the medieval concept of the king not dying. Even this must be qualified. The continuity of kingship did not mean that the death of each king was sublimated or passed over, so as to produce a seamless join. Much was made, in the ancient and medieval worlds, of a ruler's death. Rather – as Ernst Kantorowicz showed – the death of a king was regarded as different from that of ordinary mortals. The king's natural body received its rites in the normal fashion, but he had another 'body', namely his charismatic persona, the embodiment of his kingship, frequently physically manifest at his funeral in the form of an effigy. This was in some sense indestructible, and made plain to all viewers that there was more to a dead king than his corpse, or indeed his eternal soul; there was his kingship.[15]

This is, in part, merely to emphasize the fact that kings were *ex officio* charismatic individuals and thus by their nature inclined to prompt high emotion at their death, emotion in which people look around desperately for a successor. This is the situation, of course, which facilitates imposture of the sort discussed in the preceding section. Short of imposture, however, the ideal successor is one who fits the outline vacated by the departed king as well as possible, and an easy way of doing that is to have the same name.

Near the other social extreme, there are many ancient cases known of names that reflect the bearer's trade or occupation; they tend, furthermore, to be found in certain trades – particularly those involving public appearances, such as acting or sport, but also extending to doctors, who also relied on reputation. Famous names from the Roman stage – Bathyllus, Apolaustus, Pylades – had a sort of permanent existence. As the writer and moralist Seneca commented, 'How much care is taken to prevent any player's name from dropping out of use! There are whole dynasties of successors to Pylades and Bathyllus.' The same could be said of charioteers' names such as Scorpus or Scorpianus, and even of the names given to their horses: Andraemo, Passerinus, Pegasus. Type-names for animals, at least, are a phenomenon that will be recognized in the modern world.[16]

As a result of this conduct, at this distance of time, it is frequently difficult to tell whether two distinct items of information about actors, doctors or gladiators with the same name in fact relate to the same person. This ambiguity was perhaps just what the bearers of these names hoped to create: not, in all probability, an underhand method of gaining the support and popularity of a recently deceased star, but rather a public statement of piety towards a mentor or model.[17]

But the picture need not be restricted to specific trades or activities. Slaves in general followed the same practice, though not through any choice of their own. This went both for slaves acquired by capture and those born into slavery. Early Roman slave-owners had preferred simple, colourless names used throughout Italy: Salvius, Statius, Vibius. Later the fashion came in for relatively plain Greek ones – Philo, Tryphon, Nicephorus, Artemio – or refer-ences to the place of origin or purchase: Thrax (from Thrace), Milesius (bought at Miletus). Jokingly the slave might be given the name of a god or hero: Bacchus, Eros, Orpheus. In the same vein, if from the east, he might be named after a great king, Seleucus and Antiochus being especially popular.[18]

A further factor to note is that names frequently played an important part in the ancient world in indicating people's religious or mystical beliefs and even their trade or occupation. The religious change of name is well docu-mented, being most famously exemplified by Saul who called himself Paul on conversion. It can not always be easy to spot, as people often had a formal and an informal name, and it may have been the informal one that reflected the bearer's beliefs, but the formal one that was recorded. Only in the later Roman period, when tombstones began to be carved with alternative names, do we begin to see the practice in the open. Curiously, some alternative names on ancient tombstones look almost as if they were devised for the occasion: names that were never used in life, quasi-religious parting shots to accompany the deceased on their last journey. It is clear, at any rate, that the custom of religious name-change that in the modern world has become restricted to parts of the priesthood and monastic orders was widely familiar in the ancient one.

These points – the readiness with which names were changed, especially in lowly or menial social circles, or for religious reasons, and the notion of appropriate kingly names – can be taken together and throw a slightly different light on imposture in antiquity. Were the slave-born false Neros, for instance, all necessarily pretending to *be* Nero himself, in the literal sense, or merely to be a 'new' Nero; Nero in the political or social sense, so to speak? In the case recorded above, Tacitus admittedly refers to the impostor's facial resemblance to the true Nero, and it must be accepted that here at least there was an element of impersonation. But it is unnecessary to believe that in every case of imposture a hardline claim of personal identity was being made, rather than a looser one of status and policy, approach or attachment to a cause. One area where this interpretation is of great use is in the intriguing context of slave kings.

Slave revolts in the ancient world were frequently no more than mass breakouts, bids for freedom without any accompanying revolutionary or social programme (though it is regularly argued nowadays that the simple practice of running away, whether *en masse* or singly, was a conscious act of 'resistance'). The problem facing all runaway slaves in a slave-owning world, of course, is what to do next: individuals might attempt to infiltrate themselves among the ranks of the lawfully free, but this was scarcely a possibility for hundreds or thousands acting together. The huge numbers that flocked to Spartacus and his fellow leaders in 74 BC displayed notable indecision, rampaging up and down Italy, torn between escape across the Alps and the delights of pillage. Seizure of power in Rome and abolition of slavery was not, nor could it be, an option.

Accordingly, where circumstances permitted, mass breakouts frequently resulted in what was later called *grand marronage*, the collective resistance to recapture on the part of a body of escaped slaves or 'maroons'. The phrase opposes this activity to *petit marronage*, the behaviour of single runaways. Instead of running away and dispersing, those engaged in *grand marronage* would form their own social organization, either on the move or settled within the borders of the state whose citizens had enslaved them. Since there was nothing revolutionary about *marronage*, the form of social organization adopted frequently copied or resembled that of the slave-owning state in question, and it was far from unusual for the maroon leaders to be crowned kings.

There are at least two ancient examples of this phenomenon. The latter years of the second century BC saw two 'slave wars' in Sicily, one of the wildest and roughest provinces of the empire with a very high proportion of slaves. The first of these revolts, around the year 140, was led by a Syrian slave called Eunus. The historian Diodorus tells us that Eunus professed mystical powers, the ability to divine the future and a personal link with the Syrian goddess. The revolt was highly successful at first, attracting vast numbers of runaway slaves and conducting full-scale warfare against the

A copper coin ascribed to the slave-king
Eunus or Antiochus. (×2)

cities of Sicily. Eunus imposed a form of military and social order on his
rebels, with a council of advisors, and to cap it all he declared himself king
and took the name Antiochus.

A very similar outline characterizes the second slave revolt in Sicily, which
began in 104 under the leadership of a slave called Salvius. Like Eunus,
Salvius was adept in magic and divination, and gained rapid support. Revolt
was already in the air: in the vicinity of Capua, in mainland Italy, a well-born
Roman citizen called Titus Minucius had recently led a minor slave revolt
that had terminated in his self-elevation to kingship and then suicide. Salvius
followed the first of these actions, making himself king in the name of
Tryphon: an interesting choice, as it was a common slave-name in the
Roman world but, in the east, best known as the name of a usurper on the
Seleucid throne. He was joined by a rebel slave leader from another part of
the island, Athenion, who had also declared himself king but for the time
being was content to be subordinate to the new Tryphon; after the latter's
defeat in 103 he was able to resume the crown. The uprising now covered
much of Sicily and, like the first slave war a generation earlier, it saw assaults
and sieges on urban settlements large and small before its ultimate defeat.[19]

In these tales of slave kings there is doubtless no small element of dispar-
agement and exaggeration on the part of the Roman historians who relate
matters. Slaves who revolted or indulged in *grand marronage* were not
afforded much sympathy in the ancient world; even *petit marronage* was
condoned only in cases of extreme brutality on the part of the master. The
similarities between King Antiochus and King Tryphon might suggest that

Silver tetradrachm of Diodotus Tryphon, usurper king of
Syria in the period 141–137 BC. Tryphon rose to prominence
as an officer under the impostor Alexander Balas, who had
ruled 150–145.

we are dealing with a hostile stereotype: false, not to say ridiculous kings, their claims to rule largely based upon supposed magical abilities; imposture combined with charlatanism. It is perhaps significant that Spartacus, the one slave rebel of the republican era who earned respect and even-handed treatment in the historical tradition, was spared this caricature: he is nowhere described either as a king or as claiming magical powers. It might be wise, therefore, to doubt these details in the pictures we are given of Eunus and Salvius.

History, however, shows us plenty of later, better attested examples of slave kings and allows us to understand the phenomenon better. Many of these examples come from Latin America during the viceregal period, a fruitful area for maroon activity. As early as the first half of the sixteenth century, when attempts were still being made to use the native Indians as slaves, communities consisting at least partly of runaways were recorded living in the forested and often impenetrable hinterland of the white settlements of Brazil and Surinam. Later on, when African slaves had replaced the local labour, and they in turn engaged in mass or lone escape and evasion, black communities of a similar sort grew up, usually referred to as *mocambos* or hideaways. In many cases, the leaders of these societies were called kings. Thus the most durable and well-known maroon community of Brazil, Palmares, which lasted for most of the seventeenth century, was ruled by a king called Ganga Zumba and his successors, while in Colombia a *mocambo* was presided over by an ex-slave called Domingo Bioho, crowned *rey del arcaburo* (king of the craggy place). Many other examples exist.[20]

While these slave kings did not assume the names of established and powerful dynasties in the way that Eunus and Salvius did, it is natural to see their actions as imitating – if only in a selective and partial fashion – the forms and formalities of European monarchies. This idea is apparently supported by an equivalent form of activity in the earlier Indian communities. In the latter half of the sixteenth century the southern part of the Bahia region of Brazil had seen a widespread religious phenomenon known as the *santidade* movement, which grew up in settlements ruled over by ex-slaves calling themselves popes. Mixing native beliefs with Roman Catholic forms to produce a millenary cult according to which not just slavery but all manual labour would one day end, these slave popes appointed bishops to rule under them and missionaries to spread the word. It is not surprising to find that the movement had its origins in areas of sustained Jesuit activity.[21]

Cases like this seem, in short, to suggest that the 'slave kings' of the seventeenth century and later were aping the hierarchies of the west. Closer examination suggests otherwise, at least in part. An initial point is that many of the first generation of slave kings of Latin America were in fact also first-generation slaves, born in Africa and transported in adulthood. The economics of the slave trade and the realities of plantation life, furthermore, meant that the flow of Negroes from Africa to South America never really ceased, and that the proportion of first-generation slaves among maroons never dropped. This means in turn that African influences were still highly operative in maroon communities in the seventeenth and even the eighteenth centuries. Though slave-owners tried hard to keep different ethnic groups apart among their slaves, so as to make communication difficult and prevent the creation or continuation of tribal loyalties, this was not always possible, and there was in any case a large, communal central African cultural pool, about which little could be done. Among common west and central African customs was kingship, and it may well be that in many of the cases referred to above, it was African kingship, not the European model, that the slave kings were imitating.

This suggestion seems confirmed in the case of Palmares, mentioned above. Palmares was known not only as a *mocambo* but also as a *quilombo*, a word deriving from the language of Angola in Africa where many Portuguese slaves were captured. The cultural character of this region was so faithfully maintained in Palmares that the maroons living there frequently referred to it as *angola janga* (little Angola). Now in Angola a *ki-lombo* was a military community bringing together warriors from many tribes and areas, ruled over by a priest-king known by the name or title *nganga a nzumbi* – a designation that clearly explains the appearance in Brazil of King Ganga Zumba. The Palmares enterprise was evidently, at least at the outset, a recreation of African, rather than European, social forms.[22]

In the eighteenth century and later the incidence of slave kings in Latin America falls off, and maroon leaders tend instead to take titles such as 'captain', 'colonel' or 'governor', though in at least one case it is recorded that the wife of a man with a functional designation like this might herself nonetheless be a 'queen'. In fact of course these titles were no more functional and no less honorific than 'king' or indeed 'pope' had been earlier, and they did not *necessarily* reflect a Europeanized approach to the business of governing a community; but they did make an explicitly European reference, which 'king' did not.

The case of Palmares and the considerations pointed out above emphasize certain aspects of the ancient instances. Though the social system that Eunus and Salvius were escaping was part of the Roman Empire, it was to

Greek or Hellenistic models that they turned. Rome herself had no monarch at this stage, of course, and the names that each adopted as kings referred explicitly to the Seleucid kingdom of Syria. It is quite possible that Eunus and Salvius were recreating the structure of social power that they had known in their childhood. It was admittedly an act of great presumption for a runaway slave to model himself on a great Hellenistic monarch. But in doing so he was not expressing a poor and muddled comprehension of the political set-up in the Roman west. Spartacus, in turn, can perhaps be very roughly assimilated to the later maroon leaders who eschewed royal titles of the sort their predecessors had taken in favour of labels that derived from the society that had imposed slavery on them.

So the picture painted by the Roman historians of self-made kings ruling over unruly bands of escaped slaves, practising divination and other awe-inspiring activities, should not be rejected. The image certainly has elements of a *topos* about it, but that does not render it false. Two aspects of the picture in particular allow the topic to be opened out on to a broader plane: the connection between kings and magic, and the idea of the ramshackle realm of an imitation king.

Pinchbeck Princes and Mystic Kings

The imitation king is a well-known theme. Similar in some ways to the 'prince of thieves', he is often located in a criminal or near-criminal milieu, where he may be able to draw not only on authority but also on wealth (albeit ill-gotten). Other examples, like the Kings of the Gypsies and Beggar Princes, live in humbler circumstances, not actually outside the law, but certainly outside normal society. The idea perhaps stems in part from the curiously relative and subsidiary nature of authority in the Middle Ages, discussed in chapter 2. English society, to take the closest example to home, was once (and to a certain extent still is) full of barons and lords; only a small proportion of these are peers of the realm. Thus there are Lords Justice, Sea Lords, Lords President of the Council, Lords Lieutenant and Lords Mayor; Barons of the Cinque Ports and of the Exchequer. These individuals are only *functional* lords or barons, the high-sounding nature of the job description being a reflection of the dignity of their office. Parallel with this was the occasional appearance of mock or pretend lords, appointed to preside over festivities such as those at Christmas, and generically referred to now as Lords of Misrule.

To a certain extent, and in inverse proportions, we find the same phenom-

The creation of a new
Garter Principal King of
Arms, chief herald of
England and Wales.
From Vincent's *Precedents*,
an early 17th-century
manuscript in the College
of Arms.

ena in the case of the loftiest title of all in the feudal world, that of king. The
republics of antiquity knew quite a few instances of officials called 'kings'
(*basileis* in Greek, *reges* in Latin), and their existence has been explained as a
sign of the partition of kingly functions when the pre-existing monarchies
were overthrown. The medieval world, in which monarchies hung on to
their functions quite successfully, has left us few similar instances. The best
example, that of the King of Arms, is certainly the title of a high functionary
within a small department of the Crown's activities. But the evidence
suggests that the title, like the profession of herald of which it is the pinnacle,
had its earliest origin in a different milieu, where kings in fact were quite

frequent, a courtly version of the domain presided over by the Lord of Misrule. Kings of Heralds, as Kings of Arms were once known, in fact go with Kings of Minstrels, Kings of Ribalds and even, by extension, Kings of the Bean, the Summer King, the May King and other rulers from the popular English past.[23]

In these circumstances it is easy to understand how more than irony might be intended by titles such as Kings of Gypsies, Beggars or Bandits. Gypsy kings, in fact, have generally been elected and some have achieved national notoriety, such as Bampfylde Moore Carew (1693–*c*.1770). Obviously pertinent to this matter is the extent to which gypsies and other groups outside normal society regard themselves and behave as separate nations, a question that cannot be gone into here. But the relevant point to note here is the availability and currency of the supreme royal title to describe, not entirely mockingly, individuals whose position in respect of a lowly element of society was analogous to that of kings in respect of society

W. Bampfylde: Moore Carew. King of the Beggars.

The son of a Devon rector, Bampfylde Moore Carew ran away from school to join the gypsies, eventually being elected their king. He travelled abroad widely and, in 1745, was a sutler with the army of the Young Pretender.

as a whole. It is this factor that makes the concept of 'slave kings' comprehensible and gives the maroon kingship of the early modern world a certain,
misleading familiarity.

In the ancient world the same factor was present and perhaps even more
pertinent. Though there were 'kings' high up in society, as mentioned above,
there were many others of lowlier station. At Rome the *Rex Saturnalicius*,
for instance, was much like a King of Ribalds, presiding over the state
celebration of the Saturnalia, the festivities associated with Saturn. More
relevant still is the enigmatic figure of the *rex nemorensis*, the King of the
Grove of Diana near Lake Nemi, who provided a memorable point of
departure for Frazer's *The Golden Bough*: in function a priest, in name a king,
the *rex nemorensis* was a runaway slave who had killed his predecessor and
would rule until killed by a successor in turn. Frazer's tremendous essay in
the comparative study of religion and folklore does not err in identifying a
seemingly savage and outlandish practice that turns out on investigation to
have echoes throughout ancient society. It would be unusual if the slave
king of Nemi was not recalled by Romans reading of the slave kings of Sicily.

The mention of religious kingship brings us to the second aspect of those
slave kings that has broad relevance, and again we can only glance at it.
This is the involvement of kings in mystical and magical activity, and –
reciprocally – the aptness of the *magus* or wizard for rule.

The original *magi* were the members of an exalted order of priests in the
Persian Empire, into whose rites the Great King was to some extent initiated,
thus becoming a *magus* himself. Certain other kings of the near east – such as
those of Armenia – are known to have been *magi* too, and the status was
clearly of central importance to their royal position. The word however came
to be loosely used in Latin and Greek for all forms of sorcerers and celebrants
of obscure mystical rites, particularly if oriental, hence giving rise to the
word 'magic'; from this developed in turn a pejorative usage, indicating
charlatan practitioners of magic; conjurers and tricksters. It is in the first
of these broader senses that the *magi* from the east appear in the Bible, correctly translated as 'wise men', men whose prophetic and astrological
insights gave them foreknowledge of the Messiah's advent. But the alternative translation as 'kings' is a comprehensible error, in view of the ancient
associations between magic and kingship. By the Middle Ages the notion
that the *magi* who adored the infant Christ were kings was firmly established.

In bridging the gap between magic and kingship the Wise Men were far
from alone, and other figures in medieval literature are similarly ambiguous
in modern terms. On the side of Christian truth, Prester John was both a holy

The book of Matthew tells only of 'wise men' coming from the east. By the Middle Ages they had become a group of three kings, Melchior, Balthasar and Gaspar. Like other Biblical figures they were ascribed coats of arms; the versions seen here survive in a 15th-century German manuscript.

man and a man of great earthly power and riches. Marshalled against him, impostors in the spiritual sphere as much as the temporal one, were the great *magus* Muhammad and his henchmen and successors. One such imaginary henchman shared a name with one of the Wise Men: Balthasar, described in one manuscript source as 'by the grace of Muhammad King of Kings and Lord of Lords, Emperor of Babylon, Steward of Hell, Porter of Paradise, Constable of Jerusalem, flower of the whole world and cousin to the great god', with dominion over Muhammad and 'wild sprites', which his 'clerks' can summon up in any form he wishes. The same source goes on to recount how this Balthasar was by birth a Christian, who by charm, professing the Muslim faith, and advantageous marriages obtained sovereignty of first Syria and then Babylon; a usurper, in other words.[24]

This false Balthasar brings together several themes mentioned in this chapter so far, and in the book as a whole. He is an anti-emperor, a troubling and threatening figure uniting in himself opposition to the forces of Christendom. He possesses esoteric knowledge and abilities of the highest order. But he is not merely a mirror of the Christian emperor; he is almost a parody, a mock emperor like the mock kings and princes discussed above. Furthermore, even within the context of the anti-empire over which he rules, he is an upstart and a usurper. Though this factor is far from inconsistent with his magical powers, he appears at risk, ephemeral and vulnerable. Like Dr Faustus, he might find his dream at an end, his beguiling visions of earthly power evaporating before his eyes. He sheds much light on the image cast by the mystically inspired slave rulers of the ancient and new worlds: threatening parodies of kingship, at once amusing like Simnel and Warbeck, those crowned apes with their ramshackle bands of followers, and a disconcerting antithesis of true kingship.

Slave Revolt and Rebellion: the Case of Haiti

Not all slave revolts have led only to *marronage*. Some have been directed against the social structure enforcing the slavery from which the rebels have escaped. Already in the Sicilian slave wars that were discussed above there were traces of this, at least as recounted by the ancient historians: far from dwelling in secluded spots in the hinterland, Salvius and Athenion are said to have besieged cities and, like Eunus before them, waged war throughout the island. There was of course nothing 'revolutionary' about this, in a social sense, and it is easy to imagine how it might have come about as a result of the temptation of urban centres, the desire to obtain supplies in as easy a way as possible, the difficulty for the slaves of carrying on their own agriculture in the dry landscape of Sicily, and perhaps an element of revenge. Nonetheless it is worth pointing out that the picture does differ from that we have of the New World maroon communities, which lived apart, often trading with Europeans to survive. If they were successful, their fame could spread far and they could foment further *marronage* by direct activity and by their mere existence, enough to earn them the unwelcome attentions of colonial forces; but most of the guerrilla fighting they resorted to was in response to this, rather than aggressive. The inhabitants of Palmares were never likely to lay siege to Bahia.

More different still from this picture than the Sicilian revolts, however, are slave uprisings that end in the toppling and replacing of governments. An

Gold dinar of the Zanj rebellion, minted at
al-Madīna al-Mukhtarī, the rebels' 'chosen
city', in 882–3.

early model for this is the case of the Zanj in the caliphate of Baghdad, a
population of east African slaves who rose in rebellion against the 'Abbasid
caliphs in AD 869. Their assault on the city of Basra made quite clear their
intentions, namely to turn against and perhaps take over the society that
had enslaved them. This impression is confirmed by the rhetoric said to have
been used by the (non-Zanj) individual who led them. The Zanj of course
indulged in classic maroon activity before and after this attack, but as has
been pointed out, *marronage* is never absent even from overtly political slave
revolt; it is the presence of another, more ambitious aspect to their uprising
that interests us here.[25]

The revolt of 869 was ultimately defeated, though it lasted long enough to
give an idea of what was aimed at; the minting of coins and the formulae of
authority adopted appear to suggest that the 'Abbasid state itself was a
model. It was not until the end of the eighteenth century that a slave
uprising successfully led to the overthrow and replacement of a political
system. In this case it is intriguing to see how, though western models were
very consciously adopted, it was the institution of monarchy that was
repeatedly imposed.

Until 1804 Haiti – the western half of the island of Hispaniola – was
St Domingue, the most lucrative of France's colonies. But from shortly
after the Revolution in 1789 the island had been engaged in extremely
bloody civil war, the population split into three antagonistic groups: black
slaves (the vast majority), mulattos and white European settlers, the last
living both in the countryside as plantation owners and in the towns of
the coast as traders. The first slave revolt took place in 1791, a bloody
affair led by a slave called Buckman. In parts of the country the whites
now made truces with the mulattos to turn their attentions against the
slaves; elsewhere it was the slaves who forged an alliance with the mixed-
race rebels. The result was a confusingly variegated picture, with the
main black units (*les armées du roi*) interestingly declaring allegiance to the
toppled French throne: two of Buckman's lieutenants called themselves
Grand Admiral of France and Viceroy of the Occupied Territories. Gaining
support from an invading Spanish army, they declared themselves the

servants of three kings: the King of France, the King of Spain and the King of the Congo.[26]

Slightly lower down the slave rebels' hierarchy at first, but rising rapidly, was one Toussaint Bréda. Literate, highly intelligent and energetic if small and unprepossessing to look at, he was a general by August 1793 when he issued his first proclamation in the name of Toussaint Louverture. When in 1794 the combined Spanish and slave forces had all but conquered the entire colony, he defected dramatically to the republican cause and over the next two years succeeded in turning the slave revolt back on the Spanish and the other elements – including British forces – who had come to the aid of the whites and mulattos. A long struggle ensued, but by the end of the century the 'black Spartacus' was victorious. Toussaint's settlement of Haiti was carefully thought out, involving all sectors of the population who wished to make peace – whites and mulattos included. Agriculture was reorganized, with abandoned plantations nationalized and let out, the farm slaves being

Contemporary English engraving of Toussaint as governor-general of St Domingue, demonstrating not so much familiarity with his features as regard for his stance against the French republic.

TOUSSAINT L'OUVERTURE, GOVERNOR of S.T DOMINGO,
Engraved from an Original Drawing.

compelled to return to their labours as free men; Catholicism was encouraged and the clergy treated with respect, strict measures being taken against voodoo; agreement was reached with the French government whereby elected Haitian representatives were sent to the Corps Legislatif in Paris. Finally, in May 1801, a new constitution was decreed under which Toussaint was governor-general on the republic's behalf, advised by a ten-man assembly which he appointed (made up entirely of whites and mulattos). In truth his conduct was anti-republican both in spirit and form. It was scarcely surprising when the First Consul of France, Napoleon Bonaparte, decided to act; in December he sent his brother-in-law Leclerc to recapture the errant colony.

Leclerc's job was almost impossible, but Toussaint's position was weakened considerably by dissent on his own side. Terms were reached in May 1802 and broken soon after by the French. Toussaint was arrested and sent to France, where he died in prison the following April. The only satisfaction was that Leclerc had by then succumbed to fever and died in Haiti. The war recommenced.

Whether Toussaint would have declared himself a monarch is unclear. His position as governor-general was for life, and that may have been all he needed. But he was certainly not engaged in *marronage*, large or small. He had succeeded where the Zanj had failed, in turning a slave uprising into a rebellion and carrying it through to the installation of a new state.

The man who took over the leadership of the black party, another ex-slave called Jean-Jacques Dessalines, was perhaps less talented, but he managed to finish the job Toussaint had started. In November 1803 the French were defeated, and the following January independence was finally declared, a republic founded, and in true revolutionary fashion a new era instituted. The era was to endure, but the republic did not last out its first year. In September Dessalines made himself emperor of Haiti. He was crowned on 8 October, beating Napoleon to it by seven weeks. The new empire, however, was in a dire state, economically and militarily, expecting the return of the French, British or Spanish at any stage. There was no money to pay the troops and in 1806 an army mutiny in the south threatened Dessalines' position. By October he was dead, assassinated, and civil war again broke out. The *concordia ordinum* desired by Toussaint was now thoroughly destroyed; the colony split between two factions, southern mulattos and northern blacks. The former were led by Alexandre Sabès Pétion, the latter by one of Toussaint's lieutenants, a former cook and head-waiter called Henry Christophe.

Of the three individuals carried to positions of sole power in the first two decades of Haiti's bloody post-revolutionary history, Christophe is the most interesting, the most colourful and in terms of duration the most successful. Elected president of the state of Haiti (in opposition to Pétion's republic of Haiti) in March 1807, he was soon prosecuting an aggressive policy against his southern neighbours and a friendly one towards the British, while implementing further agricultural and economic reforms along the lines of those begun by Toussaint. After four years as president he may have felt he had earned a promotion, and on 28 March 1811 he declared Haiti a kingdom, himself its king.

Dessalines had done little to give Haiti the trappings of an empire. Christophe was not to repeat the oversight. One week after his proclamation he created a hereditary nobility with four princes, eight dukes, twenty-two counts and thirty-seven barons, with in addition fourteen *chevaliers* or knights. The titles, bestowed on his faithful satellites, were mainly taken from the picturesquely named estates of the inland region that had been the slaves' killing fields and were now their source of wealth; thus we have the Duc de Plaisance, Comte de Richeplaine, Comte de Crou, Comte d'Ouanaminthe and, most delightfully, the Duc de la Marmelade and the Comte de Limonade. A College of Arms on the English pattern, with kings and heralds of arms, was founded within the first fortnight of his reign, and by an edict of 15 April the heralds were given the sole right and duty of devising arms for the peers and knights of the realm. The resulting coats of arms were painted up in a splendid volume now surviving in the College of Arms in London (see Plate 3).

The edicts continued apace. Ceremonial dress was decreed for the nobility. An order of chivalry, the Royal and Military Order of St Henry, was instituted. Finally, on 2 June, in year 8 of the republic, the new king was crowned in a newly built church, and hailed as 'Henry by the Grace of God and the Constitutional Law of the State King of Haiti, Sovereign of Tortuga, Gonave and other adjacent islands, Destroyer of Tyranny, Regenerator and Benefactor of the Haitian Nation, Creator of her Moral, Political and Martial Institutions, First Crowned Monarch of the New World, Defender of the Faith, Founder of the Royal and Military Order of St Henry'.

Henry Christophe as a revolutionary leader, on a one-centime coin of the state of Haiti.

Henry Christophe as
a monarch in the
neo-classical, imperial
mould. On this coin
of 1820 only the
republican date
('L'An 17') is in French.

There is obviously something Napoleonic about all this, an impression
that seems to be confirmed by the neo-classical style of the king's portrait on
coins. But Christophe himself loathed Bonaparte; his model monarch was
rather George III of Great Britain whom, at his coronation banquet that day,
he toasted as his brother king. The format of his kingship was a western
European one. As his titulature pointed out he was the first example of
the phenomenon (with the sole, brief exception of Dessalines) across the
Atlantic: the empire of Brazil was not proclaimed until 1822.

There is also, of course, a comical aspect to the whole business. The easy
handing-out of peerages and the lofty titulature of kingship recall Evelyn
Waugh's satire *Black Mischief*. The reason for this should be understood: it is
not that the trappings of European monarchy are necessarily amusing in a
transatlantic context, or when played out by black actors. It is rather the
extreme haste with which an unfamiliar form of social order was being
imposed on Haiti, and the close attention to trivial detail that would more
normally evolve over centuries. Even these points might not in other
circumstances matter: Christophe had already spent more than fifteen years
seeing to matters of vital importance to Haiti, and doing so with great talent
and energy. The unfortunate truth was that his splendid kingdom was not
destined to last. We shall not follow its story, but nine years later it was at an
end, Christophe himself brought low by a stroke and rising unrest. In
October 1820 he killed himself, and Haiti descended once again into brutal
civil war, the ever-present violence which in fact gives Haitian monarchy the
tone not so much of satire as of Bokassa's Central African Empire.

So much for the character of his kingship: what about the nature of his rise
to power? Christophe had never been a slave himself, it seems, and was not
even born in Haiti but rather in the British colony of Grenada. There is also
some suggestion that he had a small fraction of European ancestry. From his
earliest involvement in Haiti's civil wars, however, he had made common
cause with the enslaved blacks. He was thus, in some sense, a slave king or

at any rate a king of the slaves. But, as was pointed out above with regard to Toussaint, we are here a long way from the slave kings of Brazil and South America, the leaders of maroon communities that survived precariously by retreating into inaccessible territory. That activity was at most one of resistance. If engaged in by sufficient numbers at once, it might qualify as, or entail, an uprising, but it was scarcely rebellion. The movement begun by the mysterious Buckman and carried on by Toussaint, Dessalines and Henry Christophe was undoubtedly not just an uprising; it was a rebellion.

Many writers would go further still. The chronological and causal link between events in Haiti and the French Revolution can hardly be over-looked. It is argued that revolutionary, democratic ideals and the desire to

The only known official portrait of Henry as king, by Richard Evans, 1818. Formerly in Britain (when this photograph was taken), the painting is now displayed in the Musée du Panthéon National Haïtien in Port-au-Prince.

117

transform society were at the heart of the uprising, along with a burgeoning black consciousness: this was not just a rebellion; it was revolution. Others resist this interpretation, preferring to see events of the sort that placed Christophe in power as in character the same as *marronage*, different only in degree: in particular the motives for rising remained the 'internal, intrinsic and traditional' ones of old, namely the slaves' desire to make a better life for themselves.[27]

Applying this latter interpretation too closely to the Haitian case would be a mistake. As will be clear from what has been related, there were real differences of character between it and the maroon activity of South America discussed above. But whether this particular rebellion was revolutionary is another question. This is not just because it did not advance the cause of democracy very far; revolutions do not need to be democratically inclined, still less republican or 'left-wing'. Between them, Toussaint, Dessalines and Henry managed to transform the system of power and authority in Haiti. But it seems doubtful that there was any real ideological content in the movement, or indeed enough unity of direction in their activity to merit the word 'movement'. Their political philosophy was meagre and derived entirely from the French revolution; nothing specific to the Haitian case ever developed. This may have been entirely because the business of civil war consumed too much time, energy and life for anything so refined to emerge. Whatever the reason, the only true aim of the uprising was freedom and equality for the slaves; everything else followed from that and the circumstances in which it was sought. In different circumstances it might have been obtained without any change in the political structure of St Domingue. Henry Christophe was not a revolutionary: he was a rebel king of the slaves, a mixed-blood descendant of Eunus and Salvius, King Ganga Zumba and George III. He was also a true original.

Chapter 4

Dreamers and Hoaxers

Some of the monarchic aspirations and ambitions described in this book so far may seem fairly insubstantial; little better, at times, than wishful thinking. This chapter, however, will look at individuals whose claims make those of the Stuart pretenders, false Neros and petty rebel emperors look rock-solid. For every form of subterfuge discussed so far there is a shadowy counterpart performed by individuals whose imagination ranges far beyond their station. Not all have been destined to ignominious failure, and just as those whose antics described so far shed light on authentic and uncontested monarchy, so these dreamers offer a wonderful commentary on the usurpers, rebels and pretenders.

It was discussed in chapters 2 and 3 how pretendership and imposture are two of the phenomena that arise to fill the hiatus left by a dynastic loose end. But people can be impostor-pretenders, fabricating for themselves a descent from one of the cruelly dispossessed lines or houses of the past. Certain climactic or epochal points in history, where great monarchies changed hands or even came to an end, are still capable of inspiring vivid emotions and reactions, including a sense of hurt and injustice; around these points the fantasists tend to cluster.

False Constantines

The most resounding and spectacular example of an epochal event of this sort was the capture of Constantinople by the Turks on 29 May 1453, bringing to an end the thousand-year history of the Byzantine Empire. It happened, it must be allowed, in a manner to thrill the romantic. The last emperor, Constantine XI, of the Palaeologus dynasty, was reported to have died valiantly fighting in one of the gates of the city, though others said he had fallen on his own sword in the hour of defeat. There were many conflicting versions of his end and it is not certain that his body was ever positively identified. It did not take long for the notion to grow up that he had in fact survived, first tentatively suggested in a long verse lament entitled 'The Capture of the City', composed by an unknown poet before the year 1453 was out:

> Tell me, where are you to be found ? Did you escape, or hide?
> Are you alive, or did you die by your own sword?
> The conquering sultan Mehmed, the ruler,
> When he took control of the rest of the unhappy city,
> Rummaged among the piles of severed heads
> And searched through the lopped-off bodies
> As he went round, but he never found you . . .
> I have heard them say, too, that you are hidden
> Beneath the almighty right hand of the Lord.
> Would that you were really alive and not dead.

This was really just a piece of poetic imagery, suited to the literary context, but soon the idea of the emperor who would return took root. Constantine himself, or some other, unnamed, emperor was sleeping, biding his time until he would return and drive the Turk from the city. Resembling the messianic tales of Arthur and other rulers who, having ruled, would one day rule again, this story found its proper niche in the overlap between folklore and popular literature, and has had moments of significance even in the twentieth century.[1]

Other stories told how the last emperor – in fact twice widowed and child-less – had left behind him a third wife and a child. In one version this child, a boy called Panagi, was brought up in the sultan's palace and, turning Muslim, eventually became sultan himself and begat a dynasty of sultans to succeed him: a nicely subversive account of later Ottoman history, according to which all the later rulers of Constantinople were actually of Greek, Christian stock.

In reality Constantine's heirs were two younger brothers who ruled the Morea, a tiny remnant of the Byzantine Empire around Mistra, in mainland Greece. Unable to work together or agree on where to appeal for help, they were easy prey for the Turks and were ousted in 1460. One was taken prisoner by the sultan and died a monk ten years later, with no surviving issue. The other (Thomas) fled to Rome, where he died in 1465 leaving four young children. Of these the elder son, Andreas, was a pretender in the full sense discussed in chapter 2: recognized as Despot of the Morea by the Pope, he went further and called himself Emperor of Constantinople, trying to raise funds for a new crusade to recapture his lost inheritance, but living an increasingly hopeless and penurious existence as support for and interest in his cause declined. Leaving Rome for Paris in 1494, he fell back on the pretender's last, and most pathetic, resource, and sold the King of France all his purported rights and interests in the throne of Byzantium. Even this gave only temporary respite and he died a pauper in 1502, using his will to make

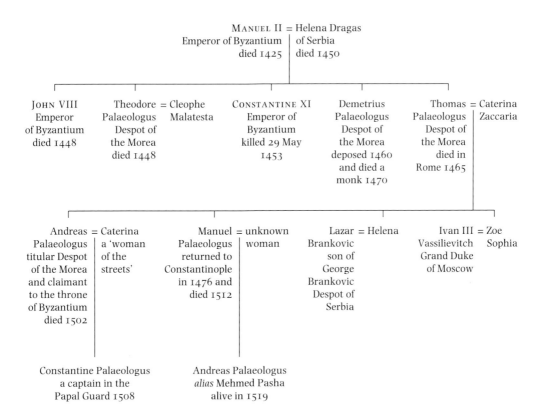

over his imperial rights once more – this time to Ferdinand and Isabella of
Spain. He left a son, last heard of in 1508: what became of him is not known.
Andreas' younger brother Manuel, disenchanted with the west, returned to
his ancestral regions in 1476 and sought Ottoman protection: at least one
son of his survived and turned Muslim, lending some slender substance to
the myth of the Palaeologus who became sultan.[2]

Thus by the start of the sixteenth century the male line of the last
emperors of Byzantium had died out or passed into obscurity. It must have
been clear by then to all but the most romantic that the empire would not be
restored – or, at any rate, not by the scions of the last reigning dynasty. In the
female line, it was true, descendants existed, and in positions of power.
Andreas Palaeologus' two sisters had married well: one to Lazar, a Prince of
Serbia; the other to Ivan III, Grand Duke of Moscow, a union of great
significance, for it assisted the Russian tsars who descended from it in
representing themselves as political heirs of the Byzantine emperors, and

in depicting Moscow as the successor state of Constantinople. Here we are back in the realm of the 'succession of empires', which was touched on in chapter 2; and it is no surprise that the fall of Constantinople spawned more than one such claim. At stake, after all, was not just the succession to the Byzantine Empire, but since Byzantium too was a successor state, the heritage of Rome herself. Venice, for instance, was one such 'third Rome'. In Constantinople itself the newly installed conqueror, Mehmed II, had no interest in claims of this nature: he had the second Rome in his power and had clear ambitions of taking the first one as well. He was now the only true emperor.[3]

The fall of Constantinople, then, prompted every kind of claim and counter-claim: messianic beliefs that the emperor was not dead; a tenuous dynastic pretendership; and the metaphysical, indeed mystical, question of *translatio imperii*. The situation was ripe for fiction, fraud and fallacy. It was not long in coming. The name Palaeologus was not rare in the Greek world, and it was naturally a temptation to anyone who bore it to believe – or allow others to believe – that it indicated a descent from the imperial dynasty. Those who did not have this option could have recourse to one of the other late Byzantine ruling dynasties with whom the Palaeologi had intermarried: Lascaris, Ducas, Angelus-Comnenus, Cantacuzenus. If details were required, there was no shortage of genealogical hooks from which one could hang a dubious line of descent: none of these families can be conclusively shown to have died out entirely, any more than the Palaeologi.

The first recorded fictions of this sort are from the sixteenth and seventeenth centuries. The Italian city of Viterbo, which had received large numbers of Greek refugees throughout the fifteenth century, of whom a proportion bore the name Palaeologus, became a centre for pseudo-antiquarian speculation quite early on. The name Viterbo itself was (entirely wrongly) said to be a corruption of the Latin *vetus verbum* (ancient word), a translation of the Greek *palaios logos*. It is perhaps no wonder that in this atmosphere of uncontrolled and unprincipled Byzantinomania, Viterbo spawned one of the most virulently partisan forgers of western history, the fiercely anti-Greek Annius (Giovanni Nanni). His epic productions quoted copiously from non-existent Greek sources to illustrate how small the Greeks' true rôle in history had been.[4]

Another Italian concentration of Palaeologi was in the east-coast port of Pesaro. It was from here that one Teodoro Paleologo set out for England, where he settled and lived until his death in 1636. His memorial tablet in Landulph church, near Saltash in Cornwall, recounts his ancestry: beginning believably enough with his father Camillo and grandfather Prospero, it then takes things back a further three generations to Thomas, Despot of the Morea, younger brother of the last emperor who 'raygned in Constantinople until subdewed by the Tvrkes'. Theodore married, the inscription adds with no sense of bathos, Mary, daughter of William Balls of Hadley, gent., and left four children. One of these, Ferdinando, emigrated to Barbados before the Civil War and lies buried there, a monument raised to his memory in 1906 similarly recounting – though in briefer form – his imperial descent.[5]

This sort of claim probably came about innocently enough: the result of a naïve and optimistic interpretation of a sonorous name, rather than calculated fraud or overweening pomposity. Things were not always thus. Jacobus Palaeologus, a notorious Greek churchman from the island of Chios, is a case in point, using his theological predications to proclaim himself grandson of the pathetic, itinerant Andreas and thus rightful heir of the last emperor. This might even then have been thought a harmless conceit, but unfortunately his theology was truly inflammatory: though a Dominican monk, he preached violent Lutheranism, and was eventually taken to Rome and burnt as a heretic in 1585.[6] A less fervently religious, but more grandiose, example from the eighteenth century was 'Prince' Johannes Antonius Angelus Flavius Comnenus Lascaris Palaeologus, a self-styled descendant of Theodore, one of the last emperor's brothers who had in fact left only female issue. This Johannes, who died in Vienna in 1738, was one of many false pretenders to claim the right of bestowing an order of chivalry supposedly in the gift of the Byzantine emperors – the Constantinian Order of St George, which is sometimes, absurdly, said to have been founded by Constantine the Great himself in AD 312.[7]

Fictions and frauds of this nature gathered force in the nineteenth century. It was not long before the contagion spread in a serious way to Britain. In part this was due to the arrival of already infected individuals from overseas, but the natives soon showed themselves equally capable of contracting the malady. Thus another Chian, a rich merchant called Demetrius Rhodocanakis, who settled first in London and then in Manchester and became a British subject in 1867, was one to take advantage of the British tendency to regard all foreigners with long names as noblemen. Claiming to be the senior male-line descendant of a marriage in 1614 between his homonymous ancestor Demetrius Rhodocanakis and the only daughter and heiress of the then head of the Palaeologus family, he main-tained that he was the rightful heir to the Byzantine throne. As such he was also head of the Order of St George, though he wisely eschewed dating it

THE IMPERIAL CONSTANTINIAN

ORDER OF ST. GEORGE.

A REVIEW OF MODERN IMPOSTURES

AND

A SKETCH OF ITS TRUE HISTORY.

BY

HIS IMPERIAL HIGHNESS THE PRINCE RHODOCANAKIS.

IN TWO PARTS.

LONDON:

LONGMANS, GREEN, AND CO.

MDCCCLXX.

back to Constantine the Great, and was content to regard the Emperor Isaac II Angelus Flavius as its real founder in 1192. For good measure, however, he traced his male line back to the imperial Ducas dynasty, explaining the name Rhodocanakis by means of an improbable etymology as a title meaning 'lord of Rhodes'. Interestingly, one of Rhodocanakis' Greek associates was the indefatigable forger Constantinos Simonides, whose extraordinary literary impostures were at least as brazen as the prince's genealogical ones, and alternately duped and entertained much of Europe. It is a fine case of being able to judge a man by his friends. [8]

The British isles, however, had other, more home-grown charlatans – though these too were doubtless partly driven by a derived form of the romantic pan-hellenism that the retreat of the Ottoman Empire had inspired across Europe. As early as 1830 Nicholas Macdonald Sarsfield Cod'd of Wexford (calling himself the Comte de Sarsfield) had petitioned the Prime Minister for recognition of his claim to the Greek throne, which he based on

124

his descent from the Palaeologi. He was unsuccessful, of course, and the crown was in fact given to the Bavarian Prince Otto of Wittelsbach. But Otto was ousted in 1862 and the kingship of the Hellenes was again up for grabs. Among those who applied this time was one Theodore Attardo di Cristoforo de Bouillon, 'Prince Nicephorus Comnenus Palaeologus', who died in 1912 and lies buried in the Greek cemetery in West Norwood, South London, his gravestone describing him as 'hereditary claimant to the Grecian throne'. The details of his genealogical claims are not known, but his immediate family were satisfied with their veracity. His daughter, Princess Eugenie, married a British artillery officer called Wickham and had four sons who all used on occasions the title and name Prince Palaeologus.[9]

There is in all this something characteristic of the age. It is worth recalling that King Otto, though a German, had been the main proponent in the mid-nineteenth century of the 'Great Idea' of reuniting all the Greeks of the eastern Mediterranean under one rule, with their capital at Constantinople. This was a period when western gentries and nobilities, viewing Hellenic affairs through a sub-Byronic haze, tinted by the nascent interest in medieval and Byzantine Greek history, were most prone to beguilement by plausible imitation Palaeologues: long-suffering but proud exiles who stoically bore the expropriation of their hereditary rights and privileges, and only sought the honourable treatment due to those of ancient, imperial lineage. In 1869 the Italian judicial body regulating matters concerning titles and coats of arms, the Congregazione Araldica Capitolina, recognized as members of the Roman nobility two separate individuals claiming descent from the family of the last Byzantine emperor: one called Prince Gerolamo de Vigo Aleramico Lascaris Paleologo and another, less extravagantly, Giovanni Antonio Lascaris. The judgements make interesting reading, accepting in both cases that the petitioners had not actually met the strict criteria in place for 'reintegration' into the nobility, but arguing that since their ancestors had enjoyed much higher titles in the past – a matter the tribunal was not actually competent to judge – they deserved admission nonetheless. It is perhaps significant that Byzantine revivalism was a widespread tendency in the new Italian kingdom of the 1860s and 1870s.[10]

But it was the twentieth century that produced the richest crop of false Constantines. A particularly brazen example was that of a Parisian lawyer, Paul Crivez, born in 1894, who as a young man got to know the widow of one Grégoire Paléologue. Like his cousin Maurice Paléologue, a distinguished diplomat and popular historian, Grégoire was descended from a wealthy Greek family living in Romania under Ottoman rule. Though there was no known link with the imperial dynasty, these 'Romanian' Palaeologi were naturally fond of the idea that some such connection might lurk undiscovered in their past, and the notion certainly informed Maurice Paléologue's view of his family background. Crivez, however, took matters far beyond this. Ingratiating himself with Grégoire's widow, he fabricated a detailed descent deducing the Greek-Romanian family from Manuel, the last emperor's Muslim nephew, and demonstrating that Grégoire himself had been senior male heir to the lost throne. It was then a relatively small matter to persuade the dying Mme Paléologue to adopt him, and invoke a completely spurious Byzantine protocol according to which the emperor's widow could, in the absence of legitimate issue, nominate her dead husband's heir. The adoption was accomplished on 11 June 1945 and Prince Paul Theodore Paléologue-Crivez, the new head of the sovereign imperial house of the east, was able to set out on forty years of ludicrous self-promotion. He died in 1984, eight years after his brother Alexandre, whom he had obligingly created Prince of the Morea.[11]

Scarcely less bold – though he is not known to have browbeaten any widows into adopting him – was an Italian tax lawyer of mediocre talents called Mario Bernardo Pierangeli. Born in Rome in 1914, Pierangeli was clearly imbued with some sense of self-importance, as testified by his loyal letters to the Duce and other elements of the fascist government (the earliest written when he was seventeen) now surviving in the Italian State Archive. He also wrote several books and articles on the historical glories of Italy's colonial possessions. But it seems to have been only after the Second World War that he began to take an interest in his own glorious genealogical past. Changing his name little by little through the 1950s, he gradually emerged as Michele Angelo-Comneno di Tessaglia, or, in full, His Royal and Imperial Highness Michael III, Prince of Thessaly and Epirus, chief of the name and arms of the sovereign house of Angelus-Comnenus. Minting gold, silver and cupro-nickel coins, and bestowing lofty-sounding titles, Michael III had acquired quite a few loyal followers by the time he died in the late 1980s.

One of a set of coins privately minted by Michael III (Mario Bernardo Pierangeli), Prince of Thessaly and Epirus. (×1.5)

It is to this côterie that we are indebted for a range of respectful works in various languages recounting not just their patron's splendid ancestry, but – more importantly – his personal merits and achievements, his democratic ideals and sense of historical obligation, his true nobility of spirit.[12] Like all genuine bluebloods, we are told, Prince Michael was dismissive of those who paid excessive attention to the details of his lineage. Well might he have been, for it was completely false.

A similarly diffident approach was taken – publicly at least – by another, much more famous, Italian who established his descent from the Emperors of Byzantium: the comic actor Totò. Born illegitimately in Naples in 1898 as Antonio Clemente, supposedly the son of one Marquess Giuseppe De Curtis, whose surname he later assumed, Totò was adopted at the age of thirty-five by another purported nobleman, Francesco Gagliardi Focas. Then began a long legal battle for recognition as heir to the Gagliardi titles; in 1945 the

Antonio De Curtis, alias Totò (1898–1967), one of the best comic actors of European cinema, but also heir to the imperial throne of Byzantium, Duke of Macedonia and Illyria, and Exarch of Ravenna.

district court in Naples granted his petition for recognition as a count, and the following year – somewhat more strikingly – as a prince entitled to the designation of Imperial Highness. Finally in 1950 the same tribunal allowed him to add six new gleaming barrels to his already noble-sounding name, and he emerged as Prince Antonio Focas Flavio Angelo Ducas Comneno di Bisanzio De Curtis Gagliardi.[13]

In Italy, as in many European countries, personal nomenclature is controlled by the law and if one wants to change one's name evidence of a good reason needs to be placed before a court. Success in this forum does not of course prove that one's lineage is as alleged, but that distinction is frequently overlooked, and the applicant – as in Totò's case – is widely assumed to have established all his claims. The press, which had followed matters closely but not critically, hailed the prince of Italian comedy as heir to the throne of Byzantium, and he himself could thereafter afford to be endearingly humorous about the whole thing. And while he lived few if any raised suspicion about the veracity of his claims.[14]

In the case of the most prominent recent British claimant to the throne of the Palaeologi, there was scarcely any need to raise suspicion. Peter Mills, of Newport in the Isle of Wight, alias His Imperial Majesty Petros I, Emperor and Autokrator of the Romans, 'the Palaeologus', was an extraordinary phenomenon. He was born in 1927, the son of Frank Mills, who came from the Isle of Ely in Cambridgeshire, and Robina, daughter of Samuel Colenutt, a plumber of Niton in the Isle of Wight. Prince Petros' Colenutt ancestry can possibly be traced on the island as far back as the early part of the eighteenth century – but no further, and this is crucial since, for some unaccountable reason, it was through the Colenutts that he derived his imperial blood. It has been suggested that a subliminal association was at work with the *theme* or province of the Byzantine Empire called Coloneia; but whatever strange thought process it was that linked his mother's interesting but decidedly English maiden name with the Emperors of Constantinople, it was entirely personal to the Emperor Petros himself. At any rate, by means of sources to which only he had access, he derived the family from one Richard Colnett who supposedly arrived in the Isle of Wight in 1525; this Richard (in truth Duke of Colnett by inheritance from his mother) was son of Prince John Palaeologus and grandson of the last emperor's brother Thomas, Despot of the Morea.

This version the *soi-disant* Petros pushed relentlessly in published and unpublished format, both under his own imperial name and as 'Count Saddington'. Bearded like a patriarch, dressed in long robes and sandals,

A rare photograph of Peter Mills, the *soi-disant* Emperor Petros. His uniform appears to include a cannibalized 'coatee' appropriate to certain officers in the British royal household.

or a Ruritanian-style uniform, he was a familiar sight in Newport, regularly visiting the Isle of Wight record office (often with his more conventionally habited father in tow) to conduct further research and tie up the loose ends of a story he was already satisfied with.[15] His early death in 1988 was marked by an obituary, accrediting him his full self-assumed titulature, in no less a journal than *The Times*.

The phenomenon shows no sign of dying out. Indeed, it proliferates. False Constantines continue to roam the globe. It is hard not to wonder what the attraction is. One answer, of course, is that it can be a way of making money. Almost all modern pretenders to the Byzantine throne have claimed to be Grand Masters of the so-called Constantinian Order of St George, and most have claimed that they have inherited the right of their imperial ancestors to bestow titles. Knighthoods and titles of nobility command high prices, even now. Nor need the exchange be crudely mercantile; it can assume the appearance of the just reward of an act of charity, if the pretender sets up a convenient and suitably vague trust for the aspirant title-holder to make a generous donation to. There are certainly several individuals using pseudo-Byzantine titles selling titles and knighthoods in this fashion at present, particularly in America.

But this is scarcely a means of acquiring princely riches. Lucrative in fits and starts, the sale of titles is doubtless a laborious business, requiring an endless round of self-promotion for uncertain returns: lectures to give, parties to organize or attend, investitures to hold, all of it to be done while creating the appearance of true, effortless, unchallenged, age-old sovereignty – just the right degree of swank – while also trying to avoid excessively close attention from the authorities or the press. No cynic, only after the money, would put up with such a life-style. Thus it follows that the pseudo-pretenders are not cynics. Self-promotion of the sort described is obviously something that appeals in itself, no matter how much the perpetrators claim that they are merely the unwilling but obedient servants of their own dynastic sense of duty. Furthermore, each time a false Constantine sells a title, not only is there an accretion to his bank balance, but there is also a new stout defender for his cause, an interested party whose own self-esteem is reliant upon the continuation of the charade.

So the title-bestowing business is a necessary part of the pseudo-pretender's activity. Yet this leaves open the question of why he is involved in this area at all. What possessed him, in short, to present himself as the true emperor of a long-lost empire?

In many cases the answer doubtless lies not in the claimant's desire for material gain at all, but in his personal proclivities, intellectual or emotional: a particular and exaggerated sensitivity to the associations and resonances of the titles and names adopted. The lost heritage of Byzantium, stretching back even to the Romans, and cruelly cut off in 1453, is an intoxicating brew of the exotic and half-familiar. Reference has already been made to the voguish fascination for Byzantine history in Italy and elsewhere in the nineteenth century, a reaction against the classicism of earlier generations. It is certainly not surprising that this attraction should be enhanced for later ages, at the dog-end of the phase of Classical education that once united Europe, when many know just enough about the Romans to disparage them. On the one hand, it seems to offer a direct connection to the

Greeks of today, in a way that studying the Classics does not. This taps into the modern movement of popular Greek nationalism. One fake Byzantine claimant, Prince Theodore Lascaris Comnenos, a Spaniard whose real name was Eugenio Lascorz, actually managed fleetingly to convince the Greek statesman Venizelos that he was the real heir to the throne lost in 1453, and was briefly held in reserve by the socialist party as an alternative to the then ruling family of Greece.[16] On the other hand, the cheek-by-jowl existence that Byzantium led with near eastern cultures opens up even more exciting vistas. The beautifully confused view of history that this can inspire is seen perfectly in the case of an individual called His Royal and Imperial Highness Georges Suleyman, Prince and Padishah d'Orléans-Bourbon d'Osman-Medjid Paléologue-Cantacuzène. Born in 1929, this prince derives his mother's lineage from the well-known 'Christian branch of the house of Osman'.[17] Again there is a hint of the playful myth of the sultan who was really a Greek prince.

It is in these entertaining fantasies – a sort of intellectual *chinoiserie* – that the attraction of setting oneself up as a Byzantine pretender largely lies. Magnified no doubt by long days and nights of solitary study, probably begun at an impressionable age, and hopelessly intertwining with personal aspirations and dreams, they can become in certain individuals a strong driving force for action. It is perhaps worth noting in this context that Totò's illegitimacy is known to have been a very painful matter for him; and interesting to observe that one of the most confident and self-assured of contemporary pretenders, who for many years has toured America and Europe bestowing titles widely and claims descent from one of the successful petitioners to the Congregazione Araldica in 1869, is said by those who have seen his birth certificate to have been born out of wedlock.[18]

Scottish Baronial and Mock Tudor

One of the themes of this chapter is that, whatever the personal motivations of the individuals whose absurd exploits and fantasies we are examining, they frequently ride some sort of wave of popular interest, fascination or trend. Indeed, it may be argued, doing so is the only way they have of getting any distance towards their aim at all. Very few of the individuals described so far are likely to have been cynical enough to have formulated their claims solely in order to court popularity; most, if not perhaps all, come across on examination like genuine, if deluded, believers in their own specialness. Some, it is true, have been entirely inadvertent riders of the popular trend. But there are certainly others who, having privately formed a wholly traditional set of beliefs about themselves, their birth and ancestry, and their inherited rights, calculate its public expression precisely so as to chime in as much as possible with contemporary ways of thinking, whether they be political or social.

This is not as difficult as it sounds, for two reasons. First, as the preceding section attempted to explain, delusions of personal grandeur frequently cluster around episodes in history that have caught the popular imagination, especially those where there is a lingering sense of injustice, or at the least of unfinished business. It is indeed likely to have been this, added to the straightforward glamour of a royal or imperial milieu, that caught the fantasist's own eye. Therefore it is no surprise if it can catch that of a wider section of the public too. Second, popular trends are not – it cannot be emphasized enough – always 'forward-looking'. Plenty of 'modern' movements are in essence or in part explicitly founded on a favourable interpretation of some aspect of the past. Nationalism, as the final chapter of this book will try to show, is in this way one of the most ambiguous sorts of political trend, sometimes looking radically new, but frequently decidedly reactionary. There is no reason *a priori* why a programme founded on traditional or long-standing, indeed long-disused principles, should not catch the public eye and therefore, in effect, become 'modern' (a meaningless word). In practice this does in fact happen, in certain circumstances, even when – perhaps especially when – the traditional concepts have been simplified and misrepresented to the point of caricature. Personal fantasists have not been slow in catching on to this.

A current example of personal fantasy that almost succeeds in riding a contemporary trend is provided by the self-styled Prince Michael of Albany, an individual of Belgian birth who believes he is the legitimate heir of Bonnie Prince Charlie (the Young Pretender) and thus the current Stuart claimant to the thrones of England and Scotland. In fact he is interested in regaining only that of Scotland. His claims are entirely traditional in their content. In a weighty tome entitled *The Forgotten Monarchy of Scotland*, which was published in 1998, the 'prince' (born in 1958) states that his mother is descended in the male line from a son and heir born to the Young Pretender in 1786, by a second marriage contracted in Rome in 1785. Both the son and the marriage were previously unknown to history, as indeed was the papal annulment by which the Pretender's first, unhappy marriage was necessarily brought to an end: this is revealed to have taken place in April 1784 and to have been recorded in the Vatican archives all along (though many have sought it there). Prince Edward James Stuart, the long-awaited heir, was brought up in secrecy and fathered a line of Princes and Counts of Albany living in exile. The sixth count of the line left only a daughter, and on his death his titles and the representation of the family passed to her son – the author of the book – who, judging the time propitious, has cast off the veil of secrecy and returned from exile to Scotland, his ancestral realm.[19]

That is the substance of his claims and, indeed, of the book. None of the sparse evidence presented in support of any of it is remotely convincing, which is perhaps unsurprising when it is considered that an earlier book (written not by the 'prince' but on his behalf) argued that he was descended, through the Stuarts and King Arthur, from Jesus Christ himself.[20] The rest of *The Forgotten Monarchy* is taken up by a highly nuanced retelling of Scottish political history before and after the Union, and a lively statement of the case for Scotland's independence. The author offers himself as a truly democratic monarch for the independent nation, humbly submitting – in what he sees as the true and ancient manner of the Scots monarchy, before it was subverted by the tyrannical ways of the Hanoverians – to the will of the people. In recounting all this, Prince Michael makes further historical revelations. The most entertaining must be the full transcript of an interview in 1782 between the Young Pretender and representatives of the government of the newly independent colonies of North America, in which they offered him the Crown of America. Unfortunately, not only is the language and content of this interview laughably anachronistic and superficial; the writer and recipient of the letter in which it supposedly survives – 'the Hon. Charles Hervey-Townshend' and 'Lady Molly Carteron, Countess of Manorwater' – never existed. There must be grave doubts about the 'Manorwater Papers' in which the letter is said to be preserved.

And yet the book – offered for sale by most reputable bookshops in their 'history' section – and its author have had a not inconsiderable amount of success, with the 'prince' being interviewed regularly both on radio and in the press. In order to explain the great support gained by one of the false Neros, Tacitus, it will be recalled, stated that people were always hungry for *nova et mira* (new things and sensational things). This explanation is not applicable in this case, and not merely because one cannot today be quite so dismissive of a popular reaction. Prince Michael's success has not been in the tabloid sphere, the rapid acquisition of enthusiastic support. It has been in not encountering opposition. This is rather odd, because if his claims were true, it would indeed be a sensation: not only the existence of a legitimate descendant of the disinherited Stuarts, but the continued and conscious

HRH Prince Michael of Albany, supposedly legitimate heir-general of Bonnie Prince Charlie. The 'prince' came to Scotland from Belgium in 1976, aged eighteen, and claims to have been the subject of intrusive and hostile investigation by the British secret services in recent years.

suppression of the truth by the Hanoverians and the house of Windsor to this day. The interviewers must sense this, and yet the true enormity of his tale remains unemphasized – and thus unexamined. Those journalists who do try to convey the essential unreliability of the prince's story are those inclined to treat the whole subject of hereditary monarchy with a degree of scorn; ignoring the fact that even in a system that apportions power by eccentric and possibly indefensible criteria, it is important that people are not deceived into thinking that the criteria have been met when they have not.[21]

And so Prince Michael has not been 'outed' and can continue to associate himself with the cause of promoting Scotland's democratic freedom from the cloying, unhealthy effects of England's hierarchical and conservative society. Is he free to do so because of a growing contemporary lack of interest in the authority of the monarchy, as opposed to its soap-operatic aspects? This might well be the case; knowledge of and sympathy with the traditional aspects of the sovereign's rôle and position are generally held to be declining. If this is so, the authenticity of the Queen's title to reign might indeed be of no interest whatsoever; her rôle is now merely that of a media star, for which the intricacies of the rules of inheritance are meaningless.

Here, however, a knowledge of history suggests otherwise. 'Prince Michael' is not the first (and will probably not be the last) to claim royal rights by virtue of legitimate descent from the Young Pretender. Others have done so with more erudition and indeed panache, gaining support at higher levels of society, attaching themselves to, indeed in some degree providing the impetus for, a change in artistic, literary and social fashion, without provoking the remotest hint of a crisis in the state.

The story of the Allen brothers, who in the early decades of the nineteenth century turned themselves bit by bit into the Princes Sobieski Stuart, claiming to be the Young Pretender's great-grandsons, has been delightfully retold by Hugh Trevor-Roper and does not need a full rehearsal here.[22] It suffices to note, first, that there was no truth in their claims whatsoever: they were from respectable middle-class stock, and though their family may have nursed certain beliefs about noble Scottish origins, the idea of the descent from Bonnie Prince Charlie was all the brothers' own. Second, though their claims were startling – like Michael 'of Albany' they stated that the Young Pretender had fathered a son who was brought up in secrecy and left a line of legitimate descendants, known to but ignored by the house of Hanover – they did not create the great constitutional or historical scandal that might have been expected. Third, instead of this, and belying the suggestion that the absence of this reaction was simply because no one believed in them, they were received with tolerance, hospitality and even warmth into the bosom of a certain section of Scottish high society. Here they continued to behave in accordance with what they saw as their station, maintaining a mini-court at their beautiful house on Eilean Aigas, an island in the River Eskadale, to which they were rowed in a barque flying the royal standard, dressing in 'revived' Highland garb adorned with orders and decorations, being referred to and addressed as princes – even by the distinguished peers and gentry with whom they associated.

Most importantly perhaps, and in partial explanation of this friendly reception, they played a central part in the early and mid-nineteenth century's attempts to resuscitate Scots traditions in literary, artistic and fashionable matters. Their rôle in this sphere was of course no less deceptive and fraudulent than in matters of genealogy. Their great publication, the

Vestiarium Scoticum, a lavish folio volume that purported to be an edition of a sixteenth-century manuscript on the tartans of the Highland clans, was an extremely expensive hoax: no such manuscript existed, nor could have done, since the system of clan-specific tartans was an invention of the nineteenth, not the sixteenth century. Their excuses and prevarications to those who wished to examine the original stood squarely in the age-old tradition of the literary fraudster. But despite this, and despite the blistering review of the book in the 1847 *Quarterly Review*, which punctured not only their literary pretensions but also their genealogical pretences, the work, packed with true and false erudition, systematic and inspiring at the same time, beautiful to look at but respectful to scholarship, continued to inform works on the history of the Highland traditions until the end of the century and beyond. The great upsurge in interest in the Highlands in the mid-1800s was a European phenomenon, and the Sobieski Stuarts were able to give some apparent substance to what would otherwise have been an entirely vapid mist of romantic visions, the haze rising from the false epics of 'Ossian' and the chivalric nonsense of the Eglington tournament. Unfortunately this substance turned out to be as illusory as the rest.

The piece in the *Quarterly Review* was, in effect, a merciless and detailed exposure of the Sobieski Stuarts, and it had a devastating effect on their career. They retired abroad for many years, venturing back to London only at the end of the 1860s, where they became familiar, studious figures in the Round Reading Room of the British Museum, still decked with stars and medals, but much lower in profile and in visibly straitened circumstances. This reversal of fortune, the tragic desserts for their earlier text-book display of hubris, might be held to show that the age in which they lived punished offenders against the established authority of monarchy much more strenuously than our own, as shown by the lukewarm tolerance accorded to Michael of Albany. In fact the difference is more likely to result from the death of a certain sort of literary *genre*, the painstaking, devastating, relentlessly and cruelly sarcastic review. Hoax-busting was an established craft in the eighteenth and nineteenth centuries, with great sledge-hammers being lovingly fashioned to crack the smallest nuts of pretension; many journals existed to provide a forum for this cruel sport, and the lettered public loved it. It is now a forgotten art, however, and would no doubt come across as unattractive and unkind if revived. If anyone were to write a detailed critical exposé of the material produced by Michael of Albany, it would be as much an essay in a lost literary style as a well-merited taking-down a peg or two.

The Sobieski Stuarts' voluntary exile and retreat into relative obscurity was in fact part of the game, the appropriate response to the onslaught on them. In truth, their romantic attraction did not suffer at all. Their appeal had never in fact been that of serious litigants ready to prove their just title to the Crown. For many of their friends and associates their achievement was a serious and holistically interpreted revival of interest in the traditions of the Highlands, however wayward the scholarship that underlay it. And even for those who believed, the brothers were attractive precisely because of the beautiful aura of romantic failure surrounding the disinherited Stuarts, that seductive vision which was discussed in chapter 2. This was, of course, undiminished by the piece in the *Quarterly Review*, which could indeed be seen as just another of the slings and arrows that Fortune had hurled at the doomed race of the Stuarts.

The truth of the matter is that pseudo-Stuarts have proved almost as frequent as false Constantines. 'Baron' Rohenstadt (1781–1854), who crossed literary swords with the Sobieskis, and lies buried in the ruins of Dunkeld Cathedral, claimed to be son of the Young Pretender's legitimated daughter, Charlotte Walkinshaw. Meanwhile, with a certain inevitability, the long exile of the Stuart Pretenders in Italy has produced at least one case of an individual claiming to represent *both* the disinherited Catholic kings of Scotland *and* the emperors of Byzantium. The so-called 'Angelos Apostolico Cantelmo Stuart' family is no doubt not alone in this.[23]

Nor are the Stuarts the only British royal dynasty from whom people claim to descend. The end of the house of Tudor did not inspire either constitutional crisis or a romantic sense of loss in the same way as the events of 1688, but the Tudor monarchs are for many heroic figures, larger than life, loved and hated in equal measure, and with plenty of significance for political and national questions that are still debated. It is not surprising therefore that several individuals have presented themselves as their legitimate descendants.

The prime example this century is that of King Anthony, a Shropshire policeman who in the course of the 1930s conceived and developed the notion that he was the legitimate male-line descendant of Henry VIII and thus the rightful king of England. Born Anthony William Hall in 1898, he served in the Royal Army Medical Corps during the Great War before entering the constabulary; he died in 1947, still protesting his right to the Crown. What inspired his curious delusion is not clear, and since his main modes of publishing his claims were the soap box and the extremely brief pamphlet, he has left little in the way of biographical material to work from.

One-pound 'banknote' produced by 'King' Anthony Hall. On some versions the reverse of the note carries a résumé of the king's ancestry.

What survives does, however, display certain interesting points. Unlike the pseudo-Stuarts, for example, King Anthony seems to have formulated no detailed explanation for the fact that he had not inherited the Crown in the normal course of events. His story was that Henry VIII had had a son, John, by Anne Boleyn, full brother to Elizabeth: why, then, did she succeed to the throne and not he? John, who was actually created Prince of Wales, married, had twenty-three children and died in 1618 at the age of ninety. Ninth in descent from him was Anthony himself.

Another telling point is the belt-and-braces method Anthony used. With the over-cautiousness of the true obsessive, he argued that the man crowned as James VI of Scotland and, later, as James I of England was not who he claimed to be, but a changeling introduced in substitution for the true son of Mary Queen of Scots, who died in infancy. This was an old tale, one of the many anti-Stuart myths that circulated in the seventeenth century. In King Anthony's case it was superfluous, for if his descent from Henry VIII was authentic he was king by right whether or not the Stuarts were descended as claimed. One result, however, was that Anthony could, with a certain degree of relish, refer to the ruling king, George VI (or Albert Wettin, as he called him) as an impostor.

In the surviving material Anthony comes across as an unsophisticated, benign patriot, less programmatic and less pugnacious than Michael of Albany. Admittedly, his fine 'proclamation', printed on a single sheet of

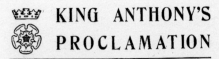

KING ANTHONY'S PROCLAMATION

COPIES OF THIS PROCLAMATION HAVE BEEN SENT TO THE ARCHBISHOP OF WESTMINSTER AND TO THE EARL MARSHAL

The Crown of England was won by our Ancestor, Henry Tudor, Earl of Richmond, at the Battle of Bosworth, near Leicester, in 1485. Henry Tudor defeated and slew Richard III, last Plantagenet King, and was crowned on the battlefield and hailed there as King Henry the Seventh. Henry VII was succeeded by his son, King Henry the Eighth, who married the Lady Anne Boleyn, by her having a 'son, John Tudor, from whom We, Anthony, are 9th in direct male line of descent, and a daughter Elizabeth Tudor, who ruled as Queen Elizabeth from 1558 to 1603.

On the death of Queen Elizabeth in 1603 a man who said he was King James VI of Scotland came to London and ascended the English throne, claiming as next legitimate heir through his supposed mother, Mary Stewart Queen of Scots, great-granddaughter of King Henry VII, Victor of Bosworth. This supposed James VI of Scotland became known as James I of England, and members of his family occupied the English throne from 1603-1714.

In 1688 James II, grandson of James VI and I, fled to France, and his nephew and son-in-law, William of Orange, came over from Holland and occupied the English throne as William III, 1688-1702. In 1701, William III gave his [supposed] royal assent to a Bill of Settlement which purported to transfer the British crown to the Guelphs of Hanover, Germany, who claimed English royal blood through Sophia, granddaughter of the supposed James VI and I; and, on the strength of their supposed English royal blood, the Guelphs occupied our throne from 1714 to 1961—George I to Victoria.

On the death of William IV in 1837, Ernest Guelph, 5th son of George III, was sent to Hanover, Germany, and his niece, Victoria Guelph, was put on the British throne. In 1840 Victoria Guelph married Albert Wettin, of Coburg, Germany; and, of their issue, a daughter, Victoria, married Fredk. Hohenzollern of Prussia and by him was the mother of William Hohenzollern, the present ex-Kaiser; the second child of Victoria and Albert was Edward Wettin, who on his mother's death in 1901 took the title Edward VII. He died in 1910 and was succeeded by his son, George Wettin (George V), who in 1917 changed his name to "Windsor" and who died 20/1/1936, being succeeded by his son, Edward Wettin or Windsor—Edward VIII. In the same year 1936 Edward abdicated and was succeeded by his brother Albert Wettin—George VI.

Thus from 1603-1714 we had the supposed Stewarts of Scotland; from 1714-1901 we had the Guelphs of Hanover, Germany; and from 1901 we have had the Wettins of Coburg, Germany. Each of these families has claimed English royal blood through James VI of Scotland.

It now appears that the **real** King James VI of Scotland, son of Mary Stewart Queen of Scots, died in infancy, and that a changeling, James Erskine, was placed in the dead King's cradle and brought up and foisted on the British people as James VI of Scotland and I of England. In 1830 a coffin containing the bones of the **real** King James was discovered in the walls of Edinburgh Castle, but the matter was hushed up. In 1928, however, a book, **Scotland's Royal Line**, by Grant R. Francis, was published by John Murray, Albemarle Street, London, at 21/-, and this book exposed the whole affair.

In February, 1931, We served a document on George V pointing out that he was not of British royal descent. In 1932 we issued a long Manifesto, and on 1st December, 1936, we served an Injunction on the Earl Marshal. On 12th April, 1937, a similar Injunction was served on Dr. Lang at Lambeth Palace. Since 1930 we have addressed over a thousand public meetings in England and Wales, and at these meetings tens of thousands of copies of our Manifestoes have been distributed.

This James VI changeling story is true. Therefore the Wettin family, now called Windsor, is out of the line of succession, the personage known as King George VI is a commoner, Mr. Albert Wettin, and the throne is vacant.

We, Anthony, are in the male line descended of the body of King Henry the Seventh, Victor of Bosworth. We are a Tudor Prince, of legitimate birth and of legitimate royal descent.

We, Anthony, hereby proclaim ourselves King of England, Emperor of India, Defender of the Faith.

TUDOR RULE.

1. Laws shall be made by the King with the assent of Lords and Commons.

2. The Judiciary shall remain independent of Executive Government.

3. All privately-owned mints, called banks, shall be confiscated, transferred to the State, and re-opened as branches of the Royal Mint of England. A draft Statute of the Mint shall be laid before Parliament.

4. As a general principle, Government will keep out of business. Business shall keep out of Government.

5. Any measures proposed by Parliament for improving the standard of living of the working classes shall receive our favourable consideration.

6. It is our intention to apply ourselves with vigour to the task of making Britain the most powerfully armed nation on earth. We are satisfied that we can fill the ranks of the British army with volunteers and that conscription will be unnecessary.

We served throughout the Great War, from September 1914 to January 1919, and it is our faithful promise that under our rule regard shall be had for the just claims of ex-servicemen.

7. There shall be no religious changes without the assent of Parliament.

Given under our hand in London this 23rd day of September 1937.

ANTHONY,
Rex-Imperator, F.D.

Proclamation, Money, etc. printed by E. Gibbon, 152 Fonthill Road, London, N.4, and published by H.M. King Anthony, 19 King's Crescent, London, N.4. Telephone, Stamford Hill 4349.

Proclamation by pamphlet. The reaction of the Earl Marshal and the Archbishop of Westminster is not recorded.

paper which was apparently sent to the Earl Marshal and, for some reason, the Archbishop of Westminster (England's senior Roman Catholic hierarch), contains quite a lot in the way of policy: recognition of the rights of ex-servicemen, confiscation of the money held by banks, and the general principle that 'Government will keep out of business' and 'Business shall keep out of Government'. He apparently also proposed the removal of Parliament to Wales; whether through respect for Wales or disrespect for Parliament is not clear. If the former, this constitutes the only known 'decentralist' element in Anthony's manifesto, and might derive from his awareness of the Welsh origins of the Tudors. In the main, though, his policies are utopian and eternal, rather than being linked to specific social or political trends. King Anthony could have lived at any period; he was not a man of his time. Neither, of course, is Prince Michael of Albany, but he represents himself as one, which King Anthony lacked the wit – or the cheek – to do.

More recent monarchs than the Tudors and the Stuarts have on occasion been claimed as legitimate ancestors by dreamers and hoaxers. The age of licentious monarchy, the eighteenth century, produced at least one 'gateway' to royal ancestry in the form of George III's supposed secret marriage as a young man to the actress Hannah Lightfoot. This is said to have produced a son, christened George and given the surname Rex. Sent to southern Africa, he lived and died in the Cape, at a beautiful spot overlooking the southern Atlantic, and where his descendants still live. A documentary on British television captured extremely well the romantic tone of the remarkable, but little-known story.[24]

If George Rex's story has failed to capture the imagination of the public, it is perhaps because his father was one of the least fondly remembered monarchs in British history. The most popular points of access for those fabricating a legitimate royal descent for themselves are those involving a monarch or prince who was loved or admired, and preferably cut off in his prime; the very same individuals most liable to impersonation, as discussed in chapter 3. A twentieth-century example will suffice. Edward VIII, that youth of excellent hope, as the Romans would have said, inspired great affection in an age which was in two minds about the monarchy. Big things were expected of his reign, but it never came to pass. Despite continual speculation about his true political inclinations – or perhaps because of this sort of controversy – it is no surprise to find that at least one individual seriously claims the handsome king that was never crowned as his father. Pursuing matters even to the extent of bringing an action in a district court for the Crown revenues of which he feels he was deprived, this person is perhaps only the first of many. As the events of the twentieth century fade into history, it will become ever easier to ignore the manifest fact that the Duke of Windsor left no children, and invoke instead the vague sense of injustice surrounding, in many people's minds, his life story.[25]

For the present, however, delusions like this are perhaps too far from the rational to detain us long. They do not admit analysis in the same way as the pseudo-Stuarts, or even the relatively crazy King Anthony. There is little difference, for the moment, between calling oneself Edward VIII's son and believing oneself to be Napoleon. The history of the royal family in the twentieth century is too familiar, and the natural home of the impostor or pseudo-pretender is, crucially, the half-familiar. Not that the unfamiliar cannot provide many openings, as the next section will show.

A Phantom Kingdom Beyond the Atlantic

For all that it has become a universal repository for myths, a peg on which dreamers and opportunists can hang their own fantasies, Byzantium undoubtedly existed. The crowns of 'Scotland' and 'England', aspired to by the likes of Prince Michael of Albany and King Anthony, were also real until the Act of Union in 1707, and could in theory be extracted once again from the mélange. The same cannot certainly be said for all the crowns to which pretenders lay claim: the kingdom of Araucania and Patagonia is one doubtful example.

For practical purposes Araucania is of one of the twelve regions of Chile, stretching from the high Andean *cordillera* in the east to the Pacific coast in the west. The indigenous peoples of this area, and in particular the Mapuche, many of whom dwell across the border in Argentina, put up a long fight both against the Spanish and then, after Chilean independence in 1818, against the post-colonial government. Chilean history books date the *guerra de Arauco* from the first arrival of the *conquistadores* in 1540 to the final pacification of the region in 1883, though from the 1840s onwards German and other European immigrants had settled in the region south of the Bio-Bio river where the Mapuche or Araucanian Indians had been contained. A brief and ephemeral incident in this long struggle is all that gives substance to the strange tale of the kingdom of Araucania.

The story goes like this. One of the European settlers was a certain Orélie-Antoine de Tounens who arrived in Chile in 1858. Born in 1825, Tounens was a lawyer from Périgord in France, of ultimately noble stock though his family had come down in the world. Wishing to make something of himself – the same desire that had prompted him to resuscitate the prefix 'de' to his family name – but also, more importantly, inspired by a humanitarian respect for the downtrodden victims of colonialism, he set out for South America and soon gravitated to the disputed region on the Chilean-Argentine border. The sturdy defiance of the Mapuches impressed him, and he offered himself as their king, undertaking to establish a sovereign state in their name and defend their frontiers against both Chile and Argentina. On 17 November 1860 a local chief accepted him in that position, and three days later he met with the representative of a Patagonian Indian tribal group who seemed acquiescent to the idea. Thus, on 20 November 1860, the kingdom of Araucania and Patagonia was born.

The new king's first act was apparently to retire to Valparaiso, where he spent the next year in a campaign for international recognition by means of

Orélie-Antoine I, King
of Araucania and
Patagonia. A portrait
made during his
imprisonment by the
Chilean authorities
and reproduced in his
1863 account of his
first expedition to
South America.

public announcements and letters to the press. The response was disappoint-
ing: a deafening silence, even from the Chilean authorities. So, returning to
his kingdom in Christmas 1861, he sought to bolster his image with some
form of democratic sanction. This was forthcoming in the form of the enthusiastic reception he received from his subjects, and Orélie-Antoine felt able to
declare he had been elected king. But the Chilean authorities were now alert
to his plans and on 10 January they arrested him and prosecuted him with
seditious activities. Found not guilty by reason of mental instability, Tounens
was committed to a sanatorium, whence he was rescued by the French
consul and sent back to France. Greeted with indifference at home, he seems
to have made further trips to the region he claimed as his kingdom: in
1869–71, 1874 and – for the final time – in 1876. Set upon by bandits
in Patagonia he was seriously injured and was again sent home in 1877,
there to die the following year.

Quite what Tounens did and did not do in Araucania in 1860–2 is hard to
tell. The main part of the story related above derives ultimately from his own

Coin of 'Nouvelle France',
alias the kingdom of
Araucania and Patagonia.
Minted in France for
Orélie-Antoine (here, as in
many other places, called
Orllie-Antoine).

book, published on his return to France in 1863. The fact that he was there
at all and got into trouble with the Chilean government can presumably be
corroborated by the records of the nine-month trial following his arrest.
But even there the question of his claim to be king of the Indians was not
at issue: the prosecution regarded it as clear proof of the charges against
him, while Tounens based his defence not on the facts, but on challenging
Chilean jurisdiction over the Araucanians, whom he argued to constitute an
independent nation-state. No contemporary Mapuche sources survive,
and a degree of scepticism is probably wise. Some parts of his story, such as
the claim that in 1860 he had travelled with two loyal associates, Lachaise
and Desfontaines, are known to be false.

What is not in doubt, however, is the extraordinary after-life that the story
has had, chiefly – though not only – in France, and the different lights in
which the original enterprise has been regarded. The tale has been partly
told by Bruce Chatwin, in his *In Patagonia*. Prior to travelling to South
America in the 1970s Chatwin paid a visit to the Araucanian 'court' at Paris
and had an audience with the pretender to the throne, Prince Philippe. From
Chatwin's account, and from various books and pamphlets published by
Araucanian royalists, not to mention the detailed website currently maintained on behalf of Prince Philippe, we learn how the claim to the 'steel
crown' of Araucania has been handed down over the decades.[26] It has been
a far from orthodox succession.

Orélie-Antoine left no children. We are told, however, that he designated
his heir before he died: Gustave Achille Laviarde, who reigned until his
death in 1902 as Achille I, known as 'the diplomat' on account of his
unrequited but unceasing approaches to national governments for recognition of Araucania. According to the 'official' history, Achille had been with
Orélie-Antoine on his third expedition and had given the founder of the
kingdom ample opportunity to assess his heroic virtues. His diplomatic
sensitivity prevented him, however, from mounting further expeditions of
his own.

On his death Achille is said to have been succeeded by Antoine II, or Dr
Antoine Cros as he was known in private life. Apparently he had served as
Secretary of State and Keeper of the Great Seal under his two predecessors, as
well as personal physician to Emperor Pedro II of Brazil. His reign was short
– less than two years – but he was active and vociferous in support of his
lost kingdom, publicly drawing a topical comparison between its fate and
that of the Boer republics, cruelly subjected by *Albion perfide*. On his death in
1903 the crown passed, for the first time by natural inheritance, to his
daughter Laure-Thérèse, and thence on her death thirteen years later to her
son Jacques Bernard, who claimed it as Antoine III. In 1951 Antoine III
abdicated in favour of the current claimant, Philippe Boiry, who as Prince
Philippe modestly eschews the kingship in the absence of any true sovereignty to justify it; though what then justifies his use of the regally derived
title of prince is hard to understand.

As the current pretender to the Araucanian throne, Prince Philippe
carries on or sponsors a large volume of activity: a journal (*The Steel Crown*,
replacing or perhaps supplementing the earlier, more scholarly *Cahiers des
Hautes Etudes Araucaniennes*), a museum of
Araucanian kingship in Orélie-Antoine's old
house in Périgord, a selection of orders and
decorations, and a small coinage (available
for purchase from the North American
Araucanian Royalist Society).

The story of Araucania combines two
obviously appealing elements, each of a sort
discussed in this book: a daring and noble-
spirited adventurer being chosen king by a
distant, downtrodden people; and a line of
unfairly dispossessed descendants. But the tale
has at different times been imbued with other
characteristics. For Orélie-Antoine the initial
enterprise seems to have been colonial in
flavour. His alternative name for Araucania
and Patagonia was 'Nouvelle France', and his
announcements and advertisements in the
press during the first year of his reign
publicized the kingdom as a haven for French
settlers, to make good the loss of Quebec and
Louisiana. He wrote of the bravery and

Part of the modern silver
coinage of Araucania and
Patagonia, produced in
the name of the current
claimant, Philippe I.

steadfastness of the natives, with imagery derived from Rousseau, but it is clear that the image of a kingdom he had in his mind was European, the form of nation-state he envisaged was, naturally enough, that of the post-revolutionary western world, and the relationship he planned between governors and governed was imperialist. His two imaginary lieutenants in 1860 were clearly imaginary Frenchmen, after all.[27]

Early in Prince Philippe's pretendership a rather different character suffused the typewritten, cyclostyled documents that passed for Araucanian national literature. One of the main spokesmen was a certain Norberto de Castro y Tosi, who was closely involved with something called the Collegio Araldico (College of Arms) of Costa Rica, and also hammered out long screeds in support of at least one false Emperor of Byzantium. For Castro and the other authors who wrote on the topic (apparently using the same typewriter as he did), the important point about Araucania was the fact that it was a monarchy; the monarchic idea was universal, they argued, and certainly predated colonialism. Indeed, by this argument, Araucania was an anti-colonial enterprise, being the natural expression by the natives of their own form of the monarchic dream. From monarchy, of course, flowed naturally the concept of nobility, and thus it was quite legitimate and in keeping with native South American traditions for the Kings of Araucania to bestow titles on deserving individuals (such as Norberto de Castro himself).[28]

Prince Philippe's pretendership has been a long one, however, and the world has changed in a few important respects. Colonialism has been replaced by post-colonialism as the bugbear of the developing world. The death of the nation-state has become a tedious truism. The rights of native peoples, associated with the land they live in but not tied to the carto-graphically defined frontiers beloved of former generations, have acquired a great prominence, frequently in close association with ecological questions. All these points apply with particular force in South America and it is no surprise that the Araucanians, or Mapuche people, should be among the interested parties. The area they inhabit, straddling the Andes, is under threat in various ways. A search on the Internet for the word 'Araucania' rather disturbingly brings up the websites of several logging companies, advertising their lucrative activities in this richly forested region. Hydro-electric schemes by the Chilean government have also resulted in various unpopular damming projects. The Mapuche have started to seek recog-nition as an oppressed people, sending deputations to the United Nations, requesting cultural and linguistic protection, autonomy or even independence; some form of freedom from the shackles of the corrupt post-colonial states between which they are split. To the clamour of this highly charged and highly contemporary political activity, Prince Philippe has added his voice. His web pages recount his untiring activities on behalf of native rights (his address to the United Nations, his approaches to the governments of Chile and Argentina) and offer a link to the main Mapuche nation site.[29] The kingdom of Araucania and Patagonia has again changed character.

There are others for whom the ideal of Orélie-Antoine is of contemporary relevance. In 1998 a Frenchman by the name of Jean Raspail caused something of a stir by depositing a flag, a set of bathroom tiles (see Plate 4A) and a car-sticker, all displaying the 'Patagonian national emblem', on the rocky and uninhabited island of Minquiers, near Jersey. In a press release he explained that he was seizing the island from Britain for the kingdom of Patagonia in exchange for the Falklands, which really belonged to Patagonia. This latter claim had, in fact, already been made in several locations on the Internet, but the actions on Minquiers were not apparently sanctioned or approved by Prince Philippe or his supporters; Raspail seems to have represented a splinter group, the hardline or irredentist Araucanian tendency. What the press interestingly failed to pick up, however, was that he is also an author of a decidedly controversial sort, whose 1973 book *The Camp of the Saints* was a novel designed to show that the white races of the world were in danger of being swamped and destroyed by the deliberate and malicious policy of the black ones.[30]

It is telling that Araucania has supported many interpretations: the colonial dream; an expression of the immanent, eternal monarchy; the homeland of a deprived people; a bulwark against the hated colonial powers of the Anglo-Saxon world. It can do this only because it lacks all substance. Whatever Orélie-Antoine de Tounens got up to among the Mapuche in 1860, and whatever justification Philippe Boiry has in regarding himself as his heir, the fact is that Araucania is now a dream, a castle in the air if ever there was one; furthermore, one whose outlines and plans are so vaguely and economically drawn as to leave everything up to the imagination of the beholder.

Araucania is not the only case of French idealism imposed on South America. In 1886 a long-running territorial dispute between Brazil and French Guyana was settled in the former's favour by a tribunal appointed for the purpose in Switzerland. Jules Gros, a French author, responded by declaring the disputed area a free state, under the name of the Republic of Counani (the Counani being a river that rises there). Before long the state

Stamps of the free state of Counani
show without fail the 'Star of
Counani' after which Jules Gros also
named the phantom republic's
main order of chivalry.

was issuing stamps and Gros was awarding the Order of the Star of Counani.
The borders of the republic were set at the Amazon and the Atlantic, a vast
area which it was argued could not fail to enclose the as yet undiscovered El
Dorado. Some observers felt that the El Dorado sought by Gros was one built
on publicity, or perhaps on the sale of stamps, decorations and titles. If so, he
was to be disappointed, as he died in December 1889, and the government
of Counani passed into military hands, namely the mysterious Captains
Trajano and Vasconcellos who presided over the grand council until 1892
when a civilian president was again elected. This was Adolphe Brezet, a
Parisian who sought to develop the stamp-issuing side of the state's activities. Issues were engraved and printed, denominated in a currency consisting
of 100 centimes to the *bengali*, and specimens donated to the great European
museums and collections by way of a network of representatives.
Approaches were made to the Universal Postal Union in which it was
claimed that the post office was a functioning enterprise in Counani itself.
Maps were produced to display the scale of its operations, which thereby
illustrated the extent of the republic's territorial claim. This was a mistake.
After tolerating the joke for almost twenty years Brazil eventually decided it
would put up with it no longer and in May 1905 made a formal complaint to
Spain about one of its citizens, a Mr Sarrion de Herrera, who was calling himself Counani's ambassador to Madrid. Sarrion was arrested and threatened
with extradition to Brazil where he would face charges of conspiracy.
Nothing is known to have come of these threats, but it is probable that after
this the game no longer seemed amusing, for from this point on we hear
of Counani as no more than an interesting philatelic by-way in stamp-
collecting magazines.[31]

The succession to republican power in Counani is doubtless as unorthodox
as that of Prince Philippe to the Araucanian crown. We do not know
whether there was any real link between Gros and Brezet; the latter may

simply have been an opportunist who came across the Counani story and realized the republic was up for grabs. But once the wind had been taken out of Counani's sails, the idea's vital momentum was lost and the notional French republic of the north Amazon was never heard of again.

Why has this not quite happened to Araucania? Its supporters would say, of course, that it is because Araucania, unlike Counani, is the true embodiment of a nation, and that a monarchy, unlike a republic, can exist in detachment from its people. There is perhaps something in this answer, to the extent that it refers to the curious mystique of monarchy, which binds the fate of nations up with that of individuals and families, so that the two become inextricably confused in some people's minds. Though Araucania is in many respects (and possibly in all respects) as airy and insubstantial as Counani, it offers a king, or at any rate a prince, as the personal embodiment of the dispossession that would otherwise have to be understood in relation to an ill-defined and shifting population. This is hard to achieve.

Hard; but not impossible. As the next chapter will show, the nineteenth and twentieth centuries have seen many attempts to turn populations into peoples, and make their justified or unjustified sense of grievance clear and comprehensible to all. This is what the Mapuche, after all, are engaged in now. Whether they are really assisted in this by the behaviour of the man who claims to be their dispossessed sovereign is open to serious doubt.

Conclusion

This chapter has focused on three main areas of pseudo-pretendership: Byzantium, Scotland and South America. There are many more. Almost every week the College of Arms in London is approached by some individual claiming to be the rightful Prince of Judah, Duke of Swabia or King of Poland. Others make it into the newspapers instead. The closing months of 1999 produced a young claimant to the title of Holy Roman Emperor (basing his claim not on any genealogy, but on the interesting argument that the position was 'vacant') and a Portuguese who maintains that his great-grandfather was the love-child of the sixty-five-year-old Duke of Wellington and the fifteen-year-old Princess (not yet Queen) Victoria.[32]

Is this phenomenon merely social climbing of an exaggerated sort? Certainly many of the people described in this chapter give the impression of being highly self-important individuals. Only one (Totò) displayed talent of a high order. Many betray the signs of deep insecurity. But others whose exploits have been recounted were at the very least obsessive, while some were evidently mad, a state of mind in which social climbing of the straightforward kind is scarcely relevant. After all, climbing so high in social terms that you rise far above all the smartest and most exalted people around you is actually not conducive to gaining acceptance among them. Calling yourself a king or an emperor is, in short, the most unsubtle and unintelligent way to get access to high society.

It is, of course, possible that all the pseudo-pretenders described in this chapter are either stupid or mad. But in some cases there is rather more to the phenomenon than mere social-climbing; something solipsistic and, at root, anti-social. Even if the historical and genealogical accounts they offer were true, the idea of the descendant of a dispossessed line emerging from centuries of obscurity and revealing himself to his people would scarcely fit with one of the main justifications for hereditary monarchy: that the destination of the throne is visible and predictable. Only in a society with an implausibly extreme legitimist approach to its own sovereignty would such behaviour be welcome. When the account is false, it is even less palatable. For all their protestations of humility, false claimants of this sort are guilty of a staggering arrogance: by means of genealogical or historical imposture they are attempting, in a quite literal and modern sense, to impose themselves on others.

Chapter 5

The Nation as Pretender

The lesson of this book is that rebels and pretenders are above all myth-makers. They have to be. They have no stores of the kinds of material capital on which real power rests and depends – money, armies, territories – to set against those of established rulers. So to compensate for this inevitable lack, they first have to manufacture for themselves *symbolic* capital to draw supporters and resources to their cause. In order to detach people from their loyalties to the established order, pretenders need to put out a more attractive story about themselves than that of the current régime in justification of their ambitious plans.

This symbolic capital may, as we have seen, take the form of a claim to dynastic legitimacy or to divine election, the pretender as rightful heir or as the Lord's anointed. These two claims may be run in tandem but the latter can operate independently of the former, on the principle that God may choose as earthly sovereign whomsoever He wishes, and does not have to keep it in the family if He does not want to. The pretender himself also needs a charismatic personality so as to convince potential supporters of the rightness, or at least the plausibility, of his claim and attract sufficient followers to be able to challenge his more powerful opponents.

But all this is history. The age of the great pretenders is now over. Dynastic monarchies are no longer the decisive factor in human affairs that they once were. Over the past two centuries or more, kings and emperors have by and large been replaced by republics. Those that remain have found themselves shorn of most of their former legal, military and religious power. In the western world at least, kings and gods have given way before laws and constitutions as the ideal focuses of communal loyalties. Yet even the secular state cannot entirely dispense with the emotive power of the myth. Legal abstractions on their own are simply not capable of exciting human passions or retaining our sympathies in times of stress or crisis. Where then is the modern state to find a myth of sufficient pulling power to equal those of the gods, kings and dynasties of the past? One of the most significant sources of post-dynastic myth-making has been the concept of the nation, and the associated ideology of nationalism.[1] Even in countries where monarchies still persist, kings and royal families have long since been displaced as the locus of communal historical narrative by the history of the community itself, of the nation. In the past the idea of dynastic succession blessed by divinity represented the theme of temporal continuity with the distant past, with all the attendant mythology that entailed. Nowadays the nation fulfils the function of the bearer of historical continuity, and therefore of political legitimacy. The mythical aspect of nation-based histories is no less crucial to their formation than it was to the dynastic histories of the past.

To an extent, of course, all history usurps the past, in that it selects certain memories with which to construct a particular kind of narrative to a pre-conceived purpose. But because the aim of nationalist history is precisely to establish the pedigree of the whole nation, to create a communal genealogy for all the people, not just a ruling family, the element of myth-making tends to be particularly intense. Nationalist history needs to assume that the 'people' have an unbroken history and a common ancestry which can be traced back into antiquity and beyond. To that end, all inconvenient evidence of foreign invasions and ethnic mixing has to be ignored, or at least interpreted as being of lesser significance than the points in favour of historical continuity with the past, particularly in settlement, language and descent.

Nineteenth-century Myths of the Nation

The nineteenth century was an especially fruitful period for the creation of mythical national histories of this kind, especially among the German communities of central Europe who were divided into a multitude of king-doms and principalities, some great, most small. There was an increasingly strong movement towards the unification of the German states into a single empire, based on the nationalist idea that peoples of the same language and culture should all belong to the same political unit. To lend historical depth and inevitability to the call for a single German state under one emperor, past precedents for German unity, and especially for a German people united through victory over foreign invaders, were sought and duly found. In the creation of nationalist narratives, exemplars from antiquity are particularly desirable because they demonstrate the nation's long, and therefore noble, pedigree. To this end, an ancient Germanic chief called Hermann (Arminius in Latin), who in AD 9 inflicted a devastating defeat upon three Roman legions, was lifted from the pages of the Roman historian Tacitus and elevated to the status of German national hero. The search for the precise location of the Teutoburg Forest, the site of the great battle, became a vital debate among German ancient historians, one which has apparently only

The *Hermannsdenkmal*, unveiled in 1875 as a monument both to Arminius, the Germanic leader who defeated the Romans in AD 9, and to the recently united German Empire.

recently been resolved. A great monument to Hermann was planned in the 1830s and, after a long gestation period, was finally completed in 1875, not coincidentally after the unification of Germany under King Wilhelm II of Prussia as emperor (*Kaiser*), which itself resulted from the Prussian defeat of the French Empire in 1870. This triumph transformed the *Hermannsdenkmal* from a merely aspirational into a celebratory monument, dedicated not just to German unity but also to the eternal martial prowess of the German nation as demonstrated by its crushing victories over both the Romans of antiquity and their present-day Romance successors, the French.[2]

The roots of the modern German, and for that matter the Italian, nation-states lie in the unification of a multiplicity of dynastic statelets over the nineteenth century. The French experience of nation-state formation was somewhat different. France had already achieved political unity under the Bourbon monarchy long before the revolution which overthrew it when the Republic was proclaimed in 1792. The various governments, republican, royal, imperial, that filled France's long nineteenth century were not faced with the problem of extensive wars of unification. Instead, the revolutionary republic and then Napoleon's empire were able to set about the conquest of the whole of Europe. Yet they were still concerned to create a unified nation-state out of a feudal dynastic kingdom in which regional sentiment was powerful, and the idea of being citizens of a French *nation* a distinct novelty for most of its inhabitants. To this end, the mythical resources of the deep antiquity of France were mobilized. The idea that the Gauls of antiquity were the ancestors of the French had been canvassed by antiquarians since the late fifteenth century, although it had always been in competition with the conception of France as the unique inheritor of Roman civilization and the eldest daughter of the Roman Catholic Church.[3] It was not till the nationalist nineteenth century that the Gauls and

Bronze medal by French artist Pierre-Alexandre Morlon made in 1907, showing the personification of Gallia in an imaginary version of ancient Gaulish costume still familiar from *Asterix* books.

their heroic struggle against the Roman invaders really came to the fore, with Vercingetorix, the leader of the unsuccessful Gaulish rebellion against Julius Caesar in 52 BC, canonized as a national hero and martyr, the very personification of Gallic virtue, ancient and modern. Monuments were erected to him as to Hermann, while archaeological attention turned to Alesia, the site of his famous stand. Extensive excavations both there and at another Gaulish site, Mont Beuvray, the ancient *Bibracte,* were patronized by the Emperor Napoleon III in the 1860s, and again in the 1980s by President François Mitterrand who at one stage even intended that he should be buried on this most crucial of sites for French national mythology.

Greece's Byzantine Inheritance

A third type of European nation-state was represented by the newly created kingdom of Greece, carved out of the European territories of the retreating Ottoman Empire in the 1830s. In the same region the first stirrings of what would later become the principle of national self-determination gave rise to a clutch of new independent states in the Balkans – Bulgaria, Serbia and Romania all achieving full independence and international recognition in 1878, and Albania in 1913. Here especially there was abundant scope and need for the creation of myths to underpin the shaky foundations of these fledgling states. The theme common to all the new national myths of this period was the continuity of the nation's history. This was easier to establish in the case of France, Germany and Italy where a plausible claim could be made to an unbroken historical record of autonomous local communities stretching back a respectably long time to later Roman antiquity and, with a leap of faith which many were prepared to take, even beyond the Roman period into prehistory. But the histories of the new Balkan nations had suffered an intermission of four hundred years or more under Ottoman Turkish domination during which they were not self-governing, let alone united.

The response of nineteenth-century Greek nationalist intellectuals to their recent experience of subjection was first to establish the eternal continuity, and quality, of the cultural life of the nation by positioning the modern Greek kingdom as the natural heir to the achievements of Classical Greece. This tendency was somewhat in tension with the other available option – the appeal to religious continuity and autonomy which had been upheld by the Orthodox Church through the centuries of the *Tourkokratia* (Turkish rule). Though Orthodox Christianity was clearly an indispensable characteristic of Greekness, the position of the Church as the focus of national identity had been rather compromised by its close cohabitation with the Ottoman establishment. The clergy were excoriated for their obscurantism and divided loyalties by Greek nationalists. In the latter part of the nineteenth century, however, as the nascent Greek kingdom found its feet and began to develop its own expansionist ambitions at the expense of the declining Ottoman Empire, the heritage of the Byzantine Empire became increasingly attractive as an encouraging precedent for Greek imperialist designs. In this period the so-called 'Grand Idea' (*Megali Idea*) of including all Greek-speaking Christian communities, who at the time were settled over large areas of Anatolia and the Black Sea littoral, in a united kingdom with its capital in the liberated imperial city of Constantinople, took hold of the Greek imagination and became the central issue in Greek political life.

The first sovereign of the new kingdom was a Bavarian prince called Otto who hellenized his name as Othon for the benefit of his new subjects, and received the title 'King of Greece'. His reign lasted from 1832 until his deposition and exile in 1862. He was replaced in the following year, this time by a Danish prince called Vilhelm who took the rather more Greek name of Georgios upon his nomination to the throne by Greece's protecting powers – Britain, France and Russia – with the new title of 'King (*basileus*) of the Greeks'. This small change in the king's title, no longer defined geographically but ethnically, was highly significant. Perhaps reminiscent of the title of the medieval Byzantine rulers, '*basileus* and *autokrator* (emperor) of the Romans', it was expressive of the nationalist dream to bring all Greeks everywhere together into a single kingdom, no longer bounded by its current arbitrary limits, but extending to wherever Greeks lived. Very much in this vein, King George's eldest son, born in 1868, was given the evocative name of Constantine. This recalled not merely the Roman emperor Constantine I the Great (AD 306–37), the founder of the imperial city, but also Constantine XI, the last Greek emperor of the Romans, who died defending Constantinople against the invading Ottoman Turkish armies in

Gold 20-drachma coin of Othon, first King of Greece
(1832–62). His youthful profile portrait is clearly modelled
on that of Alexander the Great. (×1.5)

Detail from a Greek silver 30-drachma coin, struck in 1964 to celebrate the centenary of the royal house. The bust is that of King Constantine I (1913–17, 1920–7), but the inscription calls him Constantine XII (IB in Greek), as though he were the successor to the Greek emperors of Byzantium.

1453. Popular legend had long asserted that Constantine XI had not died, and that he would one day return to his people, drive the Turk from the city and re-establish the Greek empire. No surprise, then, that on Crown Prince Constantine's accession to the Greek throne in 1913, he was hailed by many as Constantine XII, as though he were the successor of the last, immortal emperor.

Despite territorial gains in the north from the two Balkan Wars (1912–13), the dream of a Greater Greece finally foundered in the disastrous campaign of 1919–22 when an invading Greek army was thrown out of Anatolia by the Turks under Mustafa Kemal (Atatürk) and the Greek population of Turkey expelled with great loss of life. Smyrna, one of the oldest Greek towns of Anatolia with a history going back to the second millennium BC, was burnt and emptied of its Greek inhabitants. Nonetheless, the idea of the Byzantine heritage of the Greek royal family persisted. Ex-King Constantine II, who was exiled from Greece in 1974 when a plebiscite abolished the monarchy and who now lives in England, was sometimes known in his day as Constantine XIII.[4]

In chapter 4 we encountered a whole clutch of Byzantine pretenders, ranging from the frivolous to the crooked, all laying insubstantial claim to lofty titles associated with the lost empire of the Romans and inventing dynastic connections with one or other of its ruling houses. The Byzantine pretence practised by the kings of modern Greece was very different in kind, for it was not in any sense dynastic. No attempt was ever made to create family links across the centuries between the immortal emperor and King

George. In an earlier age, fantastic genealogies would undoubtedly have been manufactured to demonstrate the connections between the Danish kings of Greece and the Palaeologi of fifteenth-century Byzantium. But by the mid-nineteenth century the story of the nation had displaced that of the dynasty as the golden thread of continuity with the past, even in countries with a monarchy like Greece. Hence, the assertion of continuity and communal identity with the Greek-speaking empire of the Byzantine past came first, while the adoption of a pseudo-Byzantine numeration for the new Constantine was merely an aspect of the communal passion for the Golden Age of the Greeks' imperial past, and its longed-for revival.

Nationalist ideology required its own distortions of history to make past and present fit with one another as desired. The medieval Byzantine Empire, though Greek-speaking, had always continued to consider itself and its inhabitants Romans (*Romaioi* in Greek), not Greeks. In the Middle Ages western potentates had grown accustomed to calling the rulers of Byzantium emperors of the Greeks, to distinguish them from the western emperors, the successors of Charlemagne, who themselves claimed to be emperors (*imperatores* in Latin) of the Romans. The Byzantines, noble Romans as they were, found this highly insulting and regarded as ludicrous the idea of Frankish barbarians as Roman emperors.[5] But by the late nineteenth century the aura of the Roman name had waned drastically. Greek nationalists needed Byzantium to be Greek, not Roman. So in 1892 the then Serbian ambassador in Britain, Chedomil Mijatovitch, wrote a monograph in English on Constantine XI, dedicating it to Crown Prince Constantine of Greece, with the title *Constantine, the Last Emperor of the Greeks.*[6] The hellenization of the remnant of the Roman Empire in the east, which admittedly had begun in the Middle Ages, was thus completed retrospectively in the cause of Greek

(*Right*)
Bronze medal by Bertrand Andreu made in 1805, showing the bust of Napoleon I as Emperor of France. His image is closely modelled on that of the Roman emperor Augustus.

(*Far right*)
Brass *sestertius* of Roman emperor Augustus (31 BC–AD 14).

nationalism. The pretence involved was twofold, first that the Byzantine Empire was a nationally Greek state, and second that the modern Greek kingdom was its legitimate heir because of the unbroken continuity of the life of the nation throughout the centuries of foreign rule.

Modern Greece can at different stages of its history be fairly described as a rebel state – during the revolutionary period that led to the proclamation of an independent republic in the Peloponnese in 1822 – and as a 'pretender nation' in the late nineteenth and early twentieth centuries, when the Greek nation was figured as the rightful heir and likely resuscitator of the medieval Byzantine Empire. But what of our third category? Can national identities be impostors? Greeks claimed that Byzantium was wholly theirs and that they were its legitimate successors, both culturally and territorially. But they were not thereby asserting that they themselves were anything other than what they already believed themselves to be, that is Greeks. National imposture by contrast would be to assert that the nation's historical identity is something other than what most people both within and outside the nation have hitherto thought it was. Like the advocates of national pretendership, its proponents might appeal to more or less plausible arguments from communal and cultural genealogy: we are who and what we are now because of our unique ancestral heritage from the past. But in order to qualify as impostors, they would have to do so not merely to underpin or amplify an existing communal identity as did nineteenth-century Byzantinism in Greece, but rather to create a new identity for the group concerned, for some ulterior purpose.

North Italian Impostures

Why should a community, or a certain interest group within it, wish to fashion a different identity for itself? Perhaps in order to establish its historical distinctness with a view to translating this into political autonomy in the present. An apt example of this phenomenon in the modern world may be found in the recent political history of northern Italy. The 1980s saw the rise of regionalist political parties in the area with an ethno-linguistic agenda, seeking to establish a greater degree of autonomy for regions where the dominant language in use was not standard Italian, such as the *Union Valdôtaine* in the Val d'Aosta, where there is a significant French-speaking population, and the *Südtiroler Volkspartei*, representing the German speakers of South Tyrol, the region known to Italians as Alto Adige. The attraction of regional autonomy spread to other areas where non-standard Italian dialects were still current. A plethora of local parties sought to promote the local cultures and languages of their regions – the *Liga Veneta*, founded by the members of the Philological Society of the Veneto, in the region around Venice, *Arnassita Piemontesa* (Piedmontese Rebirth) in Piedmont, and the North-west Lombard Union, *Unolpa*, founded by Umberto Bossi in 1979, which was succeeded by the *Lega Lombarda* (Lombard League) in 1982. Throughout the 1980s these parties achieved a degree of electoral success and in 1989 a new umbrella party with the name *Lega Nord* (Northern League), led by Bossi, became the leading force in north Italian regionalist politics.[7] But there was a problem. What the League gained in strength from uniting the resources and supporters of the various ethno-regionalist parties that had preceded it, it lost in a reduced sense of cohesive regional identity as it subsumed the various smaller parties into a multi-regional federation. How then to create a sense of pan-northern identity and reconcile it with the regional diversity of local autonomist politics?

In the 1990s Bossi and the leadership of the party increasingly moved its programme away from traditional ethno-linguistic concerns with local culture and language towards a more broadly based attack on the political corruption and *partitocrazia* (party domination) associated with the Italian state. This was coupled with an appeal to the self-interested desire of the inhabitants of the wealthy north to dissociate themselves from the undeveloped, unproductive and unloved south which, they argued, was sustained solely by northerners' taxes redistributed by central government. Economic considerations such as these, together with the corruption scandals that rocked Italian politics in the early 1990s, were the main reasons behind the popularity of the Northern League as a political force, and they suffice as an explanation of its electoral success. The great northern city of Milan chose a *Lega* mayor in 1993. Nevertheless, the League felt the irrepressible urge to meddle in the politics of identity, to create a mythological history with which to buttress the idea of a distinct northern identity with antecedents in the distant past, such that it could claim chronological priority not only over the modern Italian state, which was merely an invention of the nineteenth century, but even over that state's own supposed forerunner, the Roman republic of antiquity, which had itself once dominated the whole of the Italian peninsula.

Two periods in the history of the north were hit upon as offering the desired precedent and proof of a distinct northern political tradition and ethnic identity, separate from that of the rest of Italy. In 1167 sixteen Lombard and Venetian cities supposedly swore an oath together at the town of Pontida near Bergamo to resist the invading armies of the German Holy Roman Emperor Frederick I Barbarossa, who was attempting to assert imperial control over the region in a series of expeditions across the Alps. The Lombard League was successful in withstanding imperial interference in Italian affairs, defeating Barbarossa in battle at Legnano in 1176. The wider political context of this struggle was the conflict between the Pope, Alexander III, and the Emperor Barbarossa for control of northern Italy, a game in which the League was a relatively minor player whose victories primarily furthered papal interests. Viewed more parochially, it represents for separatist-minded north Italians the unexpected triumph of a confederation of small-scale, free communities against the over-weening

500,000-lire 'note' of the Repubblica del Nord (1996), showing the portrait of Umberto Bossi, leader of the Northern League, the image of Alberto da Giussano on horseback, and the course of the *Marcia sul Po*.

power of great foreign potentates. This, not surprisingly, is precisely the perspective on the past adopted by the *Lega Nord*, whose members regard the medieval league as the inspiration for their own political struggle, and for the character of their political organization – federalist and regionalist, and resolutely opposed to outside centralizing. The historical symbolism was laid on thickly at *Lega* rallies held in the town of Pontida, where the founding oath of the medieval Lombard League was taken. One of the *Lega*'s favourite icons is the image of the medieval warrior Alberto da Giussano, leader of the Lombard forces at the Battle of Legnano, superimposed on an outline map of northern Italy. This image appears on the League's identity cards and on 'banknotes' issued in the name of the Republic of the North, or *Padania*. This was the name adopted by the League in September 1996 when assembled activists declared the whole of Italy from Tuscany to the Alps an independent federal republic, with a provisional parliament and government.

Another symbol, also appearing on the propaganda banknotes issued in the name of the League, is the *carroccio*, a medieval war-wagon that acted as the focal point in battle for the armies of the north Italian cities in the twelfth-century Lombard League.[8] In many ways Umberto Bossi, the party's leader, is the personified equivalent of the *carroccio*. He acts as the decisive source of power and authority within the party's organization. Rejecting any positioning within the conventional political spectrum from left to right, the League creates its identity as a movement around its separatist programme

One-lega 'note' of Padania (1996), illustrating the *carroccio*, the battle-standard of the free cities of northern Italy in the Middle Ages.

and around Bossi himself, as both the creator of the movement and its supreme interpreter. This is one among various aspects of the League that have led some observers to suggest that it is in fact a party of the far right, or even neo-fascist. This is somewhat ironic as Bossi is the sworn enemy of the contemporary Italian party that is often considered to be the successor to Mussolini's Fascists, the *Alleanza Nazionale* (National Alliance), dedicated centralists that they are. Nonetheless, the potent mixture of a personality cult focused on the leader with a sometimes aggressive tendency towards regional/national chauvinism and the cultivation of folkish traditionalism within the *Lega* does exhibit some parallels with the various fascist parties of earlier twentieth-century Europe.

The claim to the inheritance of the medieval Lombard League gives a touch of historical depth to the myth of a distinctly town-based and federalist character in northern Italian political life which the *Lega* advocates. This is certainly pretence, but it is not yet imposture. The element of imposture comes from the second of the League's attempts to construct a legitimate paternity for its autonomist ambitions. The problem faced by the League is that it has in a sense thrown its net too widely. The area theoretically included within the phantom Republic of the North stretches from the Alps to the southern borders of Tuscany, Umbria and the Marche. This huge area is mother to considerable cultural and linguistic diversity which is hard to distinguish qualitatively from the similarly intense variety that characterizes the rest of Italy. What is it that makes this area culturally distinct and unified? The Lombard League of the Middle Ages cannot quite suffice on its own. It excludes the Alpine regions, Liguria and the more southerly towns which did not participate in it. The River Po acts as a useful geographical symbol for much of the north, hence the name of the provisional republic (and the party newspaper), Padania, derived from *Padus,* the Latin name for the river. But again its relevance, and attraction, for voters in faraway Tuscany and Umbria to the south is less clear. The same problem also renders the Alps of only limited use as a focus of identity for the whole of the north.

An ethnic solution might provide a plausible answer. If neither history nor geography convincingly unites the whole area laid claim to by the proponents of the prospective Republic of Padania, the answer might lie in the blood. Hence the attraction of the Celtic option. For some of the more imaginative of the League's activists, and the more gullible of its supporters, have gone for the idea that northerners are, unlike other Italians, Celts, or, to give them their full ethno-historical designation, Celto-Lombards. Whence this

Celtic inheritance of northern Italians? We must go back to 191 BC, the year in which the legions of the Roman republic completed their conquest of the Po Valley by defeating the people of the Boii, the last of the local tribes of Gauls who inhabited Italy north of the Apennines. Ancient Roman historical tradition recorded how these Gauls invaded Italy at some point between 600 and 400 BC and proceeded to assault and capture the city of Rome itself in 387. Historians and archaeologists have consistently, but not necessarily rightly, asserted that they were Celts, both ethnically and linguistically.[9] *Lega* supporters have taken up this theme in an attempt to carve out an entirely new identity for north Italians, an identity of which they were previously quite unaware. It is this that makes the League's position essentially an imposture. The attractions of the ancient Celtic Gauls for the League are manifold. Just as the Gauls were the arch-enemies of the Romans in antiquity, so the League proclaims its antipathy towards the modern Italian republic. Moreover, the Gauls succeeded in destroying the city of Rome itself, an event which the League would like to transform into an inspirational group memory, like that of the Lombards' victory at the Battle of Legnano. The *Lega*'s political antagonism towards the Italian republic is thereby represented as inherited and racially predetermined, and the differences between the north and the rest of Italy a matter of millennia, not a single decade.

Celts also figure in the separatist mythologies of other European ethnoregionalist movements, in France (Brittany and Corsica), Spain (Galicia) and the British Isles (Ireland, Isle of Man, Cornwall, Wales, Scotland). A Celtic Padania can therefore adopt the emotive rhetoric of such marginalized subordinate cultures oppressed for centuries by an uncaring centralist state. There is a difference of course. While other regions where this position has been taken by regionalist or nationalist movements – Scotland, or Brittany for example – can make a reasonable case that they have fared less well both culturally and economically than the dominant region or group in their respective states, it is perhaps not quite so clear that northern Italy has suffered materially to any great extent. After all, it is obviously by far the richest part of Italy and one of the wealthiest regions in the whole of Europe. Rage at the endemic corruption in Italian politics of the early 1990s is one matter, and quite understandable. *Ennui* provoked by the spending of northern taxes by the Italian state to support the less opulent south is another, and somewhat less laudable as a separatist motive. Hence the need to establish the irreconcilable, and eternal, distinctiveness of northern Italy and north Italians from both the Rome-based state in the middle of Italy and the poor relations in the south. They are, it turns out, not related anyway. For one League activist has claimed, somewhat bizarrely, that an English scientist has proved that north Italians have Celtic DNA. The implication of this strange assertion is that they are therefore not ethnically affiliated with (other) Italians, that they have no civil obligations towards them and should therefore not belong in the same state.

The Celtic stance seems to be quite important for the symbolism of the *Lega Nord*, but just how effective has it been as a means of creating a new northern identity among northerners as a group? 'Celtic' games (*giochi celtici*) such as caber-tossing and wife-carrying races are apparently quite popular at League gatherings, and Celtic themes are regularly aired in the League's daily newspaper, *La Padania*, and its periodical magazine, *Sole delle Alpi* (Sun of the Alps). The latter is also the name of the League's logo, a flower-pattern within a circle of 'Celtic green' which appears on the flag of the would-be republic of Padania. But it would be misleading to suggest that all this mythologizing imposture really has any significant impact on the political scene in the north of Italy outside already committed League circles.

Umberto Bossi, founder and leader of the *Lega Nord*, on the *Marcia sul Po* in September 1996, holding a glass container full of water from the River Po which he carried in procession to Venice.

The limited extent of its public appeal was clearly demonstrated in September 1996 when Bossi led the so-called *Marcia sul Po* (the March along the Po). This was planned as a series of festivities to mark the declaration of independence of the republic of Padania and the proclamation of its provisional constitution. Bossi filled what was reported in the newspaper *La Stampa* as an *ampolla celtica* (a Celtic vessel), elsewhere as a test-tube, with water taken from the source of the River Po and proceeded along the length of the great river of the north in a motorized catamaran.[10] A turnout of 1.5 million to celebrate the birth of Padania was predicted. The phial of river water was eventually emptied into the lagoon at Venice before crowds estimated at about 15,000. Though the *Lega* had emerged from the elections in April of the same year as the largest party in the north, the declaration of independence, with the rediscovery of the north's Celtic roots, has yet to capture the popular imagination. The party still takes a sizeable percentage of votes cast, particularly in its heartlands in the Veneto and Lombardy, though it has consistently failed south of the Po in the regions of Tuscany, Umbria, the Marche and Emilia-Romagna.

In the declaration of independence of 15 September 1996, in the name of the 'Peoples of Padania' the League proclaimed:

We are profoundly convinced that the continued presence of Padania within the confines of the Italian State would lead to the gradual extinction of all hope of rebirth and the annihilation of the identities of its peoples ... Since time immemorial, we have lived, built, worked and protected these lands handed down to us by our forefathers, bathed and quenched by the waters of our great rivers. Here we have invented an original way of living, of developing the arts and of working. We belong to a historical area, Padania ... united by the ties which run as deep as the enduring cycles of the seasons revolving about them, as strong as the spirit of the nations that inhabit them.

This is classic nineteenth-century nationalist language. The obsession with the symbolism of the River Po, for instance, is reminiscent of Czech riverine nationalist sentiment so marvellously expressed in Smetana's symphonic poem *Vltava* in the sequence *Má Vlast* (My Country), composed in 1879, or of Germany's fixation on the Rhine as the eternal border between itself and its hereditary enemy, France.

This is one case of communal imposture which seems likely not to give rise a new identity among the mass of the population, however fervently the Northern League's supporters attempt to propagate the idea. Why? Perhaps for no more profound reason than the inherent implausibility of the notion of a Celtic 'revival' in northern Italy, coupled with the somewhat anachronistic nature of the language and symbolism adopted by the *Lega*. In the nineteenth century, the hey-day of cultural nationalism, and of Celtomania in particular, it caught on in Galicia in north-western Spain, a region which *prima facie* might appear to be an equally unlikely candidate for Celtic status.[11] Local antiquarians established the indigenous Celts, and later Germanic invaders, the Suebi, as the forefathers of the Galicians, and thus enrolled their people among the Celtic nations of Europe. The lack of any linguistic continuity between modern Gallego, the language of Galicia, and Celtic forced Galician Celtophiles to resort to archaeological evidence. The way they set about it, and their reasons for doing so, were not dissimilar to those of the *Lega Nord*. Ancient historical sources had written of a people called the Callaeci in the north-west of the Iberian peninsula who were identified as Celts by contemporary scholarship. Regionalist sentiment in Galicia sought, and found, in this ancient ethnic group a discrete and, despite all appearances to the contrary, uninterrupted cultural inheritance from prehistory. This aligned them with a pre-Roman tradition that seemed also to have survived in similarly marginalized areas elsewhere on Europe's Atlantic coast in France and Britain. The very lack of linguistic continuity merely served to underline for Galician regionalists the extent to which they had been deprived of their cultural inheritance, first by the Romans in antiquity and more recently by the Spanish state, a feeling exacerbated by Franco's nullification in 1936 of an overwhelming vote in favour of Galician autonomy. Galicia now has autonomous status, granted in 1981, and Gallego is an official language of Spain.

The myth of Celtic Galicia played an important role in defining Galician identity in the nineteenth century, and it still does. Galicians are regularly included among the Celtic peoples of Europe, together with the Scots, Welsh, Irish, Manx, Cornish and Bretons, if sometimes with a question mark. Yet Galicians have no more substantive claim to be Celts than do the inhabitants of northern Italy. Their Celtic identity is no less of a myth or invention. So why did the idea take off in Galicia in a way in which it has so far failed to do in the minds of most north Italians other than some League supporters? Perhaps because the time for the creation of new cultural identities has, for the moment, passed, in western Europe at least. The intellectual climate of the Romantic Age in the nineteenth century that gave rise to folk-cultural nationalisms reached its appalling consummation in the events of the Second World War. Since then rather more secular economic and political considerations have, for better or worse, dominated political discourse in most countries of western Europe. Public celebrations of national conse-cration, such as Umberto Bossi's *Marcia sul Po*, intended to demarcate the people's lands and dedicate them to a sacred destiny of autonomy, have a ritual character about them that recalls the style of nationalist ceremonial so popular in many countries of pre-Second World War Europe, and seems strangely out of kilter with the style of the times.

There are, however, other more modernist aspects of the *Lega*'s programme that find close affinities with contemporary trends in the politics of the European Union, in particular the idea of 'Europe of the Regions', which came to prominence in the 1980s. According to many political observers and politicians, the inevitable consequence of increased political union between the existing states of the EU and the surrendering of certain aspects of national sovereignty to its institutions – the Commission and the Parliament – was, and is, that power will also need to be devolved downwards to sub-national levels, to that of the region, in order, among other aims, to compensate for the so-called 'democratic deficit' created by the increased distance, both real and perceived, between government and most of the governed within the EU. This was of course welcome news to regionalist movements within the territories of the EU member states, as they were thereby empowered to develop their autonomist ambitions within the national context as federalist within an EU context. Regionalist parties often command fierce loyalty from their members, but characteristically fail to attract more than a significant minority of the voters within the region itself, for whom a sense of regional identity, however strong, need not necessarily entail enthusiasm for even quite limited forms of self-government. An apt recent example of this phenomenon is the tiny majority of less than 1 per cent among the Welsh electorate in favour of a devolved Assembly in the 1999 referendum. Anxieties provoked by the thought of autonomy, let alone outright independence, could however be allayed by the less disturbing prospect of co-membership in a pan-European club of autonomous regions, which might potentially enlarge the pool of voters willing to support the regionalist movement. The problem for the *Lega Nord* is that, whatever it may claim, it is attempting to create Padania from scratch. There is no historical precedent for a unitary, or even a federal, state in northern Italy covering the area claimed by Padania. The best candidate is the Cisalpine republic, created by Napoleon in 1797 after his conquest of Italy. It covered much of northern Italy but lasted barely four years before being reconstituted as the Italian republic in 1801. To our knowledge it has never been cited by the League, not unsurprisingly given its unfortunate foreign origins. One point the League insists on is the principle of self-determination. Pseudo-independence granted by invading foreigners is nothing to be proud of.

Local identities are strong, and of long standing, in the north as in the rest of Italy, and it is they that provide the viable alternative to just being Italian. The *Lega* began as an umbrella organization for the many local ethno-linguistic movements in the north that corresponded to these local identities, and at first it successfully combined their strengths within a loosely conceived northern protest movement. It has been less successful in integrating these together into a new, more concerted, quasi-national identity. The tension between the clearly nationalist language which the League employs with reference to Padania and its insistence that Padania is made up of many nations (*nazioni*), by which it means the local communities of northern Italy – Milanese, Bolognese, Venetians, Ligurians and so on – is clear, and fatal.

Belarus: a State without History?

If the political style of the Northern League is in some respects anachronistic within the context of modern western Europe, it finds many parallels in current developments within the new states of eastern Europe and the former Soviet Union. Here the politics of cultural nationalism and historical imposture are still central to public life in many areas, not least in Belarus, a country whose internal life has perhaps received little attention from western observers. Formerly known in English as White Russia or Byelorussia, it attained independence from the Soviet Union in 1991. Since then, it cannot be said that its history has been a tale of unalloyed success or civic harmony. Unlike most of the other new states carved from the moribund body of the USSR, Belarus harbours a considerable movement, which is at the moment in the ascendant, in favour of re-establishing a closer union with the Russian Federation. This tendency is led by the controversial president of the republic, Alyaksandr Lukashenka.

Quite apart from the on-going constitutional struggle between president and Parliament, one of the focal points of the conflict between Lukashenka and the Opposition has revolved around the culture-historical identity of the people of Belarus, about which there is considerable disagreement within the country. Are Belarusians merely a subspecies of Russian – their ethnic name meaning simply White Russian – whose destiny lies with their Great Russian brothers, or are they a quite different people with a unique language, a tradition of independent statehood and a distinct cultural inheritance? This internal debate is not merely a consequence of the presence of a Russian minority – estimated at 13.5 per cent of the population in 1991 compared to the 80 per cent majority identified as Belarusian – or the fact that Russian is far more widely spoken than Belarusian, even among ethnic Belarusians, though there is clearly a connection. There is importantly a lack of deep nationalist feeling among most Belarusians, for the reason that the next-door neighbours against whom the Belarusians would have to define themselves, the Russians, are not apparently perceived by most of them as very different from themselves.

How have the arguments lined up? On one level they are ideological and political. President Lukashenka and his party are mostly Communist in orientation, authoritarian in style and Russophile by instinct, while the nationalist opposition is by and large democratic, anti-Communist and anti-Russian in ideology. But the issue of the historical identity of the inhabitants of Belarus is also crucial. Both sides are in a sense arguing with fictions and historical myths. The pro-Russian tendency argues that there are no significant differences, whether cultural or historical, between Belarusians and Russians, which is clearly untrue as argued. This is backed up with the ever-malleable evidence of prehistory which, it is contended, shows that Russians, Belarusians and Ukrainians spring from a common ethnic source among the early eastern Slavic tribes and are therefore cousins, if not brothers. The Belarusian nationalist position on prehistory is that the proto-East Slavs were a motley group of warring peoples always essentially different from one another, while the proto-Belarusian element diverged still further from the others by taking in a large substrate population of Lithuanians. However, the key element in the Belarusian nationalist construction of a wholly independent past for themselves depends on what is at best a seriously partial rereading of more recent history.

The problem for Belarusian nationalists, as for the would-be Padanians of northern Italy, is that there are no long-standing traditions of independent statehood that can be clearly identified as ancestral to the current Belarusian people and state. There was a short-lived period of quasi-independence in 1918–19, but that scarcely suffices. So to fill an awkward gap, the nationalists have adopted the medieval Grand Duchy of Lithuania, later part of the commonwealth of Poland and Lithuania, as a glorious antecedent and precedent for their modern state. Not unsurprisingly, the modern republic of Lithuania has also adopted this huge state, which once stretched from the Baltic to the Black Sea, as its own historical patrimony. The most palpable expression of this potential rivalry is that both states used the same symbol as their national emblem in the 1990s. This consists of an armed medieval knight carrying a shield bearing the device of a cross with two cross-bars, sitting on a horse facing to the left which rears up on its hind legs. In

Three-talonas note of Lithuania (1991), showing Vytas, the White Knight, an emblem of the medieval kingdom of Lithuania.

Ten-rouble note of Belarus (1992), showing Pahonia, the Belarusian version of the medieval Lithuanian knight emblem.

Lithuanian he is known as Vytas (the White Knight) and as Pahonia (Pursuit) in Belarusian. This was the royal emblem of the Lithuanian dynasty that founded the great medieval empire in the late fourteenth and early fifteenth century. It is particularly associated with Grand Duke Vytautas (1401–30), the Lithuanian national hero who in 1410 won a crushing victory at Grunwald over the German Knights of the Teutonic Order who had previously dominated the Baltic region. Vytautas (Witold in Polish) established Lithuania, now united dynastically with the Polish kingdom to the west, as a great state, which dominated the Russian principality of Muscovy to the east and the Germans to the north. Natural, then, for Lithuanians to feel communal pride in this lost imperial past, and hard to see how Belarusians, whose putative ancestors were subjects of this Lithuanian state from the early fourteenth century onwards, might stake their claim.

However, as eventually happened to the Norman French conquerors of England, through extensive intermarriage with the local nobilities many of the Lithuanian conquerors took on the language and, at first, the Orthodox Christianity of their East Slavic subjects. During the period of the

Silver *grosz* of Sigismund (Zygmunt) I,
King of Poland, as Grand Duke of
Lithuania (1506–48). The reverse
shows the knight symbol from which
the modern Lithuanian and Belarusian
emblems derive.

dynastic union with Poland, between 1386 and 1569 when the Union of
Lublin joined Lithuanians and Poles together in a single commonwealth,
Polish and Roman Catholic influences from the west increasingly dominated
within the Lithuanian state. Yet its sixteenth-century statutes are written
not in Lithuanian or Polish, but in a variety of East Slavic sometimes called
Ruthenian but, predictably, claimed as medieval Belarusian by Belarusian
nationalists. By the process of nationalistic misinterpretation of medieval
history, to which the very idea of the nation, with its connotations of a
monolingual culture shared by all members, is entirely alien, Belarusian
nationalists have attempted to foist their historical narrative on the multi-
ethnic, multi-lingual Lithuanian state of a former period. Equally, however,
the modern Lithuanian nationalist claim to this inheritance is somewhat
compromised by the fact that for much of its history most of the population,
and even the ruling nobility, were not Lithuanian-speakers and, in strict
nationalist terms, were therefore Lithuanian in name only.[12]

Whatever the problems, both Lithuanian and Belarusian nationalists
claim exclusive rights to this historical inheritance. But the claim is much
less widely accepted in Belarus than in Lithuania, for a variety of reasons,
which together make it hard for most Belarusians to identify very strongly
with the grand duchy of Lithuania. Ecclesiastically it was predominantly
Roman Catholic, while the majority of Belarusians are now Orthodox,
though there is a significant minority of Catholics. Medieval Lithuania was
also the arch-enemy of the Russian state of Muscovy based in Moscow, yet
most Belarusians do not now feel significant enmity towards Russians. Both
these factors work in the opposite direction for Lithuanians who are deeply
Roman Catholic, are not by and large particularly well disposed towards
Russians and feel no sense of kinship with them. So, despite all the other
countervailing factors that weaken the case for continuity, most Lithuanians
currently find it easier to identify with medieval Lithuania than do most
Belarusians.

This question came to a head in a referendum in Belarus organized by
President Lukashenka in May 1995, in which 75 per cent voted in favour of

a range of political and symbolic measures, including economic integration
with Russia; the effective granting of autocratic power to the pro-Russian
president, allowing him to dissolve parliament in the event of a violation of
the constitution; making Russian an official language alongside Belarusian;
abolishing the new nationalist flag adopted in 1991 in favour of a version not
coincidentally rather similar to that of the Communist Byelorussian Soviet
Republic (see Plates 4B–D); and finally doing away with the nationalist
Pahonia symbol as the state emblem. Though the validity of the results was
doubted by some at the time, they clearly reflected the extent to which the
nationalist project had failed to catch the imagination of most Belarusians.
It was an implicit rejection of the idea of a distinct Belarusian nationality
constructed on the premise of an essential and enduring antipathy towards
Russia and Russians, which revealed that most Belarusians are not very
convinced of the idea that they are terribly different from their Russian
neighbours, whether culturally, linguistically or historically. This, according
to the nationalists, is clearly the inevitable result of centuries of Russian
occupation that has suppressed a once-flourishing sense of nationhood
which they are merely trying to revive in the newly independent state.
But the myth of nationhood they selected has simply failed to resonate with
their compatriots as strongly as the idea, no less mythically justified, that
Belarusians and Russians are of the same genetic stock, and are therefore
eternally and inextricably, because ethnically, connected to one another.[13]

Conclusion

On current projections, neither the *Lega Nord*'s idea of Celtic Padania nor
the Belarusian nationalist vision of the medieval Lithuanian empire as
their ancestral state is likely to convince the majority of their respective
electorates. Why is this? Is it perhaps because they are factually inauthentic?
The historical claims involved in both these particular sets of myths are
definitely very hard to accept at face value. On the other hand, they do
purport to rest on independently verifiable evidence and are certainly not
pure invention, though the constructions put upon that evidence may well
appear highly questionable to the dispassionate observer. Factual accuracy
is not the crucial issue in determining whether or not a particular myth
convinces. For a new myth to succeed, it should ideally resonate with some
aspect of the community's historical consciousness. The problem with the
idea that north Italians are ethnically Celtic is that it comes more or less out
of the blue for most northerners themselves. It adds nothing to, and has no

relationship with, their local identities as Venetians, Milanese, or whatever. Eighteenth-century antiquarians from the north flirted briefly with Celtomania, but it failed to catch on then as now. It also helps to have fertile ground, a constituency that is potentially predisposed to accepting the contemporary implications of the historical myth for their current world view which, in the cases looked at here, amounts to establishing greater political distance from a neighbouring state. But Belarusians are not generally ill-disposed towards Russians for a variety of historical reasons, not the least important of which is the vital memory of the Great Patriotic War (the Russian name for the Second World War) in which Russians and Belarusians fought side by side and died in their millions to liberate Belarus from German occupation. This is, perhaps understandably, a much more viscerally remembered myth than that of a distant and rather nebulous realm which, even on the most optimistic estimate, was only ever partly Belarusian. But things could always change. If political relations between Russia and Belarus were to deteriorate significantly, historical memories and preferred myths of nationality might alter accordingly.

This is the secret of identity myths which neither the *Lega Nord* nor Belarusian nationalists seem to have grasped. They cannot succeed as an instrument to change a people's sense of self in the absence of the right circumstances in other spheres – political, economic and social – to create the space in which a new feeling of national identity and an altered understanding of their communal history might conceivably grow. Historical myths can be highly persuasive, but without the right preconditions their seed will fall on stony ground and bear no fruit. Here is a useful lesson for all future rebels, pretenders and impostors, both individuals and nations, of whom there will no doubt be as many in the third millennium AD as in all its predecessors.

Notes

Introduction

1 Mansel 1995, 86.

2 This process is called 'overstriking' by numismatists. For more examples of Stephen Sack's innovative work in coin photography, see the catalogue of his 1999 British Museum exhibition, *The Metal Mirror*, Sack 1999.

3 For an influential collection of essays in this vein, see Hobsbawm and Ranger 1983.

Chapter 1 The Rebel in Antiquity

1 A translation is available in *Myths from Mesopotamia*, trans. S. Dalley (Oxford 1988).

2 For a classic account of the history of ancient Israel, see Bright 1981.

3 For a well-written, and well-illustrated, introduction to Roman history, see Cornell and Matthews 1982.

4 See Talbert 1984 on the Senate in the imperial period, esp. 354–8 on their role in electing emperors. On the emperor, see Millar 1977.

5 Wiseman 1992. See Levick 1990 on Claudius.

6 On the usurpers of 68 and 69, see the extensive sociological account of Flaig 1992.

7 See Levick 1999 for a biography of Vespasian.

8 On Postumus, see Drinkwater 1987; on Zenobia, Stoneman 1992; on Aurelian, Watson 1999.

9 On Carausius and Allectus, see Casey 1994.

10 In Latin, *Carausius et fratres sui*, and *Augustis cum Diocletiano*.

11 *Renovat[io] Romano[rum]* in Latin.

12 On the *Historia Augusta*, see Syme 1971.

13 For a comprehensive introduction to Hellenistic history, see Green 1990. On Cleopatra, see the brief but useful introductory works of Flamarion 1997 and Rice 1999.

14 *Orientis Graeci Inscriptiones Selectae* 53 (ed. W. Dittenberger, Berlin, 1903–5).

15 See Bowman 1990, 30–1.

16 On Mesopotamian usurpers and the Seleucids, see Kuhrt 1987, Sherwin-White and Kuhrt 1993, esp. 37–8 for the Borsippa inscription. For a recent introduction to ancient Near Eastern history, see Kuhrt 1995, esp. vol. 2, 598–603 on Cyrus and Nabonidus.

17 Matthew 1.1–17; Luke 3.23–38.

18 The standard account in English is to be found in Schürer 1973, 534–57.

Chapter 2 Kings and Pretenders

1 Thus Jones 1962. It should be noted that the Greek sources generally use *basileus* for both 'king' and 'emperor', but the Latin ones are consistent in their use of *rex*; see also the Procopius reference in note 5, which refers to Theoderic.

2 See Fabbrini 1983.

3 On the Pope and the Empire, see Muldoon 1999, chapter 1.

4 On the caliphs see Wasserstein 1993, chapter 1, Lambton 1978 and Sourdel 1978.

5 When necessary a distinction could be made: Procopius, *de Bello Gothico* i 1.26, distinguishing carefully between *basileus* and *rex* (transliterated into Greek). See generally on this topic Muldoon 1999, though Selden 1614, 18–45, is still excellent, combining the antiquarian's viewpoint with the jurist's in a way few could equal.

6 Selden 1614, 26, with other examples. For Henry VIII, see Muldoon 1999, 128–30.

7 On Iturbide see Robertson 1952. In his desperate search for an heir Maximilian of Mexico thought of adopting one of Iturbide's two grandsons, and to that end granted them princely rank in 1865: see Montgomery-Massingberd 1977, 397.

8 On Theodore of Corsica, see Colocci Vespucci 1931 and Madaro 1932, as well as the *Dictionary of National Biography* article on his son, Colonel Frederick (*c*.1725–97).

9 On regalian right, see Howell 1962. On the distinction between the king and feudal lords

inferior to him, see Reynolds 1994, 34–8. This book is of great general relevance to the question of kingship and the 'feudal system'. On the incorporation of the Duchy of Lancaster, see Kantorowicz 1957, 403–6, rightly indicating that this event (though the subject of a famous case in 1561) is scarcely mentioned by modern writers on the law and history of the peerage.

10 On the Isle of Man, see Kinvig 1975, especially 156–62. Islands are natural quasi-sovereign lordships, and the Isle of Wight was held as such from the eleventh century to the late thirteenth and again at various points in the fourteenth and fifteenth centuries. It is also stated, no doubt erroneously, in the foundation chronicle of Tewkesbury Abbey (printed in Dugdale's *Monasticon*) that Henry VI crowned his favourite Henry Beauchamp, Duke of Warwick, as king of the Isle of Wight. This event awaits attention from the Isle of Wight regionalist movement. For an interesting personal claim from the same island, see p. 128.

11 For the king of Bardsey, see Wheeler 1955, 77–80. Lord Newborough's claim is documented at the Public Record Office, ref. CRES 37/1605; also relevant is PRO T 107/2254. Recently the kingship of Bardsey has been revived and awarded to Bryn Terfel, the singer. Harman of Lundy's unsuccessful appeal to the King's Bench is *Harman v Bolt* (1931) 47 TLR 219. PRO HLG 52/1716 and 1717 contain departmental correspondence on Lundy (with references to Bardsey et al.) between 1923 and 1969, including an elegant minute by Mr V. J. Lewis of the solicitor's department of the Ministry of Housing and Local Government, dated 22 December 1959.

12 The Seborga website is at www.masterweb.it/seborga. A similar principality called Pontecorvo ('confirmed by Napoleon') can be found at www.pontecorvo.nu. The real principality of Ponte Corvo was a title granted by Napoleon to Marshal Bernardotte.

13 On San Marino, see Garosci 1967. The relativist argument for accepting states like Seborga is put (with tongue more than slightly in cheek) in an article entitled 'The Crisis of Seborga' at netspace.students.brown.edu/indy/issues/04-11-96/opinions3.html.

14 The main source of information is now the Hutt River website at www.wps.com.au/hutriver.

15 Oliver, who ran an organization called the Phoenix Foundation, was to reappear at least

twice in similar schemes: the 1973 attempt at creating an autonomous state on Abaco, an island in the Bahamas; and an equally doomed project in 1980 to turn Espiritu Santu, an island in the Gilbert group (then lately independent as Kiribati), into the Republic of Vemarana. In both cases the aim was to set up a tax haven. Information on this comes from an excellent website compiled by Jim Lerwin and entitled 'Footnotes to History', highly relevant to many topics dealt with in this book: www.gravy.net/~jim.

16 See Strauss 1984, 132–8.

17 On Henry IV's usurpation generally, see Bruce 1986. The presentation of usurpation is treated by Strohm 1998; see especially 3–4 for the 'Crouchback story'.

18 Anglo 1992, 19–20.

19 Cato, *de Occupatione* 6 (= Armstrong 1969, 94–7 with notes 129–31).

20 For Bacon's three 'titles', see the edition by Weinberger 1996, 29–33. Bacon (unlike earlier writers) concluded that, since Elizabeth of York was not made queen regnant, Henry must have decided to base his claim entirely on his Lancastrian descent. On Henry's relations with the last Plantagenets in general, see Griffiths and Thomas 1985, especially chapter 13.

21 For a graphic illustration, see table 6 ('Extirpation of Plantagenet blood under the Tudors') in Louda and Maclagan 1981, 26. See also the quotation from the Spanish ambassador printed opposite the preface in Griffiths and Thomas 1985.

22 On Henry as the red dragon of Cadwallader, see Anglo 1992, chapter 2. The whole book is highly relevant. On the function of such genealogies, see Bizzocchi 1995, 71–92.

23 The best guide to this is Montgomery-Massingberd 1977. For a specific study of pretendership in France, see Warren 1947 and, in the well known 'Que Sais-je?' series, Puy de Clinchamps 1967.

24 Lock 1995, 66–7.

25 For much of what follows, see Clark 1985. For a bibliography on various aspects of Jacobitism, see Clark 1986, appendix B.

26 Ballantyne 1743, 10, quoted by Clark 1985, 133; see also ibid. 236.

27 A complete account of Fuller and his many nefarious activities is given by Campbell 1961.

28 Campbell 1961, 186–7.

29 The standard guide to the titles, knighthoods and official appointments bestowed by the Stuart pretenders is Ruvigny 1904.

30 On the military dimension of Jacobitism, and especially the '45, see Black 1990.

31 Quoted by Clark 1986, 161, where the emphasis is naturally on the telling fact that a member of the Hanoverian dynasty, and one born so late as 1768, could feel her position undermined by the continued existence of the Stuart line.

Chapter 3 Impostors and Slave Kings

1 On the false Neros, see Tuplin 1989.

2 The classic discussion of sleeping heroes is given by Thomas 1971, 493–501.

3 There is plenty on Frederick II as a millennial figure in the main biography of him by Kantorowicz 1927–31, and the collection of follow-up articles edited by Wolf 1966, especially 617–47.

4 Bercé 1990, ch. 1. This whole book is of great relevance to all the cases discussed in this section.

5 On Ward of Trumpington and other Richard imitators, see Strohm 1998, 106–8, 245.

6 On Simnel's imposture, see Bennett 1987. For Bacon's remark, see Weinberger 1996, 54.

7 For the Warbeck episode, see now Arthurson 1994. Kleyn 1990 argues that Warbeck was the Duke of York after all.

8 Edward VI myths and impostures are recounted from primary evidence by Thomas 1971, 498–500; interestingly, one inveterate subscriber to the Edward myths was also, around 1600, peddling stories about Don Sebastian.

9 For contemporary and near-contemporary accounts of the Dmitri episode, see Howe 1916. Two very readable later accounts are Manley 1674 and Mérimée 1853, both representing Dmitri as Boris Godunov's nemesis: a theme central to Mussorgsky's great opera *Boris Godunov*.

10 *The Times*, 12 August 1999, p. 18. Another supposed offshoot of the Bourbons was Maria Stella Chiappini, who claimed to be the legitimate daughter of Louis Philippe, Duc d'Orléans, and the sister of Louis Philippe, King of the French. She married the Welsh Lord Newborough and left descendants whose claim to the island of Bardsey is mentioned above, chapter 2, note 11.

11 Two books supporting Anastasia's claims are Kurth 1983 and the less well argued Lovell 1992, which however has the attraction of including (apart from a very full bibliography of works both avowedly fictional and otherwise) an appendix listing films, plays, musicals, ballets and sound recordings based upon the Anna Anderson story. For a fierce and effective destruction of the case, see an article by John Godl at www.intlromanovsociety.org/expressions/godl.htm. It is worth pointing out that Anna Anderson was not by any means the only person to claim to be Anastasia or one of the other children of the last tsar. A supposed tsarevitch can be found on-line at www.npsnet.com/tsarevich_alexei.

12 On the significance of names in the ancient world, see now Jones 1996, especially 3–27.

13 On the Arsacids, see Wolski 1962. The ancient text on the topic of their reuse of the name Arsaces is Justin 41.5.5–6.

14 On pharaonic titulature generally, see Quirke 1990.

15 Kantorowicz 1957.

16 On actors' names, see Bonaria 1959. The Seneca quotation is from *Naturales Quaestiones* 7.32.3. For charioteers and their horses, see Syme 1977.

17 A particularly twee practice was giving two slaves (often siblings) matching names, perhaps referring to a well-known pair from mythology or history: Solin 1990. For a schematic example of the imposition of names on slaves in the market-place, see Varro, *de Lingua Latina* 8.21.

18 On religious name-change, see Harrer 1940 and Horsley 1987; on supplementary tombstone names, Kajanto 1966, 58–65.

19 On the Sicilian slave revolts and the kingship of their leaders, see Bradley 1989: also a very good introduction to the same topic in relation to the slaves of the New World.

20 In general on maroon societies, see Price 1973.

21 Schwartz 1985, 47–50.

22 Schwartz 1992, 122–8.

23 On kings of arms, see Wagner 1967, 7.

24 The quoted text is a 'letter' from Balthasar to Henry VIII, offering his daughter as a wife for

the Prince of Wales. It is a rather unexpected survival in College of Arms Ms H19/ 286–7 (a ms dating to 1563–6). The name Balthasar is merely a version of Belshazzar, last King of Babylon in the book of Daniel and the vulgate book of Baruch, where he is wrongly described as son of Nebuchadnezzar. In fact he was his grandson and a usurper of the throne.

25 On the Zanj, see Popovic 1976, citing Halm 1967.

26 On the civil wars in Haiti and all that follows here, see Cole 1967.

27 The conflicting views are best expressed by James 1963 and Craton 1982, quoted by Bradley 1989, 12–13.

Chapter 4 Dreamers and Hoaxers

1 Nicol 1992, chapter 6. Quotation from Pseudo-Gorgillas, *Threnos*, ed. Wagner 1876, 141–70, lines 825–31, 1015–17 (translation based on the paraphrase by Nicol op. cit. 99–100). On much of what follows Nicol is a sufficient introduction, and other references will here be kept to a minimum.

2 Runciman 1965, 181–4; Bierbrier 1980, 91–4; Nicol 1992, 109–16.

3 Runciman 1965, 177–8; Brown 1996, 145, 173–4; Mansel 1995, 6–7. Venice's claim to be a second Byzantium was supported by no less a personage than Cardinal Bessarion, in the quotation given by Brown, 145.

4 Nicol 1992, 117–18; Geanakoplos 1959, 17 n. 5, citing the sources. These include a letter from the thirteenth-century emperor Michael VIII Palaeologus to the Pope, and a wall painting in the Palazzo Communale at Viterbo purporting to be a portrait of the same emperor, Michael 'Viterbensis'.

5 Nicol 1992, 121–4; Shilstone 1939–40.

6 Nicol 1992, 117.

7 Nicol 1992, 119–20.

8 Nicol 1992, 120–1; Rhodocanakis 1870, esp. 21–2.

9 Nicol 1992, 121, 124–5.

10 Rome, Archivio Storico Capitolino, Lib. decret. nob. Rom. armadio 24 vol. 22, 214–18 and 219–23: Congregazione Araldica Capitolina 11/2/1869 and 2/12/1869. On Byzantium as a metaphor for corrupt and inward-looking politics in unified Italy, see Drake 1980.

11 See Sturdza 1983, 376; Gauci and Mallat 1985, 29–31, with a fairly off-putting photograph of the offender. Gauci and Mallat uncritically present a collection of genealogies of individuals claiming to descend from the imperial Palaeologi, though their introduction expressly reserves judgement on the genuineness of the claims made. Some of these are certainly startling.

12 A sample of the extraordinary literature on 'Michael III': A.N.E.G.T.I. 1967 and Macchioni di Sela 1979 (both note-form biographies listing every event in the claimant's life from his school exams onwards); Francesco 1951 and Auda-Gioanet 1953 (genealogical accounts); Auda-Gioanet 1952 (a polemical little piece in uncertain English). Pierangeli's early letters to the Duce and others are in Rome, Archivio di Stato SPD-CO 511.413.

13 I.I.G.A. 1963, 128–9. The recognition of the surnames in 1950 resulted from the clause in the Italian republic's constitution whereby legitimate pre-1922 titles of nobility could be recognized as supplementary parts of the surname. Totò had managed to squeak into the last edition of the official *Libro d'Oro* or list of the nobility of the kingdom of Italy.

14 One individual who made an unsuccessful attack on Totò's *bona fides* was another pseudo-Byzantine, one Marziano Lavarello (Emperor Marziano II), sentenced to seventeen months' imprisonment for *calunnia* (criminal libel) in December 1954. A very brief outline of the Lavarello pedigree appears in Gauci and Mallat 1985, 24–5.

15 Webster 1988. Mr Webster was the Isle of Wight County Archivist and thus had a privileged view of Prince Petros and his researches.

16 Chaffanjon and Flavigny 1982, 265–6.

17 Chaffanjon and Flavigny 1982, 269.

18 See an article at http://caltrap.bbsnet.com entitled 'The Emperor of Palm Beach'.

19 Michael of Albany 1998. For a very gentle commentary, see M. Linklater, *The Times*, 7 May 1998.

20 Gardner 1996, a book whose own genealogy is clearly a direct descent from the much better-known blockbuster *The Holy Blood and the Holy Grail* (Baigent, Leigh and Lincoln 1982), the model and ancestor of all crazy speculation in this area.

21 See an interview in the *The Guardian*, 'G2' section, 24 March 1999.

22 Trevor-Roper 1983, 31–41.

23 Gauci and Mallat 1985, 27–8.

24 Lindsey 1939. There was a connection between Hannah Lightfoot and another suppositious descendant of the Hanoverians: Dr Wilmot, the minister who purportedly married Hannah and the future George III, was uncle of Olive Ryves who later claimed to be daughter of the Duke of Cumberland, George III's brother; see Thoms 1867.

25 For purported offspring of the Duke of Windsor, see *The Times* 30 March 1996, p. 15, and 27 April 1996, p. 10.

26 Chatwin 1977, 18–23. The 'official' Araucania and Patagonia website is at www.pitt.edu/~jwcst17. Orélie-Antoine's own book is Tounens 1863.

27 As he put it in his manifesto (Tounens 1864, 3–4): 'Je commence par déclarer que j'aime trop mon pays pour songer à accroître ses embarras, et que je ne lui demande d'autre faveur que celle d'accepter de ma main une colonie douée d'un climat plus uniformément tempéré que celui de la France – où l'on intend parler ni d'épidémies, ni de fèvres, – riche en pâturages, en forêts et en mines,' with much more in the same vein.

28 Castro 1957; id. 1964; id. n.d.; Lopez 1957; Tegualda 1960. Many of the same general monarchist themes emerge in support of Eugenio Lascorz (alias Lascaris): Castro 1959.

29 Information about the Mapuche nation is available on the Internet, especially at members.aol.com/mapulink and (more cursorily) unpo.org/members/mapuche. Neither site seems to mention Araucania.

30 Raspail 1972. A later novel on Araucania's founder is Raspail 1981.

31 For Counani, see Rooke 1971.

32 In the *Independent* of 24 September 1999 a full column on the court page was taken up by an advertisement in a tiny typeface, giving the text of a proclamation by which one Karl Fredericke Von Wettinberg assumed the 'dormant' titles of Holy Roman Emperor of the German Nation, King of Germany, Supreme Defender of the Faith, 'etc.', with the motto *Christus vincit, Christus regnat, Christus imperit* (*sic*, on both occasions it appears). An interview with him appeared on p. 8 of the Review section of the same newspaper, 26 October 1999. For 'Prince' Francisco Manoel Hannover-Coburg, see the *Sunday Telegraph* 19 December 1999, and his website (www.netportugal.com/principe-manoel).

Chapter 5   The Nation as Pretender

1 For an introduction to some of the ideas relating to nations and nationalism, see Anderson 1991, Gellner 1983 and 1997, Hobsbawm 1990, Hutchinson and Smith 1994, Smith 1991.

2 On the planning and execution of the monument, see Schama 1995, 109–12.

3 Schnapp 1996, 132–3.

4 See Clogg 1992, chapter 3; Nicol 1992.

5 On this, see the enjoyable and bilious account by Liudprand of Cremona of his embassy to the Byzantine emperor Nicephorus at Constantinople in 968, available in translation in *The Embassy to Constantinople and Other Writings* (ed. J. Julius Norwich, London, 1993), 175–210.

6 Mentioned in Nicol 1992, x.

7 Levy 1996; Tarchi 1998; Stella 1996. For the official website of the *Lega*, see www.leganord.org.

8 See Voltmer 1994.

9 Williams forthcoming.

10 See Williams 1997, 78 n. 8.

11 On the modern invention of the Celts, see James 1999. On Celtic Galicia, see Diaz-Andreu 1995, 52–4.

12 For an entertaining introduction to the history and cultural politics of this little-known region, see Applebaum 1995. For an account of recent Belarusian politics, see Marples 1999. On Lithuania and the Baltic states since the break-up of the Soviet Union, see Lieven 1994.

13 On Belarusian and Ukrainian nationalism, see Wilson 1997. For a rendition of the official version of Belarusian history, see the website of the Belarusian mission to the United Nations: www.undp.org/missions/belarus. For an insight into the nationalist opposition's views, see www.belarusguide.com.

Bibliography

Anderson 1991
B. Anderson, *Imagined Communities. Reflections on the Spread and Origins of Nationalism*, London, 2nd edn.

A.N.E.G.T.I. 1967
Associazione Nazionale Economisti e Guiristi d'Italia, *Biografia di Angelo-Comneno Mario*, Rome.

Anglo 1992
S. Anglo, *Images of Tudor Kingship*, London.

Applebaum 1995
A. Applebaum, *Between East and West. Across the Borderlands of Europe*, London.

Armstrong 1969
Angelo Cato, trans. with intro. by C. A. J. Armstrong, *The Usurpation of Richard the Third*, Oxford, 2nd edn.

Arthurson 1994
I. Arthurson, *The Perkin Warbeck Conspiracy 1491–1499*, Stroud.

Auda-Gioanet 1952
I. Auda-Gioanet, *Is it really possible to Assert the Extinction of Sovereign or Noble House ? (The Angelos of Thessaly)*, Rome.

Auda-Gioanet 1953
I. Auda-Gioanet, *Une Randonnée à travers l'histoire d'Orient (les Comnènes et les Anges)*, Rome.

Baigent, Leigh and Lincoln 1982
M. Baigent, R. Leigh and H. Lincoln, *The Holy Blood and the Holy Grail*, London.

Ballantyne 1743
G. Ballantyne, *A Vindication of the Hereditary Right of His Present Majesty, King George II to the Crown of Great Britain*, London.

Bennett 1987
M. Bennett, *Lambert Simnel and the Battle of Stoke*, Stroud.

Bercé 1990
Y. -M. Bercé, *Le Roi Caché. Sauveurs et Imposteurs*, Paris.

Bierbrier 1980
M. L. Bierbrier, 'Modern descendants of Byzantine families', *Genealogists' Magazine* 20, 85–96.

Bizzocchi 1995
R. Bizzocchi, *Genealogie Incredibili. Scritti di storia nell'Europa moderna*, Bologna.

Black 1990
J. Black, *Culloden and the '45*, Stroud and New York.

Bonaria 1959
M. Bonaria, 'Dinastie di pantomimi latini', *Maia* (n.s.) 11, pp 224–39.

Bowman 1990
A. K. Bowman, *Egypt after the Pharaohs 312 BC–AD 642*, Oxford.

Bradley 1989
K. R. Bradley, *Slavery and Rebellion in the Roman World, 140 BC–70 BC*, Bloomington and London.

Bright 1981
J. Bright, *A History of Israel*, London, 3rd edn.

Brown 1996
P. Fortini Brown, *Venice and Antiquity*, New Haven and London.

Bruce 1986
M. L. Bruce, *The Usurper King. Henry of Bolingbroke 1366–99*, London.

Campbell 1961
G. Campbell, *Impostor at the Bar. William Fuller 1670–1733*, London.

Casey 1994
P. J. Casey, *Carausius and Allectus. The British Usurpers*, London.

Castro n.d.
N. de Castro y Tosi, *Idiosincrasia Nobiliaria Indohispanica en America*, n.p.

Castro 1957
N. de Castro y Tosi, *L'Independance de tous les Peuples sous le signe royal. Essai d'orientation monarchique*, Paris.

Castro 1959
N. de Castro y Tosi, *Le Prince Eugène Lascaris Comnène Grand Maitre Souverain de l'Ordre Constantinien*, Paris.

Castro 1964
  N. de Castro y Tosi, *El Reino de Araucania y Patagonia. Tercer viaje de su majestad Orelio Antonio I⁰ a la America austral*, Paris.

Chaffanjon and Flavigny 1982
  A. Chaffanjon and B. Flavigny, *Ordres et Contre-ordres de Chevalerie*, Paris.

Chatwin 1977
  B. Chatwin, *In Patagonia*, London.

Clark 1985
  J. C. D. Clark, *English Society 1688–1832*, Cambridge.

Clark 1986
  J. C. D. Clark, *Revolution and Rebellion*, Cambridge.

Clogg 1992
  R. Clogg, *A Concise History of Greece*, Cambridge.

Cole 1967
  H. Cole, *Christophe: King of Haiti*, London.

Colocci Vespucci 1931
  A. Colocci Vespucci, *Re Teodoro e l'Ordine Equestre della Liberazione*, Rome.

Cornell and Matthews 1982
  T. J. Cornell and J. Matthews, *Atlas of Roman History*, London.

Craton 1982
  M. Craton, *Testing the Chains. Resistance to slavery in the British West Indies*, Ithaca.

Diaz-Andreu 1995
  M. Diaz-Andreu, 'Archaeology and Nationalism in Spain', in P. L. Kohl and C. Fawcett (eds), *Nationalism, Politics and the Practice of Archaeology*, Cambridge, 39–56.

Drake 1980
  R. Drake, *Byzantium for Rome. The Politics of Nostalgia in Umbertian Italy 1878–1900*, Chapel Hill.

Drinkwater 1987
  J. F. Drinkwater, *The Gallic Empire. Separatism and Continuity in the north-western Provinces of the Roman Empire AD 260–74*, Stuttgart.

Fabbrini 1983
  F. Fabbrini, *Translatio Imperii. L'impero universale da Ciro ad Augusto*, Rome.

Flaig 1992
  E. Flaig, *Den Kaiser Herausfordern. Usurpation im römischen Reich*, Frankfurt.

Flamarion 1997
  E. Flamarion, *Cleopatra*, London.

Francesco 1951
  R. de Francesco, *Michele II Angelo Comneno d'Epiro e la sua discendenza*, Rome.

Gardner 1996
  L. Gardner (The Chevalier Labhràn de Saint Germain), *Bloodline of the Holy Grail. The hidden lineage of Jesus revealed*, Shaftesbury.

Garosci 1967
  A. Garosci, *San Marino. Mito e Storiografia*, Milan.

Gauci and Mallat 1985
  C. A. Gauci and P. Mallat, *The Palaeologos family. A genealogical review*, Hamrun.

Geanakoplos 1959
  D. J. Geanakoplos, *The Emperor Michael Palaeologus and the West 1258–1282*, Cambridge, Mass.

Gellner 1983
  E. Gellner, *Nations and Nationalism*, Oxford.

Gellner 1997
  E. Gellner, *Nationalism*, Oxford.

Green 1990
  P. Green, *From Alexander to Actium. The Hellenistic Age*, London.

Griffiths and Thomas 1985
  R. A. Thomas and R. S. Griffiths, *The Making of the Tudor Dynasty*, Stroud.

Halm 1967
  H. Halm, 'Die Traditionen über den Aufstand 'Ali ibn Muhammads, des "Herrn des Zanğ": eine quellenkritische Untersuchung', unpublished PhD thesis, Bonn.

Harrer 1940
  G. Harrer, 'Saul who is also called Paul', *Harvard Theological Review* 33, 19–33.

Hobsbawm 1990
  E. Hobsbawm, *Nations and Nationalism since 1780. Programme, Myth, Reality*, Cambridge.

Hobsbawm and Ranger 1983
  E. Hobsbawm and T. Ranger (eds), *The Invention of Tradition*, Cambridge.

Horsley 1987
  G. H. R. Horsley, 'Name-change as an indication of religious conversion in Antiquity', *Numen* 34, 1–17.

Howe 1916
  S. L. Howe, *The False Dmitri. A Russian romance and tragedy described by British eye-witnesses 1604–1612*, London.

Howell 1962
M. Howell, *Regalian Right in Medieval England*, London.

Hutchinson and Smith 1994
J. Hutchinson and A. D. Smith, *Nationalism*, Oxford.

I.I.G.A. 1963
Istituto Italiano di Genealogia e Araldica, *Bollettino Ufficiale della Sezione Araldica* 1.1.

James 1963
C. L. R. James, *The Black Jacobins: Toussaint L'Ouverture and the San Domingo Revolution*, New York.

James 1999
S. James, *The Atlantic Celts. Ancient People or Modern Invention?*, London.

Jones 1962
A. H. M. Jones, 'The constitutional position of Odoacer and Theoderic', *Journal of Roman Studies* 52, 126–30.

Jones 1996
F. Jones, *Nominum Ratio. Aspects of the use of personal names in Greek and Latin*, Liverpool.

Kajanto 1966
I. Kajanto, *Supernomina. A study in Latin epigraphy*, Helsinki.

Kantorowicz 1927–31
E. H. Kantorowicz, *Kaiser Friedrich der zweite*, Berlin.

Kantorowicz 1957
E. H. Kantorowicz, *The King's Two Bodies. A study in medieval political theology*, Princeton.

Kinvig 1975
R. H. Kinvig, *The Isle of Man*, Liverpool, 3rd edn.

Kleyn 1990
D. Kleyn, *Richard of England*, Oxford.

Kuhrt 1987
A. Kuhrt, 'Usurpation, conquest and ceremonial: from Babylon to Persia', in D. Cannadine and S. R. F. Price (eds), *Rituals and Royalty. Power and Ceremonial in Traditional Societies*, Cambridge, 20–55.

Kuhrt 1995
A. Kuhrt, *The Ancient Near East, c.3000–330 BC*, 2 vols, London.

Kurth 1983
P. Kurth, *Anastasia*, London.

Lambton 1978
A. K. S. Lambton, '[The caliphate] in political theory', s.v. 'Khalīfa', in *The Encyclopaedia of Islam*, new edn, various eds, vol. 4, Leiden, 947–50.

Levick 1990
B. M. Levick, *Claudius*, London.

Levick 1999
B. M. Levick, *Vespasian*, London.

Levy 1996
C. Levy (ed.), *Italian Regionalism. History, Identity and Culture*, Oxford.

Lieven 1994
A. Lieven, *The Baltic Revolution. Estonia, Latvia, Lithuania and the Path to Independence*, New Haven, 2nd edn.

Lindsey 1939
J. Lindsey, *The Lovely Quaker*, London.

Lock 1995
P. Lock, *The Franks in the Aegean*, London.

Lopez 1957
S. Lopez Pintihueque, *El Reino de Araucania y de Patagonia*, Asuncion.

Louda and Maclagan 1981
J. Louda and M. Maclagan, *Lines of Succession*, London.

Lovell 1992
J. Blair Lovell, *Anastasia*, London.

Macchioni di Sela 1979
O. Macchioni di Sela, *Mario Bernardo (Michele III) Angelo-Comneno Principe di Tessaglia e di Epiro. Note biografiche e genealogiche*, Rome.

Madaro 1932
L. Madaro, 'Documenti su re Teodoro nella Biblioteca Civica di Torino', *Archivio Storico di Corsica* 7.4, 1–8.

Manley 1674
R. M[anley], *The Russian Impostor*, London.

Mansel 1995
P. Mansel, *Constantinople. City of the World's Desire, 1453–1924*, London.

Marples 1999
D. Marples, *Belarus. A Denationalised Nation*, Durham.

Mérimée 1853
P. Mérimée, *Demetrius the Impostor*, trans. A. R. Scoble, London.

Michael of Albany 1998
HRH Prince Michael of Albany, *The Forgotten Monarchy of Scotland*, Shaftesbury.

Millar 1977
F. G. B. Millar, *The Emperor in the Roman World*, London.

Montgomery-Massingberd 1977
H. Montgomery-Massingberd (ed.) with M. Bence-Jones, H. Vickers and D. Williamson, *Burke's Royal Families of the World*, vol. 1, London.

Muldoon 1999
J. Muldoon, *Empire and Order. The Concept of Empire, 800–1800*, Basingstoke and New York.

Nicol 1992
D. M. Nicol, *The Immortal Emperor*, Cambridge.

Popovic 1976
A. Popovic, *La Révolte des Esclaves en Iraq au IIIe / IXe siècle*, Paris.

Price 1973
R. Price (ed.), *Maroon Societies: rebel slave communities in the Americas*, New York.

Puy de Clinchamps 1967
P. du Puy de Clinchamps, *Le Royalisme*, Paris.

Quirke 1990
S. Quirke, *Who were the Pharaohs?*, London.

Raspail 1972
J. Raspail, *Le Camp des Saints*, Paris.

Raspail 1981
J. Raspail, *Moi, Antoine de Tounens, Roi de Patagonie*, Paris.

Reynolds 1994
S. Reynolds, *Fiefs and Vassals. The medieval evidence reinterpreted*, Oxford.

Rhodocanakis 1870
The Prince Rhodocanakis, *The Imperial Constantinian Order of St George*, London.

Rice 1999
E. E. Rice, *Cleopatra*, Stroud.

Robertson 1952
W. S. Robertson, *Iturbide of Mexico*, Durham, N.C.

Rooke 1971
H. F. Rooke, 'Remember Counani', *The Cinderella Philatelist* 11, April 1971, 25–9.

Runciman 1965
S. Runciman, *The Fall of Constantinople 1453*, Cambridge.

Ruvigny 1904
Marquis of Ruvigny and Raineval, *The Jacobite Peerage, Baronetage, Knightage and Grants of Honour*, Edinburgh and London.

Sack 1999
S. Sack, *The Metal Mirror*, London.

Schama 1995
S. Schama, *Landscape and Memory*, London.

Schnapp 1996
A. Schnapp, *The Discovery of the Past. The Origins of Archaeology*, London.

Schürer 1973
E. Schürer, *A History of the Jewish People in the Age of Jesus Christ (175 BC to AD 135)*, trans and new edn by G. Vermes and F. G. B. Millar, vol. 1, Edinburgh.

Schwartz 1985
S. B. Schwartz, *Sugar Plantations in the Formation of Brazilian society: Bahia 1550–1835*, Cambridge.

Schwartz 1992
S. B. Schwartz, *Slaves, Peasants and Rebels. Reconsidering Brazilian Slavery*, Chicago.

Selden 1614
J. Selden, *Titles of Honor*, London.

Sherwin-White and Kuhrt 1993
S. Sherwin-White and A. Kuhrt, *From Samarkand to Sardis. A New Approach to the Seleucid Empire*, London.

Shilstone 1939–40
E. M. Shilstone, 'Ferdinand Palaeologus', *Journal of the Barbados Museum and Historical Society* 7, 160–9, with supplementary note in vol. 8, 101–2.

Smith 1991
A. D. Smith, *National Identity*, London.

Solin 1990
H. Solin, *Namenpaare: eine Studie zur römischen Namengebung*, Helsinki.

Sourdel 1978
D. Sourdel, 'The history of the institution of the Caliphate', s.v. 'Khalīfa', in *The Encyclopaedia of Islam*, new edn, various eds, vol. 4, Leiden, 937–47.

Stella 1996
G. A. Stella, *Dio Po. Gli Uomini che fecero la Padania*, Milan.

Stoneman 1992
R. Stoneman, *Palmyra and its Empire. Zenobia's Revolt against Rome*, Ann Arbor.

Strauss 1984
 E. W. Strauss, *How to Start your own Country*, Port Townshend.

Strohm 1998
 P. Strohm, *England's Empty Throne. Usurpation and the language of legitimation, 1399–1422*, New Haven and London.

Sturdza 1983
 M. D. Sturdza, *Grandes Familles de Grèce, d'Albanie et de Constantinople*, Paris.

Syme 1971
 R. Syme, *Emperors and Biography. Studies in the Historia Augusta*, Oxford.

Syme 1977
 R. Syme, 'Scorpus the charioteer', *American Journal of Ancient History* 2, 86–94 = *Roman Papers* vol. 3, Oxford 1984, 1062–9.

Talbert 1984
 R. Talbert, *The Senate of Imperial Rome*, Princeton.

Tarchi 1998
 M. Tarchi, 'The *Lega Nord*', in L. De Winter and H. Türsan (eds), *Regionalist Parties in Western Europe*, London.

Tegualda 1960
 G. de Tegualda, *Un Centenaire franco-américain. 1860, Orélie-Antoine de Thounens fondait le Royaume d'Araucanie*, Paris.

Thomas 1971
 K. Thomas, *Religion and the Decline of Magic*, London.

Thoms 1867
 W. J. Thoms, *Hannah Lightfoot, Queen Charlotte and the Chevalier d'Eon, Dr Wilmot's Polish Princess*, London (reprinted from *Notes and Queries*).

Tounens 1863
 Orélie-Antoine [de Tounens], *Orllie-Antoine* (sic) *1ᵉʳ, roi d'Araucanie et de Patagonie. Son Avènement au trône et sa captivité au Chili*, Paris.

Tounens 1864
 Manifeste d'Orllie-Antoine 1ᵉʳ Roi d'Araucanie et de Patagonie, Paris.

Trevor-Roper 1983
 H. R. Trevor-Roper, 'The invention of tradition: the Highland tradition of Scotland', in Hobsbawm and Ranger 1983, 15–41.

Tuplin 1989
 C. J. Tuplin, 'The false Neros of the First Century AD', in *Studies in Latin Literature and Roman History* vol. iv, ed. C. Deroux, Brussels, 364–404.

Voltmer 1994
 E. Voltmer, *Il Carroccio*, trans G. Albertoni, Turin.

Wagner 1876
 W. Wagner (ed.), *Mediaeval Greek Texts*, London.

Wagner 1967
 A. R. Wagner, *Heralds of England*, London.

Warren 1947–55
 R. de Warren, *Les Prétendants au Trone de France*, 2 vols, Paris.

Wasserstein 1993
 D. J. Wasserstein, *The Caliphate in the West*, Oxford.

Watson 1999
 A. Watson, *Aurelian and the Third Century*, London.

Webster 1988
 C. D. Webster, 'The Palaeologos legend', *Genealogists' Magazine* 22, 367–70.

Weinberger 1996
 F. Bacon, ed. with notes and interpretive essay by J. Weinberger, *The History of the Reign of King Henry the Seventh*, Ithaca and London.

Wheeler 1955
 M. Wheeler, *Still Digging*, London.

Williams 1997
 J. H. C. Williams, 'Celtic ethnicity in northern Italy; problems ancient and modern', in T. J. Cornell and K. Lomas (eds), *Gender and Ethnicity in Ancient Italy*, London, 69–81.

Williams forthcoming
 J. H. C. Williams, *Beyond the Rubicon. Romans and Gauls in Republican Italy*, Oxford.

Wilson 1997
 A. Wilson, 'Myths of national history in Belarus and Ukraine', in G. Hosking and G. Schöpflin (eds), *Myths and Nationhood*, London, 182–97.

Wiseman 1992
 T. P. Wiseman, 'Killing Caligula', in *Talking to Virgil – a Miscellany*, Exeter, 1–13.

Wolf 1966
 G. Wolf (ed.), *Stupor Mundi: zur Geschichte Friedrichs II von Hohenstaufen*, Darmstadt.

Wolski 1962
 J. Wolski, 'Arsace II et la généalogie des premiers Arsacides', *Historia* 11, 138–45.

Illustration References

British Museum objects (indicated BM) appear by courtesy of The Trustees of the British Museum and the Photographic Service. British Library objects (BL) appear by kind permission of the British Library Board. College of Arms objects appear by permission of the Kings, Heralds and Pursuivants of Arms.

Frontispiece: BM, PD 1859-8-6-643

Colour Plates (between pages 96 and 97)
1:    College of Arms Ms Arundel 23
2:    Photograph by Stephen Sack
3:    College of Arms Ms J. P. 177
4A: Jersey Heritage Trust
4B–D: The Flag Institute

Page
Introduction
7:    College of Arms Ms Arundel 23
10: BM, CM 1919.10-1.1
11: BM, CM PM 232
13: BM, CM 1996.2-17.239; BM, CM 1979.10-39.20
15: By courtesy of the Dean and Chapter of Westminster

Chapter 1
18: BM, BMC Diodotus I 1; BM, CM 1926.4-2.1
21: BM, CM 1995.4-1.1
22: BM, BMC Balbinus and Pupienus 94; BM, BMC Claudius 8
23: BM, BMC Galba 156
27: BM, BMC Otho 24

29: BM, BMC Vitellius 27; BM, BMC Vespasian 566
31: BM, CM 1860.3-27.273
34: BM, CM 1977.9-3.1; BM, CM 1967.9-1.1; BM, CM 1900.11-5.10
35: BM, CM 1841.7-30.318; BM, CM 1998.4-1.1
40: BM, BMC Seleucus I 25; BM, BMC Ptolemy I 23
41: BM, EA 24
42: BM, WAA 90920
43: BM, WAA 90837

Chapter 2
46: BM, CM 1882.4-5.1
48: College of Arms Ms M5b (Hyghalmen Roll) folio 5v
50: BM, CM 1859.7-8.50
51: BM, CM 1870.5-7.9087
53: BM, CM SSB 1736.144-111; BM, CM 1995.7-18.122 and 1992.5-5.102
54: BM, PD 1851.3-8.733
55: BM, CM 1981.5-16.1; BL Philatelic Collections, Chinchen Collection
56: BM, CM 1995.8-7.2 and 1995.8-7.6
60: BM, CM 1999.1-20.1; BM, CM 1999.1-20.2
61: Rouge Dragon Pursuivant
67: BM, CM M 245
71: BM, PD 1868.8-22.2392
78: BL, 111.c.27
81: BM, PD 1864.8-13.220
82: BM, CM 1957.10-2.20
83: BM, CM M 8542
84: BM, CM 1906.11-3.422

Chapter 3
86: BM, BMC Nero 236
88: BM, CM C2809
91: BM, CM Walker 204
93: BM, PD 1896.11-23.8
96: BM, CM 1909.2-2.80 and 1862.9-15.1
98: BM, CM unregistered

103: BM, CM 1868.7-30.156; BM, CM 1858.11-24.80
107: College of Arms Ms Vincent 151 page 30a
108: BM, PD 1851.3-8.157
110: College of Arms Ms M5b (Hyghalmen Roll) folio 2v
112: BM, CM unregistered
113: BM, PD 1926.4-12.250
115: BM, CM 1870.5-7.15385
116: BM, CM 1866.3-23.3
117: College of Arms

Chapter 4
124: BM, CM Library
126: BM, CM 1956.2-1.1
127: ANSA (Rome)
129: Photograph in private collection
134: Photograph by Murdo Mcleod
138: BM, CM CIB 8551.E1
139: BM, CM 8549.1937
142: BL, 9772.dd.12
143: BM, CM 1906.11-3.3672 Parkes Weber Gift
144: BM, CM 1999.2-1.1 and 1999.2-1.2
147: BL, Philatelic Collections

Chapter 5
152: Deutsche Presse-Agentur GmBH (Frankfurt am Main)
153: BM, CM 1985.3-29.39
155: BM, CM 1842.11-29.1
156: BM, CM 1981.5-15.46
157: BM, CM 1898.1-2.46; BM, BMC Augustus 565
160: BM, CM unregistered
161: BM, CM unregistered
164: ANSA (Rome)
170: BM, CM unregistered; BM, CM 1998.9-1.38
171: BM, CM SSB 1547.93-148

Index

Countries or regions either ruled or claimed by individuals named in the text are indicated in brackets.

References to illustration pages in italics